Patience, Compassion, Hope, and the Christian Art of Dying Well

Patience, Compassion, Hope, and the Christian Art of Dying Well

CHRISTOPHER P. VOGT

A SHEED & WARD BOOK

ROWMAN & LITTLEFIELD PUBLISHERS, INC.
Lanham • Boulder • New York • Toronto • Oxford

A SHEED & WARD BOOK

ROWMAN & LITTLEFIELD PUBLISHERS, INC.

Published in the United States of America
by Rowman & Littlefield Publishers, Inc.
A wholly owned subsidiary of The Rowman & Littlefield Publishing Group, Inc.
4501 Forbes Boulevard, Suite 200, Lanham, Maryland 20706
www.rowmanlittlefield.com

PO Box 317
Oxford
OX2 9RU, UK

British Library Cataloguing in Publication Information Available

Library of Congress Cataloging-in-Publication Data

Vogt, Christopher P., 1970–
  Patience, compassion, hope, and the Christian art of dying well / Christopher P. Vogt.
    p. cm.
  "A Sheed & Ward book."
  Includes bibliographical references and index.
  ISBN 0-7425-3185-6 (cloth : alk. paper) — ISBN 0-7425-3186-4 (pbk. : alk. paper)
    1. Death—Religious aspects—Christianity. 2. Suffering—Religious aspects—
Christianity. I. Title.
  BT825.V568 2004
  241'.4—dc22   2004014060

Printed in the United States of America

♾™ The paper used in this publication meets the minimum requirements of American
National Standard for Information Sciences—Permanence of Paper for Printed Library
Materials, ANSI/NISO Z39.48-1992.

In memory of my grandmother,
Ruby E. Meng,
Whose dying led me to begin this work

Table of Contents

Acknowledgments

As I looked back on the experience of writing this book, I realized that it taught me a great deal about the meaning of grace. I used to think that it was incredibly corny for athletes to blurt out "I'd like to thank God and Jesus Christ" the moment an interviewer would extend a microphone toward them to ask how it felt to have accomplished some great athletic feat. Now here I am doing much the same thing; my first words are that without God's help, and a deep awareness that God was assisting me in this endeavor, I would never have finished this book.

I am deeply thankful for the many people who have shaped me intellectually and personally during my years of academic formation, and guided the progress of my work. I offer special thanks to my wife, Jennifer, whose ministry to the dying inspired my research. Special thanks also goes to my teacher and mentor, James F. Keenan, SJ, for teaching me the importance of studying the virtues, for his patient guidance and generosity, and for living as a model of how one should serve the church and the academy. Thanks to Daniel Harrington, SJ, and Lisa Sowle Cahill for the insightful, constructive criticism they offered of my writing on this topic as it progressed, and for inspiring me by the great examples of their own work. I am indebted to John O'Malley, SJ, for his useful advice on navigating the historical tradition of the *ars moriendi.*

I am grateful to Jeremy Langford, editorial director at Sheed & Ward, for backing this project, and for his kind assistance in guiding me through the process of publishing my first book.

The fourth chapter of this work is based upon a paper I delivered at the annual meeting of the Society of Christian Ethics in 2002, which was subsequently published in the society's journal. I am grateful to the editorial board of the *Journal of the Society of Christian Ethics* for generously granting me permission to include that material here.

The support of my colleagues at St. John's University has meant a lot to me. I am particularly grateful to Marilyn Martone for her helpful advice on how to improve the manuscript, and to Patrick Primeaux, S.M., for his collaborative leadership as department chair, his strong support of my professional development, and his good humor.

It has been my good fortune to have very loving, supportive parents. I am grateful to them for their encouragement, for their editorial advice, and for the many ways in which they are models of virtue. Finally, I wish to offer my thanks to my children, Abigail and Bryan, for helping me to keep the relative importance of academic pursuits in perspective, and for all the joy they have given to me.

Chapter 1

A Context for the Task of Dying:
Christian Virtue Ethics and Dying Well

Joanne Lynn has observed that in the past one hundred years the approach to terminal illnesses found in medical textbooks has changed markedly. In the nineteenth century, considerable attention was paid to how the course of any given disease was known to affect people. For example, Sir William Osler's textbook in medicine specified what people experienced as they suffered from various illnesses, listed signs that the disease was getting worse, when death was near as well as what if anything could be done to aid or comfort the patient. A century or more ago, little could be done to stop a disease, but doctors were well attuned to their patients' experience of dying.[1] In contrast, today's textbooks rarely even mention that people sometimes die of a given disease. Dr. Lynn laments, "Congestive heart failure is one of our most common lethal illnesses, but a modern American textbook did not acknowledge that it regularly caused death and certainly did not say what people look like as they come near that death. How do they die? How can we make their dying better or worse? How can we best care for these patients? None of these issues is addressed."[2]

A similar criticism could be made of the textbooks used to teach bioethics. It would be wrong to contend that contemporary bioethicists and moral theologians bury or ignore death. However, most textbooks in bioethics focus on the complex quandaries faced by medical professionals whose patients are near the end of life and who have usually lost the capacity for autonomous decision-making (e.g., "When is it morally justifiable to discontinue medical nutrition and hydration?" "Are continued efforts to revive a victim in the ER justified?").[3] The same is true for much of the literature in bioethics as a whole, and the theological scholarship on death and dying.[4] The intended audience of these texts is professional and their focus is usually discreet questions of right or wrong action. Although there are many notable exceptions to this pattern, it remains true that

1

typically a substantial consideration of the existential *experience* of dying is absent.[5] In this sense the deficiencies of the bioethical literature mirror those in the medical literature as described by Joanne Lynn.[6]

The relative inattentiveness of the contemporary literature to the existential and experiential aspects of dying is brought into greater relief by comparing it with the theological literature on the end of life written a few centuries ago. Beginning in the fifteenth century, a new genre of theological literature known as the *"ars moriendi"* (which can be translated as "art of dying") emerged which sought to prepare readers for the task of dying. The authors of these works viewed dying as a task or an art—a *learned* behavior that one could perform either well or badly.[7] As social historian Philippe Ariès has observed, these authors—and all of the early-modern European societies in which these texts emerged—recognized "there was a moral importance in the way the dying man *behaved* and in the circumstances surrounding his death."[8]

The main purpose of this book is to recover a fundamental insight of the *ars moriendi* tradition, namely that the key to preparing for a good death is the development of virtues throughout one's entire lifetime. Rather than argue for the importance of "the virtues" in general, I will focus on three virtues that are essential for a contemporary development of the Christian art of dying well: patience, compassion, and hope.[9] Pieces of the argument that is at the heart of this book can be found in ongoing scholarly conversations on death and dying, especially in the theological literature. Some authors have helpfully recognized the importance of the virtue of patience for the sick and dying.[10] Others have skillfully explored the virtue of compassion and its importance for the Christian life.[11] Still others have provided a helpful treatment of Christian hope.[12] What will be added here to this conversation is some historical insight into the importance of these virtues for Christians in the context of death and dying (in the *ars moriendi* tradition) and a careful exploration of the interaction of patience, compassion, and hope as a mutually interdependent set of virtues.

What Is Christian Virtue Ethics?

This book is a work in contemporary virtue ethics. Readers who are not familiar with the field of ethics may not know exactly what is meant by this label or understand how this particular way of approaching the moral life stands in relationship to other approaches.[13] Although it has a very long history, it was only relatively recently that the study of virtue has regained much prominence in ethical scholarship.[14] Since the eighteenth century, the study of ethics often focused upon determining whether particular acts are morally acceptable. These acts were condemned or promoted on the basis of an examination of their consequences or by appealing to a set of ethical principles.[15] In roughly the last quarter-century, a number of ethicists grew dissatisfied with these dominant approaches, and turned to the thought of Aristotle, Augustine, Thomas Aquinas, and others to recover an alternative framework for moral inquiry.[16]

For many years, there was substantial debate in academic circles regarding the wisdom of returning to a virtue-based methodology.[17] Although these discussions continue, virtue ethics has grown to the point where it no longer assumes a position of marginality within the field.[18] Therefore, I do not find it necessary to revisit the arguments justifying virtue ethics here. Instead, this brief section is intended merely to give a rough sketch of virtue ethics for readers whose interest in reading about dying and virtue ethics is not coupled with any background in ethical theory.

One of the defining qualities of virtue ethics is its focus on moral character. This approach defines the central task of ethics as coming to know what constitutes good character and a life well lived, rather than passing judgment upon whether this or that particular act is right or wrong. The fundamental question shifts from "Is it right for me to do this act?" to "What sort of person should I become?" Thus, virtue ethics is a teleological approach to morality. It develops a rich description of what constitutes a good human life, which serves as the *telos* or end toward which we should strive. It then goes about describing the dispositions, practices, and ways of living (i.e., the *virtues*) that both constitute and lead to that life. Joseph Kotva summarizes this dynamic well when he writes that virtue ethics begins with an examination of human nature as it exists, develops a vision of human nature as it could be, and describes the habits, capacities, and inclinations that would lead from point A to point B.[19]

The morally good life is a complicated reality. It should not be conceived of as a thing to be acquired so much as a harmonious way of living. Furthermore, perfecting this way of living is not a matter of mastering one task, activity, or virtue so much as developing several virtues at the same time. Each of the virtues describes one facet of the good, well-ordered human life.

The virtues serve both as a way of describing a good life and as a roadmap of sorts for moving oneself toward living such a life. A virtue describes a good state of character that a person has already attained. This is what Jean Porter has in mind when she writes that a virtue is "a trait of character or intellect which is in some way praiseworthy, admirable or desirable. When we refer to somebody's virtues, what we usually have in mind are relatively stable and effective dispositions to act in particular ways."[20] Here a virtue refers to a quality of character that inclines someone to feel or act in a particular, good way. For example, a person who is compassionate will consistently *feel* the pain of other people and be inclined to *act* with those people to relieve their suffering. The virtue of compassion refers not to an isolated act but rather to a particular kind of person. One who is compassionate will consistently feel and respond in this manner; this is what Jean Porter means by the "stability" of a virtue.

Although perfectly accurate, the definition that we have so far provides an incomplete account of the place of virtues in the moral life because it does not explain how one goes about becoming more virtuous. It is helpful to be able to say that a virtuous person will be just, temperate, courageous, prudent, and so forth, but one must also be able to answer the question of how one develops these stable qualities of character.

The vision of moral development that predominates in virtue ethics is rooted in a strong sense of the importance of habituation. One cannot become good merely by coming to know what is good or right; it is necessary to engage consciously in practices that concretize the good in order to become virtuous and move oneself closer to embracing the good life. Reading a series of books on the virtue of temperance might help me to see that the amount of food that I eat is not consistent with good living. However, that insight will not make me more temperate so long as I regularly choose to pull into the drive-thru lane of fast-food restaurants. In order for my character to take on a stable quality by which I do what is morally right for the right reasons, I must consciously and repeatedly act in a way that manifests a particular virtue.

The term "habituation" should not be misconstrued to imply an unthinking or rote repetition of good behavior.[21] A crucial dimension of becoming virtuous lies in the development of the faculty of practical reason. Discerning what particular action would be courageous, patient, and so forth, in any given situation requires a high level of moral development. Prudence is the virtue which names this ability to perceive all of the morally relevant features of a situation, and then to act appropriately. It is by the virtue of prudence that the general demands and principles of morality are translated into good specific actions. This requires a proactive approach to the moral life. The key questions of virtue ethics have an orientation toward the future: "Who should I become?" and "What must I do to become that person?"

Virtues are not qualities that can be switched on instantly by sheer force of will. This implies that if you wish to be patient and hopeful at the hour of your death, you should have endeavored to become patient and hopeful during the more active stages of your life. Thus, while the reflection on dying and the virtues in this book should be helpful for understanding how we should strive to live out the final days and moments of our lives, it must also serve to focus our attention on the consideration of how we can become patient, hopeful, and virtuous in other ways long before our last hour comes.[22]

The Importance of Patience, Compassion, and Hope for Dying Well

Many virtues pertain to the experience of dying; let me explain why I have chosen patience, compassion, and hope as focal points. First, in the literature on death and dying it is acknowledged that whether a person will "die well" is often determined by how that person deals with suffering and sadness.[23] Here I refer not to the endurance of physical pain so much as the suffering associated with the sorrow one experiences when facing the prospect of being separated from loved ones, and indeed from life itself; in short, what is to be endured is the suffering that results from anticipatory grieving of one's own death. Patience is the virtue most suitable for addressing this sort of difficulty. As Stanley Hauerwas has observed, "Patience is fundamentally about dealing with sadness—persevering in sadness and not allowing it to deteriorate into despair."[24]

If patience is the virtue appropriate for dealing with hardships faced by oneself, compassion is the virtue which should guide one's response to the suffering of others. We face the moral dimension of dying not only when we ourselves face death, but more frequently when someone we know and love is dying. Many writers in the field of death and dying have recognized the importance of shifting the context of dying from the hospital to a supportive family setting at home.[25] The importance of compassion is rooted both in the recognition that even the most patient of patients needs support, and in the claim that part of living well as a Christian is being a person who is compassionate toward those who are suffering and those who are dying.[26]

Hope is a virtue that cannot be ignored when developing a contemporary Christian approach to dying well. This third virtue unifies the other two in the sense that it is required by both. Whereas patience is primarily for the dying and compassion for the supportive family and community, hope is important for *both* groups. A further connection between patience and hope arises from the fact that Christian patience or endurance is not an end in itself; rather, it is a secondary virtue. For example, in St. Thomas Aquinas's scheme of the virtues, patience serves the greater virtue of justice (*ST* II-II:136.2). In the context of death and dying, patience instead is more closely related to hope. Patience and hope are related in that patience both serves hope (that is, it is the good toward which patience is directed) and is dependent upon hope for its strength.

It would be impossible to understand fully the dynamics of Christian patience without any reference to hope. For example, the *ars moriendi* tradition points to the importance of patience or endurance in sustaining hope. Most Christians living in the early modern period believed that one's disposition at the moment of death was decisive for one's eternal fate—a soul in despair was easy prey for the devil.[27] Therefore, Erasmus and many of his contemporaries encouraged readers to stave off despair (i.e., to keep *hope* alive) through the development of patience or endurance. At the same time, Erasmus sought to fortify the patience of the dying by nurturing their hope in Divine compassion and forgiveness.[28] It is by our hope in God's mercy and love for us that we find the strength to endure—that is, to be patient.

Compassion and hope are also closely interrelated. Wendy Farley has described this connection quite well. In her work on developing a Christian "tragic vision" as a way of dealing with the problem of evil, she describes compassion as a way of seeing the suffering of others in such a way that we are empowered to give comfort and aid to them and to generate a resistance to their suffering.[29] While such resistance can emerge among those with an atheistic worldview (Farley cites the example of the character, Dr. Rieux, in Albert Camus's novel, *The Plague*), *Christian* compassion is necessarily marked by the virtue of hope. Christian compassion draws its energy and power from the hope that in the end, God's love and justice will prevail. The importance of hope is apparent in Farley's description of the effects of compassion:

> In this world, in an order "shaped by death," the penultimate victories in which the degradation of suffering is even temporarily defeated are signs of the nonfinality of evil. Compassionate power enables the terminally ill person to defy the despair which her condition would seem to demand. It empowers parents to survive the suffering or death of their children. Nothing can take away the cruelty or pain of such suffering, but compassionate power makes it possible for meaning, healing, or love to transcend tragedy. Through it the hollow absurdity of Camus' cosmos may be superseded by a beauty that survives even the ravages of radical suffering. And when we participate in the work of alleviating human anguish we can taste something of the empowering presence and beauty of the divine life as it is perennially incarnate in the redemption of this world.[30]

Hope is thus an extremely important virtue for those who would also seek to be compassionate toward the dying.

The Difficulty of Dying Well

In her aptly titled work, "Dying Well Isn't Easy," Patricia Beattie Jung warns of the temptation to romanticize the "good death" or underestimate the sometimes personally debilitating suffering that accompanies it. She notes that while patient endurance of the suffering that accompanies death can be educative, it can also "separate us from the humanizing roles and relations that bear witness to the blissful communion for which we were made. . . . Suffering can break spirits, crush relationships and brutalize communities."[31] This insight is not new. Indeed it is the same one William Perkins had four centuries ago when he wrote that a person's manner of death should not be regarded as indicative of his or her prospects for salvation; he recognized that even good and virtuous people sometimes die a difficult death.[32]

Even though this insight into the difficulty and painfulness of death is not new, it is worth repeating for at least two reasons. First, it highlights the ambiguous nature of death itself. The authors of the *ars moriendi* literature struggled with the question of whether death is always to be resisted because it is purely evil or if it might be conceptualized as a part of life that sometimes should be embraced; historically, this discussion usually centered upon the question of whether death was willed by God "from the beginning" to be a fact of human life or if it was a punishment resulting from original sin.[33]

A similar discussion on the question of whether death is an evil or a natural part of life persists today, although on different terms. Vigen Guroian provides an interesting analysis of this contemporary discussion in his book *Life's Living Toward Dying*.[34] He finds the view that death is an ultimate evil and must therefore be stopped at all costs to be as unsatisfactory as the view that death is a neutral, natural part of life. Guroian argues instead for maintaining a tension between the insights that death is in some ways evil and in some ways natural. I would locate myself alongside Guroian and others who find death ambiguous, and in opposition to those who seek to describe dying well wholly as a matter of the acceptance or embrace of death as "the final stage of growth."[35] Accepting the inevitability of death and enduring it well is not necessarily the same thing as embracing death as a good.

Another reason to begin this book with a reminder about the pain, difficulty, and messiness of dying is to emphasize the modesty of my aims here. This effort to explore patience, compassion, and hope in the context of dying well should not be construed as an effort to "solve" the problem of dying. Although I have undertaken to show that the well-formed virtues of patience, compassion, and hope are invaluable for dying well (and living well), this is not to say that their cultivation will make dying *easy*.

An Overview of What Follows

The main body of this work will begin by setting an historical context for Christian theological reflection on the question of how one might endeavor to die well. As noted above, during the late fifteenth through the mid-seventeenth century a vast array of devotional literature was produced on the subject of dying well. In chapter 2, it will become clear that the authors of the *ars moriendi* literature encouraged their readers to prepare for dying well primarily by living well. That is to say that they saw the Christian life well lived to be the best preparation for death. They called readers back to the fundamentals of Christian spiritual life—nurturing faith and trust in God, living one's life in imitation of Jesus Christ, and so forth. These authors saw the development and practice of virtues—especially patience, compassion, and hope, all supported by faith—to be an effective way to instruct readers about practices crucial for living the good Christian life and thus to prepare for death as well.

Chapter 3 shifts from the historical to the contemporary literature on death and dying. The focus of discussion in recent years has often been upon the question of exactly what it means to respond compassionately to the suffering of people who are dying. There has been a great deal of public discussion of this question in the context of the ongoing debate over the legalization and normalization of physician-assisted suicide (PAS). Many proponents of the idea have sought to draw a close connection between "compassion" and PAS, going so far as to suggest that compassion for the dying *demands* the legalization of that practice.[36] The third chapter critically explores this understanding of compassion by analyzing the work of Dr. Timothy Quill, a physician noted for his reasoned discourse, years of experience in hospice care, and strong advocacy of the legalization of PAS. It then goes on to contrast Quill's notion of compassion with an understanding of compassion that draws upon sources in contemporary Christian ethics.

I conclude that much is to be said for Quill's view of compassion; many parallels can be drawn between his understanding and one rooted in Christian ethics, most notably the importance of developing a deep relationship with those who are dying in one's care, recognition of the centrality of listening, and the uniqueness of each patient's path to dying. At the same time, the understanding of Christian compassion developed in this book differs fundamentally from Quill's view. Quill's compassion is used primarily to support the absolute autonomy of his patients—to help them to be in complete control until the end and to die "on their own terms." In contrast, Christian compassion should support the development of patience and hope in the dying. Thus, Christian compassion differs in the sense that it is part of a more comprehensive web of virtues (most notably, faith, patience, and hope) that give a very different shape to compassion itself.

The fourth chapter addresses the issue of whether the Gospel depiction of Jesus' death can clarify how patience, compassion, and hope should be practiced in the context of dying well today. All of the theologians examined in chapter 2 recommend that their readers should imitate Jesus in their dying. It remains a common pastoral practice among Catholics and other Christians to encourage the dying to turn to Jesus as a source of comfort and inspiration, and as a model for dying well.[37]

These pastoral practices raise important questions that deserve reflection here. What exactly is it about the way in which Jesus died that should be imitated by Christians today? Does the practice of encouraging people to imitate Jesus in dying lead to an unhealthy pursuit of suffering for its own sake? Holding Jesus up as a model might lead some people to think that since Jesus died an agonizing death, they likewise should not seek remedies for their own pain.[38]

An examination of Luke's passion narrative in chapter 4 shows that despite the potential dangers of misinterpretation, it is appropriate to hold up the Lucan Jesus as a model of dying well. Throughout his ordeal, Jesus never ceases to practice compassion toward all the people that surround him. He maintains a deep sense of hope and a prayerful connection to God despite the tragic death he must endure. In his practice of compassion and hope, Jesus is a model for all Christians. His practice of patience also is an inspiration, but how Jesus embodies this virtue requires more careful analysis. It is explained in chapter 4 that we must shift the focus away from Jesus' willingness and ability to endure physical pain onto his willingness to endure the suffering that comes with refusing ever to seize absolute control of his destiny (choosing instead to share that control with God). It is in that way that Jesus' modeling of patience is illuminative for contemporary Christians.

In the final chapter, the insights of the three main chapters of the book are brought together into a synthesis that names some key practices that would be necessary components of an *ars moriendi* for our time. The chapter is not comprehensive in scope but rather is limited to two main points. First, Christians today should take seriously the insight that the best *ars moriendi* is an *ars viviendi*. A lifetime of the pursuit of Christian virtue is the best preparation for death. Second, Christians should support communal expressions of compassion that nurture patience and that emphasize some of the fundamental understandings of a Christian anthropology. Most significantly, these practices must make clear that human beings are fundamentally relational creatures who retain their full dignity even in situations where their independence and physical capacities are impaired.

These two steps are just part of what must be a concerted effort to help one another once again entertain the very possibility of dying well. In contemporary western culture, it is widely held that the process of dying is an unspeakable horror that is always to be avoided. Christians should embrace an alternative view. Taking Jesus as a model, it is necessary for Christians to come to see their own dying as a venue where the possibility exists to find deepened self-understanding and to bear witness to God. In other words, dying must be made a part of living in the sense that one's efforts at discipleship persist through this stage of life. Dying is not a time or a task that is devoid of meaning, divorced from God's presence. The practices of prayer and attentiveness to God's ongoing presence in one's life are crucial here as well.

The task of dying is very difficult, to be sure. The suffering that can accompany our journey to death can be enough to break even the strongest person and cast even the most holy men and women among us into despair. But from this fact it does not follow that all dying must be sheer horror. It is still possible for some people to die well. In what follows I hope to make that possibility clear and to begin to illuminate the practices that might support making it a reality.

Notes

1. Joanne Lynn, "Caring for Those Who Die in Old Age," in *Facing Death: Where Culture, Religion and Medicine Meet*, ed. Howard M. Spiro, Mary G. McCrea Curnen and Lee Palmet Wandel, (New Haven, Conn.: Yale University Press, 1996), 91.

2. Lynn, "Caring," 93.

3. These examples are from the chapter on death and dying in Thomas A. Shannon, *Bioethics*, 4th Ed. (Mahwah, N.J.: Paulist Press, 1993), 167–212. Similar questions are the focus in Tom Beauchamp & James Childress, *Principles of Biomedical Ethics* (New York: Oxford University Press, 1994), 4th ed. (New York: Oxford University Press, 2001), for example, in their chapter on nonmaleficence. See also James Childress, *Practical Reasoning in Bioethics* (Bloomington: Indiana University Press, 1997), where discussion of death and dying focuses on the termination of life-sustaining treatment. Also similar is Robert M. Veatch's collection of essays, *Medical Ethics* (Sudbury, Mass.: Jones and Bartlett, 1996) where the lead issues of the chapter on death and dying are life-support withdrawal decisions and moral difficulties surrounding the incompetent patient.

4. Daniel Callahan makes this assertion in his book, *The Troubled Dream of Life: In Search of a Peaceful Death* (New York: Simon & Schuster, 1993), 13, where he agrees that too much emphasis in bioethics has been placed on "law, regulation, moral rules, and medical practice" to the neglect of discussion of the meaning of death and people's experience of dying. Callahan's book is itself an exception to this trend. I make note of that fact to indicate my awareness that there is not a complete lack of attention to the experience of dying in the literature, but rather a relative inattentiveness to that topic.

5. M. Therese Lysaught makes the observation that the bioethical literature typically ignores the experiential dimension of dying. Citing Beauchamp and Childress' *Principles of Biomedical Ethics* and H. Tristram Englehardt's *The Foundations of Bioethics* (New York: Oxford University Press, 1986) as prototypical, she argues that these authors divide the moral life into public and private spheres, locating their own work in the former. As such they see their work as properly secular and neutral vis-à-vis particular moral or religious communities—a neutral, reasoned analysis whose aim is the peaceful resolution of controversies. It is Lysaught's position that these philosophical commitments make bioethicists inattentive to patients' experience of suffering, and especially to the importance of the religious/moral interpretations patients give to their own suffering. See "Patient Suffering and the Anointing of the Sick," in *On Moral Medicine: Theological Perspectives in Medical Ethics*, 2nd ed., ed. Stephen E. Lammers and Allen Verhey (Grand Rapids, Mich.: Eerdmans, 1998), 356–64.

6. I do not mean to overstate my case here. Some excellent work has been done in bioethics on the experiences of suffering and dying. My point is simply that this line of ethical inquiry has suffered from relative neglect in the field. Some of the more notable works that defy this trend include the following: Arthur Kleinman, *The Illness Narratives: Suffering, Healing, and the Human Condition* (New York: Basic Books, 1988). Eric J. Cassel, "The Nature of Suffering and the Goals of Medicine," *New England Journal of Medicine* 306, no. 11 (March 18, 1982): 639–45. Margaret Mohrmann, *Pain Seeking Understanding: Suffering, Medicine, and Faith* (Cleveland, Ohio: Pilgrim Press, 1999).

7. Arthur E. Imhof, "An *Ars Moriendi* for Our Time," in *Facing Death* (see note 1), 116.

8. Philippe Ariès, *Western Attitudes Toward Death from the Middle Ages to the Present* (Baltimore: Johns Hopkins University Press, 1974), 39.

9. I wish to emphasize that these three virtues are not of *exclusive* importance, especially given the inherent unity of the virtues. This book will explain why these three are of critical importance while merely alluding to the importance of various other virtues.

10. Stanley Hauerwas and Charles Pinches, *Christians Among the Virtues: Theological Conversations with Ancient and Modern Ethics* (Notre Dame, Ind.: University of Notre Dame Press, 1997), chapter 10.

11. For example, Diana Fritz Cates, *Choosing to Feel: Virtue, Friendship and Compassion for Friends* (Notre Dame, Ind.: University of Notre Dame Press, 1997).

12. Jürgen Moltmann, *Theology of Hope: On the Ground and Implications of Christian Eschatology* (New York: Harper & Row, 1967). Karl Rahner "Towards a Theology of Hope," *Concurrence* 1 (1969): 23–33. Schubert Ogden, "The Meaning of Christian Hope," *Union Seminary Quarterly Review* 30 (1975): 153–64.

13. James F. Keenan's book *Virtues for Ordinary Christians* (Kansas City, Mo.: Sheed and Ward, 1996) provides a good introduction to Christian virtue ethics for a general audience.

14. Lee H. Yearley, "Recent Work on Virtue," *Religious Studies Review* 16 (1990): 1.

15. William Spohn, "The Return of Virtue Ethics," *Theological Studies* 53 (1992): 60.

16. One of the earliest and most important theological works in this contemporary revival of virtue ethics is Stanley Hauerwas, *Character and the Christian Life: A Study in Theological Ethics* (San Antonio, Tex.: Trinity University Press, 1975). One should note that although deontological and consequentialist ethics predominated throughout much of the twentieth century, some excellent work in virtue ethics was also produced. For example, Gérard Gilleman, *The Primacy of Charity in Moral Theology*, trans. William F. Ryan and André Vachon (Westminster, Md.: Newman Press, 1959).

17. The fact that a major monograph series such as Georgetown's *Moral Traditions and Moral Arguments* perceived the need to publish Joseph J. Kotva's book, *The Christian Case for Virtue Ethics*, as recently as 1996 indicates that the validity of a virtue-based approach remained an open question for many in the field. This book is an excellent piece of scholarship, both for its defense of the natural fit between virtue ethics and the Christian moral life, and for Kotva's thorough and accessible description of contemporary thought on virtue ethics. See Joseph J. Kotva, *The Christian Case for Virtue Ethics* (Washington, D.C.: Georgetown University Press, 1996).

18. The inclusion of a chapter on virtue ethics in the recent *Cambridge Companion to Christian Ethics* is but one indication of mainstream status. See Jean Porter, "Virtue Ethics," in *The Cambridge Companion to Christian Ethics*, ed. Robin Gill (New York: Cambridge University Press, 2001), 96–111.

19. Kotva, *Christian Case*, 17.

20. Porter, "Virtue Ethics," 96.

21. Jean Porter, "Virtue," in *The Harpercollins Encyclopedia of Catholicism*, ed. Richard P. McBrien (San Francisco: HarperSanFrancisco, 1994), 1316.

22. When I say that this reflection on dying and the virtues might help us to know how we should strive to be at the end of life, I mean not only that it should help us to understand what state of character might be conducive for dying well, but also that it might rule out certain behaviors as contrary to the vision of Christian living developed here. For example, I find physician-assisted suicide to be generally incompatible with Christian compassion and patience. Thus, I would not place virtue ethics in strict opposition to an approach to morality that utilizes moral rules and principles. As Joseph Kotva

explains, "Virtue ethics is concerned with rules at many levels. To begin with, virtue theory admits that communities and societies must set minimal rules or laws. This admission makes sense based on the communal nature of the *telos*. We seek not only to become virtuous individuals, but also to become a certain kind of community. However, any community seeking a common good must stipulate when someone's actions have placed him or her outside the common pursuit. That is, a group seeking a common end must identify the kinds of behavior that excludes one from the group precisely because it impairs the group's movement toward the end." See Kotva, *Christian Case*, 34–35. William Spohn agrees that it is unnecessary to oppose virtue ethics and moral rules or principles. He argues that in fact both are needed for ethics to be practical. See Spohn, "Return of Virtue," 66.

23. Ira Byock, *Dying Well: Peace and Possibilities at the End of Life* (New York: Riverhead Books, 1997), 60. See also Elisabeth Kübler-Ross, *On Death and Dying* (New York: Macmillan, 1969).

24. Hauerwas and Pinches, *Christians Among the Virtues*, 174. Aquinas takes a similar view in his discussion of patience, stating that patience is fundamentally about enduring hardships (especially evils committed against oneself) and specifically enduring grief. See the *ST* II-II 136:3.

25. Eric L. Krakauer, "Attending to Dying: Limitations of Medical Technology," in *Facing Death* (see note 1), 22–31. In the same volume, see also Sherwin B. Nuland, "The Doctor's Role in Death," 38–43.

26. Hauerwas and Pinches have an interesting discussion of this subject, asserting that a willingness to be with friends when one is suffering (i.e., to be a recipient of compassion) and also to be with friends who are suffering is a vital and necessary mark of Christian friendship. This is in contrast to an Aristotelian mode of friendship for example wherein one seeks heroically to shield one's friends from one's own hardships and suffering and expects them to do the same. See Hauerwas and Pinches, *Christians Among the Virtues*, 70–88.

27. Ariès, *Western Attitudes*, 36.

28. Desiderius Erasmus, *Preparing for Death* (*De praeparatione ad mortem*), trans. John N. Grant, in *Spiritualia and Pastoralia*, vol. 70, *Collected Works of Erasmus*, ed. John W. O'Malley (Toronto: University of Toronto Press, 1998), 399.

29. Wendy Farley, "Natural Suffering, Tragedy, and the Compassion of God," *Second Opinion* 18, no. 3 (October 1992): 25. See also Wendy Farley, *Tragic Vision and Diving Compassion: A Contemporary Theodicy* (Louisville, Ky.: Westminster John Knox Press, 1990).

30. Farley, "Natural Suffering," 28.

31. Patricia Beattie Jung, "Dying Well Isn't Easy: Thoughts of a Roman Catholic Theologian on Assisted Death," in *Must We Suffer Our Way to Death? Cultural and Theological Perspectives on Death by Choice*, ed. Ronald P. Hamel and Edwin R. DuBose (Dallas: Southern Methodist University Press, 1996), 183.

32. William Perkins, *A Salve for a Sicke Man*, in *The English Ars Moriendi*, ed. David William Atkinson (New York: Lang, 1992), 131.

33. For example, see Perkins, *Salve*, 127–30.

34. Vigen Guroian, *Life's Living Toward Dying: A Theological and Medical-Ethical Study* (Grand Rapids, Mich.: Eerdmans, 1996).

35. Lucy Bregman has noted that many who write in the field of death and dying insist upon seeing death in an unqualified positive light, such as "the final stage of growth" (a phrase borrowed from Elisabeth Kübler-Ross, a pioneer in this field). While she does not criticize this position on theological grounds, Bregman suggests its inadequacy by noting that there is a huge gap between the view of dying as growth in the death and dying literature and the view of death as hurtful separation from which one never recovers, which pervades the literature on mourning and grief. See Lucy Bregman, "Current Perspectives on Death, Dying and Mourning," *Religious Studies Review* 25, no. 1 (January 1999): 29–34. For a more extensive and theological critique see George Kuykendall, "Care for the Dying: A Kübler-Ross Critique," *Theology Today* 38 (1981): 37–48.

36. For example, a national advocacy group promoting the legalization of "aid-in-dying" has named itself "Compassion in Dying." See their website, www.compassion indying.org (Jan. 5, 2004).

37. For example, see National Conference of Catholic Bishops (USA), Bishops Committee on the Liturgy, *A Ritual for Laypersons: Rites for Holy Communion and the Pastoral Care of the Sick and Dying* (Collegeville, Minn.: Liturgical Press, 1993), 89.

38. This logic is apparent in Catholic Church, Sacred Congregation for the Doctrine of the Faith, *Declaration on Euthanasia* (Washington, D.C.: United States Catholic Conference, 1980), 2.

Chapter 2

Dying Well in Historical Perspective: The *Ars Moriendi* Tradition of the Sixteenth and Seventeenth Centuries

The human struggle to face death is not new. There is a long history of writing on this fundamental aspect of human life. However, it is not readily apparent why one should investigate any of these earlier works as part of an effort to articulate an effective contemporary approach to dying. In fact, current trends in scholarship so heavily emphasize the importance of each individual's cultural and historical context for moral reflection that a move toward history becomes almost counterintuitive.[1] At the very least, it becomes necessary to speak to the issue of why one should turn to history when taking up the topic of dying well, and to make a determination as to which particular works should be examined.

An important reason why it is wise to begin this investigation by turning to history can be found in the widely held opinion that contemporary approaches to dying are seriously adrift.[2] Even some experts whose lives have been dedicated to offering insight into medical moral quandaries admit that many in the field have fallen short when it comes to offering contemporary people the intellectual resources they need to come to terms with mortality. For example, Daniel Callahan, a leading bioethicist, has written that bioethicists have neglected a discussion of the meaning of death and people's experience of dying.[3] David E. Stannard, a historian, casts the contemporary situation in particularly stark terms. In the epilogue to his insightful study, *The Puritan Way of Death*, Stannard argues that contemporary Americans "no longer possess the conceptual resources for giving believable or acceptable meaning to [death]."[4] He goes on to assert that religion has been exhausted as a resource for making sense of the world or for offering comfort, leaving contemporary men and women in a world bereft of ultimate meaning either in life or in death.[5]

The position that we have lost the ability to deal conceptually with death implies that at one time people were better equipped. It is not my purpose to prove this fact historically. I will rely upon the work of social historians who have shown that the experience people had of dying centuries ago was significantly eased by the intellectual, cultural, and religious traditions of those times. [6] Assuming this to be true, what I seek to examine is whether these same traditions might be of help to people today.

As a theologian, my task differs from that of most historians. For example, David Stannard undertakes a vigorous and careful attempt to understand the Puritan worldview and how the Puritan approach to death fit into it, but in the end he places a chasm between contemporary readers and the Puritans. In Stannard's view, concepts such as Providence and even belief in God (key aspects of the Puritan approach to dying) are incompatible with contemporary sensibilities. On the basis of this assumption, the traditions and beliefs that gave the Puritans comfort are dismissed as being of exclusively historical interest. [7] In contrast, as a theologian I seek to entertain more seriously the possibility that the theological and ethical tradition that deeply informed the lives of the Puritans and other religious communities in the sixteenth and seventeenth centuries retains some credibility today. [8] Understanding the teaching of the religious writers of centuries past on death and dying can enrich contemporary theological thought and religious practice. To put the matter differently, the turn to history can be seen as a wise practical move at a time when current ways of approaching death are less than satisfying.

Once we have some sense of the logic of turning to history, the next question to be answered is what specific texts or tradition should be examined. I have chosen to focus upon the *ars moriendi* ("art of dying") tradition of the sixteenth and seventeenth century. This is a genre of devotional literature written for the laity with the primary aim of preparing faithful Christians for the difficult experience of dying. [9]

Although the tradition does have medieval precursors, the genre, as developed by the authors I will examine, has its origin more properly in the work of Erasmus. [10] His *Preparing for Death* is regarded as the seminal work in this area, decisively shaping the genre as a whole. [11] Building upon Erasmus's work were countless others. In addition to Erasmus, this book examines the work of three of the most notable theologians who contributed works to this genre that appeared in English: the English Puritan, William Perkins (1558–1602), the Roman Catholic theologian Robert Bellarmine (1542–1621), and Jeremy Taylor (1613–1667), an Anglican. These three theologians are prominent representatives of each of the major branches of Christianity in England during this period. Taken together (with Erasmus), theirs were the most influential works in this genre across the spectrum of Christianity in the English speaking world.

The *ars moriendi* tradition is significant for a number of reasons. First, it was widely read in both Catholic and Protestant lands, and thus is not particular to any one denominational mode of piety. Furthermore, some of the most prominent theologians of this period are among the authors of the *ars moriendi* literature. These works not only enjoyed a wide geographical distribution, but were also very widely read. Erasmus's *Preparing for Death* ran through twenty Latin editions in six years as well as four in French, two in Dutch and Spanish, one in German, and one in English.[12] The popularity of these works was such that their influence was widespread; the *ars moriendi* literature not only affected intellectual reflection on death, but also had a profound impact on the practices people undertook in the face of death.[13]

Another important reason to examine this historical tradition is that it seeks to locate discussion of the subject of dying within the context of the whole of the Christian life. In *Preparing for Death* and in one of his earlier Colloquies (*The Funeral*), Erasmus makes clear his view that it is too late to prepare for death when one has already reached one's deathbed.[14] In other words, beginning with Erasmus this body of literature focuses on how to live one's entire life so as to be ready for death; it is in many ways about the art of living as much as it is about the art of dying.[15] To give a more contemporary frame of reference, this tradition falls in the category of virtue ethics with its focus upon the questions of character ("Who am I becoming?"), and the development of good habits and dispositions necessary for living a moral life—and dying a good death.[16]

Foundation of the Tradition:
Erasmus's *Preparing for Death* (1533)

The intended audience for Erasmus's work is not easy to pin down. The text's dedication indicates that it was prepared for the private consolation of Thomas Boleyn, earl of Wiltshire and Ormand and father of Henry VIII's second wife, Anne.[17] However, in addition to the commissioning audience it is clear that Erasmus intended this work to be read for general edification by a wide public.[18] Theological writing during this period reflected the fact that this was an era of intense political, military, and intellectual struggle between Catholics and Protestants. However, there is a noticeable lack of polemics in this work, both in tone and content, suggesting that Erasmus desired to construct a work that could be edifying to all people of his day (both Catholics and Protestants). Indeed, it is a mark of Erasmus's work in general to seek to find a middle way between extremes and to reconcile people with each other.[19] Finally, although he is not himself an "audience" in the true sense, it is interesting to know that Erasmus wrote this work with a view to his own death. Erasmus remarked that the work was written for his own comfort and composed when he was becoming frail with old age.[20] He died merely three years after its completion.

Preparing for Death is a work of about sixty pages, approximately twice the length of the medieval *ars moriendi* tract. The tone of the work is rather intimate, reading more like an extended reflection on death from a wise and intelligent old friend than a formal treatise in theology or philosophy. Erasmus achieves this intimacy immediately by referring to himself in the first page of the introduction as among those who are terrified of dying and in need of the lessons to be unfolded in this work. Thus, although Erasmus primarily plays the role of teacher in writing this essay, he approaches the audience as one who shares their weaknesses and offers to accompany them in their struggle with this question rather than with an air of superiority.

Erasmus's intimate tone should not blind the reader to the truly learned nature of his work. The great depth of the author's learning is fully evident in *Preparing for Death* as he includes quotations, images, and reflections on death from a wide array of classical, patristic, and scriptural sources. Scripture is the source Erasmus draws upon most heavily. Hardly a page goes by without a scriptural reference and many pages include several references. Erasmus draws upon images and assurances from the Psalms, Pauline letters, and all four Gospels to build the basis for the consolation he seeks to offer his readers.

The structure of *Preparing for Death* is not obvious. There are no divisions into chapters, sections, and so forth, but a deliberate method of organization can be discerned. Erasmus begins with a reflection on anxiety concerning death, and then shifts quickly to Christ as the remedy. Assurance here is direct: "There is no part of human experience that is so terrifying that it cannot be overcome through the help of Christ."[21] These direct assurances are supported by an extended reflection upon how Christ has conquered the forces that can separate human beings from God, most notably sin and "the world," but also Satan, death, and hell. Having established the centrality of Christ in one's approach to death, Erasmus turns explicitly to what it is within one's own power to do to prepare for dying (chiefly to strive to live one's entire life in whole-hearted repentance for one's sinfulness and in pursuit of a deeper love of God). Finally, Erasmus turns to practical advice that would be of use as death approaches. For example, he advises the seriously ill to prepare a last will and testament, and gives advice regarding how to respond to the temptations visited upon the dying by Satan. He concludes the work by reiterating the importance of a deep devotion to Christ and of the development of the virtues of faith, hope, and love.

One need not read far into Erasmus's text before his overarching concern in composing the piece comes into view. On the very first page of the text, Erasmus expresses his dismay that "there are so many people like me; although they have learned and profess the complete Christian philosophy they are nevertheless terrified of death."[22] It is an effort to understand and allay this fear that guides Erasmus in the entire work. His concern is fundamentally pastoral: how can one offer consolation and hope to those fearfully approaching their deathbed? Erasmus follows the quick description of his primary concern with an equally quick diagnosis of its ultimate cause: a lack of hope rooted in insecure faith or imperfect knowledge of God and God's promises. He writes that those who live in terror of death typically either do not know God, or do not know of God's mercy or compassion. The two are much the same thing in his view since he writes that to know God is to know God's compassion.[23] In other words, Erasmus highlights the development of the theological virtues (especially faith and hope) as fundamental to any effort to overcome the fear of death.

Supplementing Erasmus's primary objective of offering consolation to his audience is a deep concern for their salvation. Neither Erasmus nor any of the writers to be examined here express the least bit of agnosticism concerning the existence of life after death. The continuation of life beyond the grave is taken as given. What remains in doubt merely is whether one is to spend eternity with God or in painful torment.[24] Concerns about the salvation of the dying are closely connected to concerns about their emotional dispositions. A corollary of the prevailing assumption regarding the certainty of life after death in the late Middle Ages was the belief that one's dispositions on one's deathbed were determinative of one's eternal fate.[25] Satan was believed to visit the deathbed in an effort to tempt the dying toward five deadly sins of unbelief, despair, impatience, pride, and avarice. The medieval *ars moriendi* tracts center on this belief in the deathbed temptations of Satan and their eternal consequences, seeking to offer resources such as prayers and inspirational examples from scripture that would be useful to the dying in this final battle.[26]

Erasmus revises the tradition in a way that indicates his dissatisfaction with the medieval focus on the temptations of the deathbed. He unequivocally refutes the notion that falling into despair or impatience or any manner of difficulty upon one's deathbed can be determinative of one's eternal fate. He writes, "No matter what kind of death befalls us, we should never be judged by it. . . . Sometimes those who expire in the most peaceful manner move on to eternal torture, while those who suffer a most torturous death sometimes escape into peace."[27] Although the aim of the book remains to assist people in their dying, the focus of activity shifts noticeably away from the deathbed toward preparation for death throughout life. As William Perkins would later summarize this crucial shift in the tradition: "[a reformed life] alone will be sufficient means to stay the rage of our affections, and all inordinate feare of death."[28] This shift in the context of activity determinative of a good death and consequent eternal life changes the very nature of the book from one which outlines techniques (sharing with the reader skills to be used upon facing various modes of satanic temptation) to one which illuminates the nature of virtuous living and the good Christian life.

Given that Erasmus's fundamental concern is to help his readers to avoid despair, hope emerges as a central virtue in *Preparing for Death*. Indeed, Erasmus argues that the development of hope, joined with faith and love, is the central task Christians should undertake in preparation for death. He writes of the necessity of lifelong preparation for death and that "the spark of faith must be continually fanned so that it grows and gains strength. Love, joined to it, will attract hope" and the development of these three together will diminish our fear of death as our confidence in God's promise of victory over death grows.[29]

The content of this virtue for Erasmus is theological, personal, and largely eschatological. It is fundamentally theological in the sense that hope in this treatise always draws its power from God, and consists in the ultimate promise of union with God. That is to say that hope can be understood best as confidence in the promises of God—promises that Erasmus writes consist of "promised victory over death, victory over flesh, the world, and Satan."[30] Hope here is personal in the sense that the continued life of the individual's soul with God rather than in perpetual torment in hell is the overwhelming concern here.[31]

This concern with salvation points to the primarily eschatological nature of the virtue of hope for Erasmus. Erasmus grounds his discussion of hope primarily upon God's power to save the individual definitively beyond the grave. At the same time, hope is not entirely otherworldly. In his discussion of the sacrament of the anointing of the sick, Erasmus strongly emphasizes that those being anointed should find not only their hope for salvation strengthened (because the sacrament heals "spiritual sickness" or sin) but also hope for recovery from illness.[32] Furthermore, hope remains rooted in "this world" in the sense that it is to be nurtured and developed throughout life.[33] Erasmus is concerned with despair among the living and the dying, not among the dead.

The shape of hope for Erasmus cannot be fully understood by its "content" or object alone; the connection of hope to other important virtues is crucial for understanding both its shape and how it is to be cultivated. Thus, we now turn to some of the other virtues that Erasmus highlights, not only to gain some insight into the breadth of virtues Erasmus saw as crucial for dying well, but also to develop a deeper understanding of hope, each virtue that follows, and how they are mutually interrelated.

One of the virtues most closely related to hope in *Preparing for Death* is faith. Erasmus makes the connection between hope and faith by grounding the basis of hope Christologically. Repeatedly, Erasmus reminds his readers that the basis of hope in eternal life does not lie in one's own righteousness, but rather in the promises of Jesus Christ. He writes, "Christ is our righteousness, Christ is our victory, Christ is our hope and security, Christ is our triumph and our crown."[34] Moreover, he exhorts, "faith is the victory that conquers the world. Fight therefore, with faith, placing all confidence in your Lord, and do not doubt that you will come off the victor under his auspices and protection."[35]

The only effective solace or means to hope is to transfer all confidence from oneself to God. Erasmus calls his readers to recognize the futility of relying upon one's own abilities or merits as a means of salvation, calling them instead to ground their hope in faith in the ability and willingness of God to save them. Thus, in this work faith and hope are mutually reinforcing. There can be no hope without secure faith in Jesus Christ; the content of faith, or the knowledge of God one achieves through it is often referred to as "promises and blessings of God" or alternatively as the power of God to save us through Jesus Christ.[36] Thus, a lack of hope is a sign of a lack of faith.

A substantial section of *Preparing for Death* (nearly six pages of the fifty-seven page work) is devoted to fortifying the dying in faithfulness.[37] Here the shape of faithfulness expands beyond its status as the foundation for hopefulness. A primary concern for Erasmus here is to assist the reader in professing a faith that corresponds to the creed and to "what the church, taught by the Holy Spirit, has handed down to us."[38] Following in the medieval tradition of the *ars moriendi*, Erasmus depicts Satan visiting the deathbed to perform a scrutiny of faith. A full array of questions is posed to the dying by Satan (Was Christ both God and man? Was he born from a virgin? Will he rise again?) with the aim of finding a teaching of the church that the dying person does not believe or uphold.[39]

At first, this emphasis on the importance of right doctrinal belief seems to contradict what I have said above about the intimate connection between faith and hope. Here it first appears that the content of faith is more a set of propositions that must be believed in order for one to be considered worthy of eternal life (i.e., that its content is extrinsic to its function as the basis of hope). However, further along in Satan's interrogation it becomes clear that the attack on faith is at once an attack on hope. Satan seeks to trip up the dying believer into finding a contradiction of faith in order to dash his or her hope in God's promises, with the logic being that if one aspect of the faith is untrue (e.g., the virgin birth), then the whole of the faith and its promise of eternal life are insecure.

The fact that hope is as much the target of Satan's temptation as faith becomes clearer when faith as belief in the promise and willingness of God to save us is attacked directly. The following exchange, found in the section on Satan's efforts to tempt the dying to *unfaithfulness* bears out this point well:

[Satan]:	How do you hope for the reward of righteousness, when you are wholly unrighteous?
[Moriens]:	Christ is my righteousness.
[Satan]:	Will you pass into rest in the company of Peter and Paul, when you are covered with sin?
[Moriens]:	No, but in the company of the thief who on the cross heard, "Today you will be with me in paradise."
[Satan]:	Where do you find that confidence when you have done nothing good?
[Moriens]:	Because I have a good Lord, a judge who is easily moved and an advocate who looks kindly upon us. . . .
[Satan]:	Many legions of demons await your soul.
[Moriens]:	I would have no hope, if I did not have a protector who has crushed your tyranny.
[Satan]:	God is unjust if he gives eternal life in return for evil deeds.
[Moriens]:	He who keeps his promises is just, and because of his justice I have long since called upon his mercy.[40]

Satan seeks to push the dying toward despair by severing the proper connection between hope and faith. Here in this imagined dialogue between Satan and the dying, Erasmus urges the reader constantly back to the consideration of God's mercy, and to faith in the fact that she or he has been forgiven by God through Jesus Christ. These two—faith and divine mercy—become the twin pillars of support for Christian hope.

Mercy emerges as a virtue closely connected with both faith and hope. Mercy is especially connected to faith understood as true knowledge of God. Erasmus suggests that we come to hope not simply by believing in a transaction of forgiveness in the atonement (Jesus who was without sin died for our sake and thereby atoned for our transgressions making possible our salvation). The knowledge of faith is rooted more deeply in a growing awareness of God's fundamental nature as merciful. Thus, the development of the virtue of hope through faith becomes in large part an exercise in increasing our awareness of the importance of mercy and compassion.

The extreme significance of knowledge of God's mercy is presented in both subtle and overt ways by Erasmus in this work. At the level of subtlety, it is significant to note that although Erasmus wisely counsels those who minister to the dying to exercise prudence in determining whether to offer the dying encouragement and consolation or admonishment and a sense of God's justice, this treatise leans very heavily toward the former.[41] Indeed the tone of the entire work is one of consolation—its very composition an act of compassion designed to relieve the distress of the dying. Passages from scripture are frequently and explicitly chosen to direct the reader toward contemplation of God's mercy. For example, in the section of the work in which instruction is offered for those who would minister to the dying, Erasmus suggests reminding them of the numerous examples from the scriptures in which "the mercy of God shone most brightly."[42] Examples here are numerous and taken from both the Old and the New Testaments (e.g., God's forgiveness of David, the forgiveness of the people of Nineveh, the prodigal son).

One of the most significant ways in which Erasmus encouraged readers to grow in their knowledge of divine mercy was through frequent examination of conscience and sacramental reconciliation. He laments the tendency common in his day to delay full confession until the very last moments of life, asking "why do we desire to receive only once what we ought to and can receive every day?"[43] Instead of delaying until one's last breath, Erasmus urges readers to undertake an examination of conscience each day before retiring for sleep, and "to purge your conscience three or four times or more in a year in sincere confession before a priest."[44]

There is at least a twofold basis for Erasmus's encouragement of daily examination of conscience and regular confession. The uncertainty of the timing of one's death (far greater in the time of Erasmus than in our own) combined with a fear of dying in a state of mortal sin is one of these bases. Erasmus writes,

"What a great risk there is in falling asleep in that state in which we shall perish for eternity if death, the sister of sleep, should follow her brother and come upon us unexpectedly!"[45] The other and seemingly more important factor for Erasmus is the importance of habituation as part of one's preparation for death. That is to say that repeated examination of conscience and repentance are not important merely to increase the chances that one will not be in a state of sin when death strikes; rather the repetition of these acts themselves is important because of their effects upon our ability to perform them and upon our very identity.

The importance of repetition and habituation should be understood at two levels. First, repetition of an activity such as the examination of conscience and sacramental confession is perfected through repetition as a sort of technique or skill. As with any activity, the more time one dedicates to practicing it, the higher one's level of skill, familiarity, and comfort with the activity. Erasmus has this benefit of habituation in mind when he writes that through frequent penance one can avoid intimidation and anxiety that can sometimes come with confession on one's deathbed.[46]

A deeper and more significant effect of habituation occurs at the level of character and identity. The depth and nature of this effect becomes clear when Erasmus speaks of the importance of frequent contemplation of the death of Jesus and the communion of the church combined with the frequent penance recommended above. Erasmus writes:

> It will be to your advantage to contemplate both; an action continually repeated will become a habit, the habit will become a state, and the state become part of your nature. This will happen if your conscience is purged of all desire to sin and if we take frequently the sacred bread and drink from the sacred cup, since this sacrament commends two things to us: the unmatched love of the head for its members and the very close fellowship of the members themselves.[47]

Here Erasmus has used sacramental theology quite effectively to communicate the importance of habituation in the spheres of reconciliation and worship. The importance of worship is highlighted here not simply as something owed to God, but also in terms of its significance for the character and identity of the faithful. Frequent reception of the Eucharist, contemplation of the communion of the church, (Erasmus has in mind especially the power of prayer of the full church for each member here) and repentance make one more deeply Christian—a fact expressed powerfully here in the image of the individual as incorporated into the body of Christ and the church.[48]

The final component of Erasmus's reflection on the importance of mercy can be found in his emphasis on the importance of forgiving the sins of others. For Erasmus, an important way in which one comes to know the importance of mercy and God's compassion for oneself is through the practice of mercy toward others. Erasmus makes a direct connection between the practice of mercy and knowledge of God's mercy directed toward oneself when he writes, "Accordingly, let no one reflect upon how badly he has been injured by this person or that, but rather how many things he asks God to forgive in himself. . . . No deed is more efficacious for obtaining the Lord's mercy than to consign sincerely whatever sins others have committed against us to the grace of Jesus Christ."[49] The frequent and repeated practice of mercy not only transforms one into a merciful, forgiving person, but also serves as a mode of making known the depth and value of God's mercy for us, which in turn helps those who forgive not only to become more merciful but also to fall more deeply in love with God.[50]

The importance of habituation for Erasmus is not limited to the areas of worship and repentance. From a contemporary point of view, one of the more significant practices he proposes is to spend time frequently with the dying. He writes:

> Examples have great power to stir our resolve, since they show, as in a mirror, what is proper and what is not. In non-spiritual matters we are more powerfully affected by what we see than by what we hear; similarly, we shall profit greatly by being frequently at the bed of the dying. We will then avoid what we have seen to be detestable in them and will imitate what is righteous and holy.[51]

Erasmus goes on to recommend attention to the manner of Jesus's dying as well. The point that he is making here is one fundamental to contemporary virtue ethics, namely the importance of role models in the development of virtue.[52] Who we are becoming is shaped by our actions and habits which in turn are influenced by our contemporaries whom we hold in high esteem. For Christians, of even greater importance than the example of our contemporaries is the example of Jesus as conveyed through the scriptures.[53]

Erasmus does not specify the exact shape of the virtuous behavior exemplified in the deaths of others, nor their specifically "detestable actions." However, he does give briefly some indication of the specific aspects of the mode of Jesus's dying to be imitated. While some of these uses of the passion are a bit strained (e.g., Erasmus sees Jesus's words to Mary, "Woman, behold your son" and to his disciple John, "Behold your mother" (Jn 19:26–27) as indicating the importance of having a final will and testament), others are more substantial.[54] In particular, the importance of forgiving others when dying is given added weight by repeated reference to Jesus's forgiveness of the sinners on his right and left on the cross.[55]

Erasmus sees in Jesus's approach to death a model for a final virtue: patience. However, since patience is taken up more directly in the work of William Perkins, Erasmus's treatment of that virtue will be treated below in comparison with Perkins. But before moving on to Perkins's work, I wish to point out that when one juxtaposes Erasmus's claims concerning the centrality of mercy with his treatment of the importance of habituation, an unmistakable tension comes into view.

On the one hand, Erasmus holds that we achieve righteousness and develop hopefulness not by our own works but by the grace of God. He writes: "Do not calculate your strength but that of your helper. . . . The anchor of our hope is Jesus Christ."[56] On the other hand, his writing is clearly exhortative and he implies that one's ability to be hopeful, or patient, or to call upon God's mercy is heavily dependent upon whether one has consciously and actively pursued virtue throughout life (e.g., by regular examination of conscience or visitation of the dying). This is a tension that Erasmus does not resolve or even acknowledge. Furthermore, it is a tension that persists in each of the authors examined below. The ways in which Taylor, Perkins, and Bellarmine emphasize one side of this equation or the other will be one of the distinguishing characteristics of their work.

A Puritan *Ars Moriendi*:
William Perkins's *Salve for the Sicke Man* (1595)

A Salve For A Sicke Man was one of the most popular works on dying well written in English, appearing in at least six editions between 1595 and 1632. It was also included in many of the editions of William Perkins's *Workes* that were published during the same period.[57] Perkins was very influential and prolific in areas beyond the subject of dying well, most notably as a moral theologian and preacher. He is indisputably the father of British reformed casuistry and he is widely regarded as the most popular English preacher of the late sixteenth century.[58]

Like the work of Erasmus, Perkins's tract is intended for a wide audience, directed to all the faithful.[59] Although his inclusion of some condemnatory material on what he saw as erroneous Roman Catholic approaches to dying makes this a less ecumenical work than that of Erasmus, its tone is not generally polemical.[60] Rather, it focuses how one should approach death in light of a very fundamental understanding of Christian faith.

A Salve for a Sicke Man is a work of about thirty pages, making it somewhat more compact than Erasmus's tract. The work is conceptually well organized, although it is not formally divided into chapters. Perkins begins with an extended reflection on a verse from Ecclesiastes (7:3), "The day of death is better than the day that one is born." In this section, Perkins discusses how the death of human beings differs from that of animals and also explores various meanings for death in a human context (spiritual death, bodily death, etc.). He also uses this section as a place to argue that seeking to die well is compatible with the Christian life; if Solomon (thought then to be the author of Ecclesiastes) says that death can be greater than birth, then there must be a way to die well and Christians should seek it out. Perkins's decision to begin his work with scripture signals his belief in the importance of right belief or theology grounded in the Word of God, combined always with concern for practicality or the living expression of faith.[61]

Perkins divides the remaining two-thirds of his work into two major sections: preparation for death "in general" (i.e., to be carried out throughout life) and "in particular" (i.e., behavior and dispositions as death draws near). Perkins summarizes the general preparation as "the actions of a repentant sinner."[62] After discussing his understanding of the centrality of ongoing repentance before God, Perkins highlights five crucial aspects of one's general preparation for death: meditating on death throughout life; striving to remove the power of death (i.e., sin) from one's life; allowing Christ to guide one's thoughts, will, and affections; exercising patience; and finally, living vigorously (doing all one can to serve the church and the commonwealth).

In the final section on particular preparation, Perkins organizes his discussion under the categories of duties to God, to oneself, and to one's neighbor. Duties to God include examination of conscience, seeking reconciliation, and renewing one's faith. Duties to self include exercises one should undertake to restrain any tendency toward fear or despair. Finally, in the section on one's duties to others, Perkins discusses the importance of forgiveness and reconciliation as well as the more practical matters of justly dividing one's estate.

Faith is the virtue at the center of Perkins's work. One of the distinguishing marks of *A Salve for a Sicke Man* in relation to the *ars moriendi* tradition as a whole can be found in Perkins's decision to avoid discussion of the specific deathbed temptations as found in the medieval tract in favor of emphasizing the vital importance of faith and God's mercy.[63] Perkins writes that the most important disposition at the time of death is to die in or by faith.[64] He explains his meaning as follows: "To die by faith is when a man in the time of death doth, with all his heart, rely himselfe wholly on God's speciall loue and fauour and mercie in Christ, as it is reuealed in the word."[65] As was the case in Erasmus's work, faith, hope, and the mercy of God are closely connected and mutually interdependent in Perkins's understanding as well. One develops hope for salvation through faith in the promise of God through Jesus Christ to have mercy upon sinners.

Two characteristics of faith as understood by Perkins are important to recognize here. First, faith in Christ is not rooted in an egocentric concern for one's eternal fate, but rather is a fundamentally relational virtue rooted in love. On the side of the human being, the relationship of faith rooted in love is characterized by devotion and a deep attachment to the figure of Christ.[66] This fact is apparent in the following lines from the *Salve* where Perkins writes that the foundation of our very comfort is that

> Although the body be seuered from the soule in death, yet neither body nor soule are seuered from Christ, but the very body rotting in the graue . . . abides still united to him, and is as truly a member of Christ then as before. . . . Now, then, considering our coniunction with Christ is the foundation of all our joy

and comfort in life and death, we are in the feare of God to learne this one les-
son, namely that while we haue time in this world, we must labour to be vnited
unto Christ that we may bee bone of his bone and flesh of his flesh.[67]

The language used here calls to mind the grief one might experience at the separation from one's beloved at death. Similarly, the image of "bone of his bone
and flesh of his flesh" derives from Christian marital imagery, suggesting that
the proper relationship to Christ in faith is not simply a matter of confidence in
Christ's willingness and power to save one's soul, but also a matter of love and
attachment to Christ. Thus, although Perkins does not explicitly connect faith to
charity (the virtue of love for God), his emphasis on the importance of loving
God makes such a connection implicit.

The second important characteristic of faith as understood by Perkins is its
fundamentally active quality. Genuine faith in Jesus Christ leads inevitably to
action, for as Perkins writes, "true faith is no dead thing."[68] In the Puritan view,
one finds assurance that faith is genuine through the examination of the fruit it
produces in one's mode of living.[69] Perkins writes,

> We must shewe our selues to be members of his mystical body by the daily
> fruits of righteousnesse and true repentance. And being once certainly assured
> in conscience of our being in Christ, let death come when it will, and let it cru-
> elly part asunder both body and soule, yet shall they both remaine in the coue-
> nant, and by meanes thereof be reunited and taken up into life eternall. . . . La-
> bour that your consciences by the Holy Ghost may testifie that ye are liuing
> stones in the temple of God and branches bearing fruite in the true vine."[70]

The importance of bearing fruit for faith points to a corresponding importance of
particular practices geared toward nurturing and developing it.

Perkins highlights frequent examination of conscience and continual repentance as crucial for the development of faith, and as a preparation for death. He
writes that death derives its strength and power from our own sinfulness. Were it
not for our sins, death would have no sting because human beings would pass
always into eternal life with God at the time of their death, making it a moment
of joy rather than pain and sorrow.[71] This being the case, it is the duty of every
Christian to endeavor to remove the sting and power of death as much as possible by frequently and humbly confessing one's sins before God, and "to carry a
purpose, resolution and endeavor in all things to reform both heart and life according to God's word."[72] This duty of repenting for sins is joined by Perkins to
the positive exhortation to endeavor to follow always the will of Christ in ordering one's own life rather than one's own will; he urges his readers to be able to
echo Paul's words (Gal 2:20) that "I live not, but Christ lives in me." These ex-
hortations to action under the heading of building up faith make clear the fact
that Perkins understands faith not strictly as belief in a set of propositions so
much as a habitual activity—a virtue. Faith is indeed right belief, but it is

equally an activity characterized by striving to reform one's life according to God's will and God's word, and to become more closely attached to Jesus Christ in charity (to become "bone of his bone and flesh of his flesh"). Faith and repentance are inseparable for Perkins.[73]

The tension between divine mercy and human initiative that was evident in Erasmus's work can also be found here in Perkins's writing. On the one hand, it is clear that Perkins was a devoted Puritan who sought to affirm Calvin's view that human beings are saved only by faith and grace. This perspective underlies Perkins's assertion that the dying must put their confidence in the "pure mercy of God."[74] At the same time, Perkins's awareness of the importance of practices and habituation for the development of virtue (even virtues such as faith and hope) lead him simultaneously to recommend that readers should pursue conscious activities in order to grow in virtue and prepare for death (e.g., learning to bear life's little crosses so as to patiently bear their ultimate demise).[75] Erasmus and Perkins are in agreement that neither divine mercy nor human initiative can be removed from the formula guiding Christian preparation for dying well.

A final virtue that Perkins emphasizes in his work is compassion. Erasmus makes note of the consolation that can come to the dying through the prayers of the full communion of the church, and also asserts that all Christians should be frequently at the bedside of the dying. However, whereas Erasmus encourages Christians to visit the dying for their own moral education, Perkins links the importance of this duty to development of the virtue of compassion.[76]

According to Perkins's understanding, compassion is a virtue that ought to be developed as a preparation for dying. However, developing compassion is a mode of preparation undertaken not primarily for oneself, but for one's family, friends, and neighbors. The context of dying here is unmistakably social.[77] This fact is made clear in Perkins's articulation of two related duties: the duty of the dying to invoke the help of others in renewing their own faith and repentance, and the duty of all Christians to come to the aid of the dying.[78] The purpose of both of these duties is to bring comfort to the dying, and to move them toward greater depths of faith and repentance.

Whereas Erasmus encouraged visiting the dying to learn the art for oneself, Perkins stresses that such visits have as their primary purpose to show compassion to the dying—to be with them in their suffering and to bolster their faith.[79] Here the connection between faith and compassion becomes clearer. Compassion—the activity of "suffering with" the suffering and seeking to bring them comfort—ultimately finds itself redirected toward the renewal of faith. This is so because the only true comfort to the dying is the hope of salvation, which in turn can only be derived from the assurance of true faith and repentance. Perkins writes, "Death joined with reformed life hath a promise of blessedness as adjoined unto it, and it alone will be sufficient means to stay the rage of our affections, and all inordinate fear of death."[80] It is for this reason that Perkins describes the duties of visitors to the dying as bolstering their faith through the use of appropriate prayers and reference to God's word. The exercise of compassion toward the dying thus not only requires the development of dispositions of concern and attachment toward the suffering, but also requires the very concrete preparation of nurturing one's own faith so that one is able to provide comfort through appropriate prayers and reference to scripture. This preparation is also essential for one to be able to communicate a deep personal sense of hope in God's mercy. Thus, the visitation of the dying is a key practice because it illustrates the deep interrelationship of faith, hope, and compassion, and because it points to the necessity of conscious, concrete activity to nurture those virtues and make them of value in the context of dying.

No discussion of Perkins's *A Salve for a Sicke Man* would be complete without attention to one additional virtue: patience. Indeed, if faith (joined with repentance) stands as one foundational pillar of Perkins's approach to dying, the development of patience stands as the other. In his discussion of the particular duties of Christians on their deathbed, Perkins names three: to die in faith, to die in obedience, and to render our souls into the hands of God.[81] The first of these has been discussed at some length above, but the importance of these latter two (which seem in fact to be much the same thing upon further analysis) should not be overlooked.

Perkins explains that to die in obedience is to be "willing and ready and desirous to go out of this world whensoever God shall call him, and that without murmuring or repining, at what time, where, and when it shall please God."[82] Rendering our souls to God is a particular mode of "dying in obedience," namely to "render up our souls into the hands of God, as the most faithful keeper of all" through repeating the words of Jesus on the cross: "Father, into your hands I commend my spirit [Lk 23:46]."[83]

Perkins recognizes that giving up one's soul willingly to God—willingly enduring death and the suffering associated with it—is no easy task for anyone. For this reason, Perkins urges lifelong preparation for one's final trial. He writes:

He that would be able to beare the crosse of all crosses, namely death itselfe, must first of all learne to beare small crosses, as sicknesses in body & troubles in mind, with losses of goods and of friends, of good name, which I may fitely tearme little deaths . . . we must first of all acquaint our selues with these little deaths before we can well be able to beare the great death of all.[84]

What Perkins is advocating here is the development of the virtue of patience.[85]

According to Perkins, the effect of developing the virtue of patience is at least twofold. As the quotation above makes clear, one of the primary benefits of patience is that it enhances a person's ability to overcome the ill effects of suffering and adversity. That is, it increases a person's ability to endure hardships; it enables a person to have strength of character such that his or her other virtues and very identity remain intact despite misfortune or suffering, even to the point of death. The true threat posed by pain and suffering is that it will transform a person from one who is marked by faith, hope, and charity (i.e., a good Christian) into one marked by infidelity or despair or resentment and hatred toward God. Patience is a virtue that serves to protect these higher virtues.

For Perkins, however, patience entails more than increasing one's endurance for suffering; it also involves the development of a disposition to embrace suffering and even death willingly. That is to say that the virtue of patience involves the development of a disposition of obedience to God. This component of patience makes more sense if one realizes the centrality of Providence in Puritan thought. In the Puritan view (shared by many others at that time as well), nothing occurred by chance, but rather always by God's divine will. Thus, sickness was not the result of random contact with germs, but typically seen as the result of sin (i.e., divine punishment).[86] Sickness and death come to be seen as events visited upon a person by God, and one's response to those events seen as a response to the divine will. Erasmus took a similar view. He proposes the following patient disposition toward suffering (one of which Perkins would have likely approved):

> Misfortunes become profit if, free of sins, we bear them with endurance, giving thanks to the Lord for all; they become medicine if anything resides in us that has to be purged either by surgery or cautery or by bitter drugs. Such misfortunes are disease, poverty, old age, loss of our loved ones, and the other countless troubles by which all human lives are beset on all sides. . . . If we accept these misfortunes with compliance and even with an expression of thanks—as if they come from the hand of a kindly disposed parent—and consider that we have deserved much more grievous things and the Christ, though innocent, suffered horribly for our sins, these are no longer afflictions but either health-giving remedies or the means of increasing our heavenly rewards.[87]

Patience thus entails not only an enhanced ability to endure suffering, but also a disposition to do so willingly. This aspect of patience (i.e., that it contains an element of obedience to the Divine will) reconnects it to the virtue of faith and repentance as developed by Perkins. Patience becomes a particular mode of seeking to allow Christ to guide one's thoughts, affections, and will.[88]

A Roman Catholic *Ars Moriendi*:
Robert Bellarmine's *The Art of Dying Well* (1619)

The *ars moriendi* tradition, reshaped from its medieval form by many theologians, did not see any decline in its popularity in the seventeenth century.[89] One of the more popular works on preparing for death in the seventeenth century was Robert Bellarmine's *The Art of Dying Well*. Over fifty-six editions of this work were published in a variety of languages including French, Italian, German,

Spanish, English, and some others.[90] As in the case of the works already examined, the intended audience for Bellarmine's *Art of Dying Well* was very wide, encompassing virtually all Christians from every walk of life.[91] This wide intended audience is consistent with Bellarmine's work in theology as a whole.

Bellarmine was a priest of the Society of Jesus, ordained in 1570. Soon after ordination, he taught controversial theology at the new Jesuit college at Louvain during a time of religious wars and intense theological conflict. In 1576, he moved to the Roman College where he continued his work in controversial theology. Bellarmine's work in this field is notable for its lack of *ad hominem* attacks or mud slinging when such tactics were widespread.[92] Although he was widely known for very precise work in controversial theology, and later for his revision of the Latin Vulgate, Bellarmine was also a dedicated archbishop (named archbishop of Capua in 1602) with a strong pastoral sensibility.[93] He had a reputation for being a mild and kind preacher who used simple language so as to reach as many members of his flock as possible.[94] These two facets of Bellarmine's vocation as theologian and pastor are both evident in his work on the art of dying well.

The Art of Dying Well is a lengthy work for this genre, spanning about one hundred fifty pages (approximately two to three times longer than the work of Perkins or Erasmus). Bellarmine organized this work meticulously, dividing it into two books of about sixteen chapters each. Book I focuses upon the preparations for dying well that one should undertake while in good health throughout life, while Book II provides preparations specific to the time when death draws near. Each chapter is a largely self-contained "rule" that typically suggests an activity Bellarmine saw as an essential component of living well (and thus of preparing to die well). The rules in book one are devoted largely to the theological and moral virtues (six chapters) and to the sacraments (seven chapters). In book two, the rules are heavily derived from the medieval *ars moriendi*, centering upon the deathbed temptations of Satan and remedies for the same (six chapters). The second book also provides six eschatological meditations (e.g., a meditation on hell, a meditation on the last judgment) and reprises three sacramental rules on confession of sins, Holy Viaticum, and Extreme Unction. The book concludes with a rule summarizing the whole of the work.

Although Bellarmine was writing for a general audience, his style seems to derive more from his work in controversial theology than his popular preaching. The language of the work is not overly technical, but it is filled with "proofs" of the validity of Bellarmine's assertions taken from scriptural and patristic sources. The sheer quantity of scriptural references in particular combined with Bellarmine's elaborate dissection of the text into thirty-three chapters makes for choppy reading, and at times obscures the overall flow of his argument. In addition to authoritative proofs, Bellarmine also often includes colorful anecdotes to illustrate his points. These are drawn mostly from the lives of the saints, but also from everyday experience. The anecdotes range from the apt to the amusing with some bordering on the bizarre, but in all cases they add color and some vitality to his writing.

The mood of Bellarmine's work is generally dark, with his emphasis typically falling upon the need to remedy the human tendency toward sinfulness (whether through avoidance of sin to begin with, or through making satisfaction for sin through penance), or the need to endure hardship in this life so as to preserve one's stake in eternal life after death. However, one does occasionally catch a glimpse of the beauty of God's mercy and love and of the bliss associated with union with God in charity. For example, the chapter on Viaticum includes a very beautiful prayer of devotion indicating Bellarmine's deep attachment to Christ and his sense of its importance in Christian spirituality (Book 2, chapter 7). However, in general, this work does not set its spiritual sights very high. In the introduction to his translation of this work, John Patrick Donnelly writes that Bellarmine was not writing here for mystics or others at an advanced level of prayer.[95] Indeed, that is true. One leaves this work with a sense that the best that one can generally hope for is to avoid sin in a world pervaded by it. Intimate union with God and spiritual perfection are well beyond the horizon.

Bellarmine's fundamental concern or the organizing principle behind his work on the art of dying is a very Augustinian insight into the ultimate importance of God, and the decidedly secondary importance of the things of "this world."[96] Following this theological insight is its logical moral corollary, namely that one of the fundamental moral tasks for human beings is to order their lives in a fashion based upon the recognition of a hierarchy of goods with God at its peak. Bellarmine summarizes the process of recognizing God as the greatest good in one's life as "dying to the world."[97]

The Art of Dying Well consists primarily of Bellarmine's description of how one might most readily reorient oneself from a life dedicated to "the things of this world" to a life oriented wholly toward God. Of particular importance to him are the sacraments and the cultivation of virtue. Bellarmine writes that it is not enough merely to die to the world; a Stoic life is not necessarily a Christian life. In place of the false gods of riches, power, etc. one must substitute the true God as the proper end of human life. For this reason, the pursuit of the theological virtues is of primary importance to Bellarmine. Faith, hope, and charity direct people toward their true end of knowing God, trusting God, and loving God.[98]

Bellarmine's treatment of the theological virtues is quite compact. Following the traditional order of generation among these virtues, Bellarmine first takes up faith. Here he emphasizes the importance of the truth and sincerity of faith. That is, he argues that true faith requires both right knowledge and right action. Those who adhere to unsound doctrine (unbelievers, pagans, heretics, and so forth) lack faith as do those who profess true doctrine, but contradict their belief through sinful action.[99] Faith (understood as knowledge of God and belief in God's power) serves as a foundation for the virtue of hope, which Bellarmine does not define explicitly here, but which can be understood as a trust in God.[100] Bellarmine describes genuine hope as rooted in friendship with God through faith, in contrast to "empty hope" that is held by those who live in sin while planning to be reconciled to God at some point later in life.[101] Finally, Bellarmine describes charity as love of God from a pure heart.[102] That is, the mark of charity is love of God unmixed with worldly desires or sinfulness (filthy love, vainglory, hatred for neighbor, etc.).

What stands out most noticeably in Bellarmine's description of the theological virtues is how they are kept at some distance from God's compassion. Whereas in Perkins and Erasmus, faith, hope, and charity were dependent upon and drew their strength and meaning largely from a deep awareness of God's mercy, there is some ambiguity on this matter in Bellarmine's chapter on the theological virtues. Instead, Bellarmine makes faith, hope, and charity largely dependent upon the purity and righteousness of the individual. He does so by linking charity to "purity of heart" and hope to "good conscience."[103] The following quotation is illuminative:

> The second virtue of the just man is hope, or a good conscience, as our teacher, the Apostle Paul, thought it should be called in this passage [1 Tm 1:5]. This virtue arises from faith, for one who either does not know the true God or does not believe that he is powerful and merciful cannot hope in God. A good conscience is very important for exercising and strengthening hope so that it can be called not merely hope, but also trust. For with what attitude can one approach God and ask favors from him, if he is aware of a sin he has committed against God, but has not yet expiated by true penance? For who asks favors from an enemy? Who is confident of being helped by someone he is sure is angry with him?[104]

Bellarmine makes a connection among faith, hope, and God's mercy, but then goes on to make the matter of whether one has purified oneself of sin via penance the test of whether hope is genuine. One is not transformed from being an enemy of God into a friend of God by throwing oneself upon God's mercy in faith, but rather by a prior action of purification through sacramental penance. Oddly, one must be free from the stain of sin in order to hope in God's mercy.

The emphasis in Bellarmine's *Art of Dying Well* is more upon human purity and an almost mechanical removal of sin via penance rather than upon the free exercise of divine mercy. Bellarmine's description of penance is not mechanical in the sense of being false or rote. He emphasizes the importance of true contrition and even of tears of sorrow. However, his scheme is mechanical in the sense that one must employ the proper means (*mechanism*) of contrition. This point is made clear by comparing Erasmus's view that priests should be satisfied with the confession of the chief misdeeds of the penitent and not inquire deeply into the details of every sin when hearing the confession of the dying with Bellarmine's stress on the importance of confessing the full details of one's sins.[105]

A further example can be found by comparing Erasmus's view that faith and love and repentance take priority over the "visible rites" with Bellarmine's view of the importance of a *complete* sacramental confession.[106]

In addition to highlighting the importance of the theological virtues, Bellarmine also recommends the moral virtues of piety, justice, and sobriety as three "which wonderfully assist men to live and to die well."[107] Bellarmine writes that the selection of these three is scripturally based, deriving from the letter to Titus (2:11–13), which includes an exhortation to live "soberly, justly and piously in the world."[108] However, Bellarmine's treatment of these virtues indicates that the selection of these three also suits his overarching theme of the need to reorder one's life toward love of God (and away from love of worldly things).

The virtue of piety fits most easily into Bellarmine's theme of the importance of placing God at the center of one's life. He points to this theme when he defines impiety as turning away from God and a simultaneous turn toward creatures in an embrace of "worldly lusts."[109] Here, though, it is important to note that Bellarmine is not equating piety and charity, but rather suggesting that pious activity is conducive to placing God at the center of one's life. The opposition here is not between love for God and love for the world per se, but between activities that direct one toward the former (Mass daily, listening to preaching, etc.) or the latter (swearing, blasphemy, etc.). As in the theological virtues, Bellarmine focuses a bit excessively on sinfulness and upon the need for utter purity before God. On the one hand, his general point is well taken that pious activity does little good if one's life is equally filled with impious activity.[110] The Christian life must consist of more than worship on Sunday followed by all manner of sinfulness outside of church; here, Bellarmine rightfully points to the highly demanding *metanoia* that is true moral conversion. However, Bellarmine goes beyond this when he writes again of how "God is present and sees all and notes even the slightest sins."[111] In doing so, Bellarmine shifts the image of God to taskmaster rather than One calling sinners forward toward moral and spiritual growth.

Bellarmine's treatment of justice and sobriety are closely joined. Bellarmine provides the standard definition and understanding of justice (to give to each his due), but quickly gives an added dimension to this virtue as well by insisting that "worldly lusts can in no way be joined to true justice."[112] Thus, justice too is joined to Bellarmine's main theme of turning away from "the world" as a preparation for living and dying well. Bellarmine goes on to connect justice to sobriety as well. He defines this third moral virtue as living "according to reason rather than desire" and consuming only what is necessary for the care and preservation of the body.[113] In addition to again tempering worldly desires, Bellarmine notes that sobriety also is exemplary because it gives testimony to the fact that "wealth beyond our needs is not ours, but belongs to the poor," thus serving justice as well.[114]

Following his discussion of piety, sobriety, and justice, Bellarmine offers three chapters on practices or activities: prayer, fasting, and almsgiving. These practices correspond to and build up the virtues just discussed (prayer for piety, fasting for sobriety, and almsgiving for justice). Of these three chapters, the first (on prayer) is the most interesting and significant from the perspective of virtue ethics, and therefore I will focus exclusively on that chapter here.[115]

Although Bellarmine does not name prayer as a singularly crucial practice for living well and dying well, it emerges as invaluable in light of the many virtues it supports. Bellarmine writes that prayer nourishes faith and trust, kindles love of God, increases humility, and leads to "contempt for all temporal things."[116] Exactly *how* prayer provides these benefits is not specified or discussed at any length. However, a clue can be found in the fact that Bellarmine also specifies the possession of several virtues as necessary conditions for praying well: faith, hope, charity, humility, devotion, and perseverance. That is to say, the proper practice of prayer requires the exercise of these virtues, and it is in their exercise that they grow and are made stronger (i.e., they grow through habituation).[117]

Bellarmine's writing on these virtues and their development is not very extensive or unique. His innovation or contribution to this genre lies rather in his emphasis on the importance of the sacramental life, and in his use of meditation as a method of preparing for death. However, since my focus is upon the question of dying and the virtues, I will leave discussion of these aspects of Bellarmine's work to others.

An Anglican *Ars Moriendi*:
Jeremy Taylor's *Rule and Exercises of Holy Dying* (1651)

Jeremy Taylor's *Rule and Exercises of Holy Dying* was one of the most popular tracts published in English in the *ars moriendi* tradition. By 1710, the book was in its twenty-first English edition, and enjoyed considerable popularity well into the eighteenth century. A revival of interest in *Holy Dying* also came during the Victorian period when conduct books regained their popularity.[118] In addition to achieving high popularity in its own time, Taylor's work has enjoyed some acclaim in literary circles up to the present day, being regarded by many as the most sophisticated work (from an artistic and literary perspective) of the *ars moriendi* tradition.[119]

Like Erasmus's work, Taylor's *Holy Dying* was commissioned by a wealthy benefactor. In this case, the Earl of Carbury recruited Taylor to write a tract on dying for his wife.[120] Unfortunately, Lady Carbury died about a year before Taylor completed his work and it proceeded immediately to publication. As with the three works above, Taylor's intended audience is quite wide, with the author targeting not only clergy but also a broad lay audience.

This tract is perhaps the least ecumenical of the four works under consideration here. Taylor strongly condemns Roman Catholic approaches to dying well
by (wrongly) asserting that Catholics disregarded the importance of a life well
lived and instead relied entirely upon the absolution of the priest via sacramental
anointing. He labeled Catholic tracts in the *ars moriendi* tradition as riddled with
"great errours" and "huge folly."[121] Although Taylor does not include a polemical attack on Puritan efforts in the *ars moriendi* tradition, it is unlikely that he
held them in very high regard. In fact, Taylor is quite dismissive of these works
when he asserts boldly and contrary to fact that his own work is "the first entire
body of directions for sick and dying people that I remember to have been published in the Church of England."[122] Beyond this slight, it is unlikely that Puritans would have been particularly receptive to Taylor's sense of the importance
of the sacraments in his writing (particularly auricular confession). Thus, this is
a work written by a devoted Anglican primarily for Anglicans.

Taylor's *Holy Dying* is the lengthiest treatise under consideration here, fill-
ing well over two hundred pages. The book is carefully organized into five chapters that are each subdivided into several sections. In contrast to Bellarmine's
work, however, Taylor's elaborate organizational structure actually contributes
to the coherence of his overall argument because chapters are generally thematic
with their subsections elaborating upon various details relevant to the main
theme.[123]

The first chapter is devoted to preparation for death "by way of consideration" in which Taylor provides numerous meditations on the brevity of life and
the universal reality of mortality for human beings. It is characteristic of Taylor's work to approach the same topic "by way of consideration" (i.e., through
contemplation) and then again by way of "practice" in which Taylor suggests
exercises and modes of living to reinforce what has been learned through meditation, or suggests behavior appropriate in light of what has been learned.[124] Indeed, this method is one of Taylor's most original and powerful contributions to
the *ars moriendi* tradition. The alternation between meditation and the discussion of its practical implications is most pronounced in the first chapter, which is
an extended meditation on the brevity of human life. Here Taylor weaves together poetic metaphors on the shortness of life with confirmation of this fact
drawn from everyday life, leading the reader to two key conclusions. First, life is
brief and one can never know when the end is near, therefore it is imperative
that one live piously throughout life in preparation for one's final reckoning;
when death strikes it is often too late to reform your life adequately and prepare
yourself to die well.[125] Second, life is often filled with misery, so patience and
fortitude are essential, and death is not always one's enemy.

The second chapter focuses on preparation for death "by way of exercise."
Here Taylor highlights the particular importance of the practice of remembering
the fact of mortality throughout life, daily examination of conscience, and the
practice of charity throughout life. Chapter 3 examines temptations one encoun-

ters in sickness and death (especially impatience, and an inordinate fear of death) as well as some remedies for the same. Chapter 4 takes up the practice of various virtues in the context of sickness and death: patience, faith, charity, and justice. This chapter includes many prayers (designed to be read by the dying along or more likely during the visitation of a priest) organized thematically around the virtues (e.g., prayers for patience and for mercy) and draw heavily upon the Psalms. The final chapter is devoted to the discussion of the proper role of the priest in the visitation of the sick and dying (i.e., it is primarily a chapter in pastoral theology aimed at clergy).

The tone of Taylor's work throughout is somber. Taylor's primary focus is upon the need for Christians to engage in a life of constant repentance and to embrace the cross of Christ (i.e., to practice patience and faithfulness and avoid frivolity), and the tone of the text matches the difficulty and severity of this task. The mood here seems to match what one would find on the road to Golgotha.[126] There is hope here and a sense of God's mercy, but always in a context colored deeply by the pain and difficulty of dying and by a profound sense of the fragility of human life (both in a physical sense, and in the sense of human suscepti-bility to sinfulness). Taylor assumes a formal but not an authoritarian tone with the reader; he endeavors to instruct by way of persuasion rather than coercion.[127]

The guiding theme underlying Taylor's work is the metaphor of the way of the cross as the proper model for Christian life. A broad sense of Taylor's un-derstanding of the shape of a life lived in the way of the cross is captured in the following quotation:

> He that desires to die well and happily, above all things must be careful, that he do not live a soft, a delicate and a voluptuous life; but a life severe, holy and under the discipline of the cross. . . . Let him confesse his sin and chastise it; let him bear his crosse patiently and his persecutions nobly, and his repentances willingly and constantly. . . . He that would die holily and happily, must in this world love tears, humility, solitude and repentance.[128]

Given the fact that such a life is marked by difficulty and (more than) its share of suffering, the central virtue that emerges in Taylor's *Holy Dying* is pa-tience.[129]

Taylor's understanding of patience is not unlike that of William Perkins. That is to say that he sees it as a virtue that is crucial both for enabling a person to withstand the suffering associated with dying, and also as a virtue closely associated with growing in obedience to the will of God. In a section entitled "Constituent or integrall parts of patience" (chapter 3, section 3), Taylor explic-itly includes obedience. Toward the end of this section, he writes:

> He is patient that calls upon God, that hopes for health or heaven, that believes God is wise and just in sending him afflictions; that confesses his sins and ac-cuses himself, and justifies God; that expects God will turne this into good; that

is civil to his Physitians and his servants; that converses with the guides of
souls, the ministers of religion; *and in all things submits to God's will*; and
would use no indirect means for his recovery; but had rather be sick and die,
than enter at all into Gods displeasure.[130]

The theme of obedience is reprised in a later section on prayer as it relates to
patience (chapter 4, section 2) where Taylor advises that those suffering should
behave "as sons under discipline" and exhorts his readers to "humbly lie down
under [God's] rod."[131]

Taylor's account of patience is distinguished from that of Perkins by his use
of the way of the cross as the central metaphor for the practice of patience and
the use he makes of the suffering of Jesus (i.e., portraying the suffering of Jesus
as something to be imitated).[132] Here patient suffering takes on a dual function.
Not only does one demonstrate a willingness to submit obediently to the will of
God (out of recognition of God's status as divine, and out of an attempt to
rightly order one's will). Patient suffering takes on additional soteriological significance as an imitation of Jesus Christ; in Taylor's view, any part in suffering
sent by God implies a share in Jesus's suffering and therefore in his glory.[133] By
seeking to see one's own sufferings as an occasion for imitation of Jesus Christ
in his suffering, Taylor believes that one can make affliction a "school of virtue"
and an opportunity to grow in holiness.[134]

A final interesting aspect of Taylor's treatment of the virtue of patience is
found in the practices he suggests in its support. A particularly interesting innovation is his suggestion to the dying that they employ meditation to bolster their
patience. Taylor urges his readers to think back upon a particularly powerful and
holy death scene they witnessed or upon a sermon that struck them passionately
and to keep those images at the center of their minds. Taylor reasons that meditating on such an image that deeply engages one's emotions is more capable of
arousing one's ability to endure patiently than even the most cleverly reasoned
discourse.[135]

Taylor provides more than an ample supply of heavily scriptural prayers
(drawn mostly from the Psalms) designed to bolster one's patience and also to
be effective entreaties to God for mercy. Many of these are quite eloquent and
moving. However, of equal interest is Taylor's suggestion that patient suffering
itself is a form of prayer. He writes, "Do not think that God is only to be found
in a great prayer, or a solemn office; he is moved by a sigh, by a groan, by an act
of love; and therefore when your pain is great and pungent, lay all your strength
upon it, to bear it patiently."[136] Here spiritual practice becomes more than a resource employed to bolster one's endurance in suffering; the very experience of
suffering itself is transformed into a spiritual practice.

As was the case in all of the authors examined here, patience is not a virtue
practiced or nurtured in isolation, but rather one supported by other virtues—
especially faith and hope. Taylor specifically states that hope is designed by God
to support patience.[137] The interconnection among patience, faith, and hope is

repeatedly made manifest in the many prayers Taylor includes in this work. In particular, prayers for hope and against despair are common in prayers for patience.

Taylor is particularly effective in indicating the fundamental importance of God's mercy as the basis for hope. It is in Taylor's section on exercises against despair that it is most apparent that God's mercy is the foundation of Christian hope. Taylor writes that hope rises up in proportion to an awareness of God's great mercy, and that hope should always be sustained by the awareness that God's mercy exceeds one's own sinfulness.[138] Of equal importance is the way in which Taylor ultimately makes patience subordinate to the mercy of God. Despite the fact that Taylor's work focuses on what human beings can do to prepare themselves for holy dying (especially the importance of developing patience and embracing a way of life marked by the cross), he does remind readers that no effort can bear fruit in the absence of God's mercy. Even devout Christians cannot trust in the worthiness of their life for salvation or in their own strength in the face of the agony of death. Taylor writes, "But all that I can do, and all that I am, and all that I know of my self is nothing but sin, and infirmity, and misery; therefore I go forth of my self, and throw my self wholly into the arms of thy mercy, through Jesus Christ."[139]

Rather than point to the futility of one's own efforts, this reminder of the centrality of God's abundant mercy for salvation instead serves as a reminder of the proper ordering of the virtues important for dying well (i.e., that faith and hope are primary). In addition, the centrality of mercy serves as a consolation to those who find themselves failing the test of patience put before them by God despite their sincere, even lifelong effort. In a simple, but moving prayer, Taylor writes, "If I suffer and am broken here, in your mercy gather me up in eternity."[140] Thus, the priority of faith and hope and the abundance of God's mercy have pastoral as well as theological importance.

Recovering the Tradition for Today

In all four works examined in this chapter, hope emerged as a centrally important virtue for dying well. Furthermore, all four authors pointed to the importance of a particular type of hope, namely one rooted deeply in faith. Indeed, the hope described by these authors is one that draws its strength from faith that God's compassion and mercy are more powerful than human sinfulness, and from faith that neither sinfulness nor death itself is enough to cut us off from the love of God through Christ.[141] This connection of hope to faith is perhaps its most salient feature to keep in mind for comparison as we move forward in this study and take up contemporary understandings of hope in the context of death and dying (in the next chapter). There is a marked difference between hope rooted in the expectation of some kind of eschatological salvation and hope rooted in a sense of the worthiness of the life one has lived, for example.[142]

Compassion figures most prominently in the *ars moriendi* tradition as an activity of God in the context of discussion of the dependence of Christian hope upon God's compassionate forgiveness of sinners. However, it also emerges in this tradition as an important virtue both for the dying and those who care for them. For the one who is dying, these authors indicate the importance of forgiving the sins of others (an act of compassion) throughout life and in preparation for death.[143] The ongoing practice of compassion toward others is significant as a way in which one comes to know the compassion God shows unto oneself. The practice of compassion not only transforms one into a compassionate person, but also serves as a means of growth in the knowledge of God's compassion for us, which in turn supports our development of Christian hope.

The practice of compassion is also important for those who attend to the dying. Since Christian hope is rooted ultimately in God's mercy, it is imperative that caregivers bring God's compassion to the minds of the dying. Erasmus and Perkins suggest that caregivers and visitors recount appropriate passages from scripture that testify to God's enduring compassion. I would add that in their very manner of caring, family and friends should try to embody (however imperfectly) God's own compassion and care for the dying.

Finally, all of these authors saw a strong need for the development of patience as a lifelong preparation for dying well. As Perkins aptly puts it, those who would endure well the greatest loss of death must first become adept at enduring lesser suffering and loss.[144] Furthermore, these authors all highlighted the importance of finding meaning in suffering as a component of developing the ability to endure suffering patiently. Contemporary theologians may disagree morally and theologically with these authors in their advocacy of taking the obedient stance of a child under the correction of a stern but loving parent; however, this component of finding meaning in suffering as a step toward patiently enduring it cannot be overlooked. Indeed, either embracing this explanation for suffering or finding a viable substitute for it in support of patience will be one of the more urgent issues faced in subsequent chapters.

A full discussion of how this tradition might be appropriated will be postponed to the concluding chapter where I will attempt to bring the *ars moriendi* tradition, contemporary death and dying literature, and a biblical perspective on dying all into dialogue and move toward some synthesis. For now, I will merely highlight some of the features of these texts that I suspect will prove to be a valuable resource for articulating a contemporary Christian approach to dying well.

The audience each of these theologians chose to address in their work is an important feature of this tradition. Erasmus, Perkins, Bellarmine, and Taylor all directed their work not only to their intellectual colleagues but also to ordinary clergymen and indeed to all members of the laity. This union of audiences is matched by a similar breadth in the content of the work itself. There is no sharp division here between pastoral theology, fundamental theology, and moral theology or even between theology and devotional literature. In fact, the interrelationship is not merely a happy coincidence, but rather one of the authors' key points. Right action and right belief are mutually reinforcing, and so systematic reflection on each should be joined. Reintegrating these often separate streams of thought in contemporary theology emerges as an imperative suggested by these texts.

Among the key practices put forward by these authors is the discipline of "*momento mori*" or remembering the fact of one's mortality. Perkins and Taylor were particularly emphatic on the importance of this practice.[145] At a strategic level, these authors saw the constant remembrance of mortality as a way of highlighting the uncertainty of one's days and the corresponding need to waste no time in turning to a life of virtue and repentance. Along these same (strategic) lines, remembering one's mortality was seen as a fundamental prerequisite for a conscious, lifelong preparation for death. As Philippe Ariès has observed, many in the contemporary Western world live as though they were immortal, taking some practical precautions against dying (e.g., buying life insurance), but not acknowledging the reality of death existentially.[146] The effort by these authors to integrate a deep awareness of death into their articulation of basic Christian spirituality is something for which a contemporary equivalent is needed.

A third theme highlighted by three of the authors examined here (all except Bellarmine) is the importance of being present at the death of others. The practice of visiting the dying serves many functions. It is an important act of compassion in support of one's friends, family, and acquaintances.[147] It is a means by which the visitors can be reminded of their own mortality, and also an opportunity to be witness to the holy death of others that they might be role models to be remembered when we later find ourselves engaged in the dying process.[148] All of these factors point to the importance of exploring the social and interpersonal aspects of dying in a contemporary context, and how that social dimension is to be logically and practically integrated into a comprehensive contemporary Christian spirituality and approach to dying well.

Some aspects of these texts from the *ars moriendi* tradition are likely to prove problematic or of questionable value. Although they do so to varying degrees, all four authors tend to oppose the Christian life and life "in the world." Many contemporary theologians have put forward good reasons to be skeptical of spiritualities that tend toward such dualism, making the attractiveness of this aspect of the *ars* tradition somewhat suspect.

Finally, the theology of suffering found in the *ars moriendi* tradition is problematic, or at least likely to be the source of much controversy in a contemporary context. Submission and obedience to God's corrective hand are the dominant responses to suffering suggested here. Many contemporary theologians have called into question theologies of suffering such as these, which are closely linked to traditional theodicy, and which struggle primarily to understand the reason for suffering rather than struggle against it.[149] Some key questions that emerge are: "Is this theology of suffering viable in a contemporary context?" and "If not, what credible alternative can be substituted in its place?" In addition, one must ask whether patience in the face of death described in this literature is dependent upon the theology of suffering they assume, or if some other viable basis for patience can emerge. We must keep these questions in mind as we turn to an examination of some contemporary perspectives on patience, compassion, and hope.

Notes

1. I have in mind here the work of Richard Rorty among others. His view that human thought and speech are vocabularies and opinions determined by historical circumstance is especially to the point here. See "The Priority of Democracy to Philosophy" in *Prospects for a Common Morality*, ed. Gene Outka and John P. Reeder (Princeton, N.J.: Princeton, 1993), 265–66. Michel Foucault's influential work on the history of sexual morality as a construct that serves as a very subtle and deeply entrenched locus for the exercise of power also casts a dark shadow over the possibility of a historical resourcement. See Michel Foucault, *The History of Sexuality*, vol. 1 (New York: Vintage Books, 1990). For an interesting perspective on the contemporary hesitancy to articulate cross-cultural or cross-historical norms see Martha Nussbaum, "Human Functioning and Social Justice: In Defense of Aristotelian Essentialism," *Political Theory* 20 (1992): 202–16.

2. Arthur E. Imhof sees the medicalization of dying as the fundamental problem with the contemporary approach to death. He also calls for a renewal of the historical understanding of death as an art to be learned. See Arthur E. Imhof "An *Ars Moriendi* for Our Time: To Live a Fulfilled Life; to Die a Peaceful Death," in *Facing Death: Where Culture, Religion and Medicine Meet*, ed. Howard M. Spiro, Mary G. McCrea Curnen and Lee Palmet Wandel (New Haven: Yale University Press, 1996), 114–20. See Vigen Guroian, *Life's Living Toward Dying: A Theological and Medical-Ethical Study* (Grand Rapids, Mich.: Eerdmans, 1996).

3. Daniel Callahan, *The Troubled Dream of Life: In Search of a Peaceful Death* (New York: Simon & Schuster, 1993), 13.

4. David E. Stannard, *The Puritan Way of Death: A Study in Religion, Culture and Social Change* (New York: Oxford University Press, 1977), 194.

5. Stannard, *Puritan Way*, 230. See note 38 where he defends this assertion briefly.

6. One of the best, most concise works on this topic is Philippe Ariès, *Western Attitudes Toward Death: From the Middle Ages to the Present* (Baltimore: Johns Hopkins University Press, 1974). See also Ariès's longer work, *The Hour of Our Death* (New York: Knopf, 1981).

7. History is not a matter of trivia for Stannard, but the conclusions he reaches are at the level of sociological patterns (e.g., how cultural changes that the Puritans found alarming affected their ways of dying, funeral customs). This is not the same task as en-

gaging the beliefs and traditions of the period as a possible source for our own contemporary understanding of death and the way humans should approach it.

8. I am not suggesting the historically naïve position that such traditions can simply be appropriated without interpretation or modification. Rather, I am suggesting that the historical particularity of these texts does not preclude the possibility that they might remain meaningful in our own unique circumstances. To use the hermeneutical language of Hans-Georg Gadamer, a fusion of perspectives or worldviews is possible. For more on this hermeneutical question, see Hans-Georg Gadamer, *Truth and Method* (New York: Crossroad, 1991), especially 306–7 and 374–75.

9. For an excellent, concise introduction to the *ars moriendi*, see Carlos M. N. Eire, "*Ars Moriendi*," in *Westminster Dictionary of Christian Spirituality*, ed. Gordon S. Wakefield (Philadelphia: Westminster Press, 1983), 21–22.

10. The origins of the *ars moriendi* can be traced to two late medieval tracts on dying which serve as a common source for this genre of literature. These two tracts are actually different versions of a single text. One version is a lengthier five-part text focusing on the temptations one faces on one's deathbed. The other version has the same focus, but consists primarily of woodcut illustrations with only an abbreviated supplemental text. Mary Catherine O'Connor's work remains a valuable study on the development of the *ars moriendi*. She describes not only the germinal works of the tradition, but also briefly examines how a wide array of authors over time developed their own version of it. See Mary Catherine O'Connor, *The Art of Dying Well: The Development of the Ars moriendi* (New York: Columbia University Press, 1942). A shorter, but helpful introduction to this genre focusing on its development in the English language can be found in David W. Atkinson's introduction to his collection of primary texts in the *ars moriendi* tradition. See David W. Atkinson, *The English Ars Moriendi* (New York: Lang, 1992), xi–xxxiv.

11. John W. O'Malley makes this assertion in his introduction to the volume of the collected works of Erasmus that includes *Preparing for Death*. Erasmus shaped the genre and the work of subsequent authors by shifting the focus of the *ars moriendi* from deathbed temptations to the importance of living a good life. The importance of this fact will be examined and developed below. See John W. O'Malley, ed., *Spiritualia and Pastoralia*, vol. 70, *Collected Works of Erasmus* (Toronto: University of Toronto Press, 1998), xxix. David Atkinson and Peter G. Bietenholz agree with O'Malley on the importance of Erasmus's tract in shifting the nature of the genre as a whole. See David W. Atkinson, "Erasmus on Preparing to Die," *Wascana Review* 15, no. 2 (1980): 3. Peter G. Bietenholz, "Ludwig Baer, Erasmus, and the Tradition of the 'Ars bene moriendi,'" *Revue de littérature comparée* 52 (1978): 159.

12. O'Malley, Introduction to vol. 70, xxvi.

13. Carlos Eire makes this argument that a sharp division between intellectual and social history (e.g., theology over and against faith and piety or practice) or between the practices and beliefs of the elite vs. the masses is a false dichotomy. See the prologue to his book, *From Madrid to Purgatory: The Art and Craft of Dying in Sixteenth-Century Spain* (New York: Cambridge University Press, 1995), 5.

14. Desiderius Erasmus, "The Funeral (*Funus*)," trans. Craig R. Thompson, in *Colloquies*, vol. 40, *Collected Works of Erasmus*, ed. John W. O'Malley (Toronto: University of Toronto Press, 1997), 763–95.

15. O'Malley, Introduction to vol. 70, xxviii. See also Carlos M. N. Eire, "*Ars Moriendi*," 21.

16. See Joseph J. Kotva, *The Christian Case for Virtue Ethics* (Washington, D.C.: Georgetown University Press, 1996), especially chapter two where the teleological nature of virtue ethics and the priority of character ("Who are we morally") are discussed.

17. Shortly after the work was produced for Boleyn in December 1533, it was published as a book by Froben press in Basel in early 1534. See "Introductory Note" to *Preparing for Death*, trans. John N. Grant in *Spiritualia and Pastoralia*, vol. 70 of *Collected Works of Erasmus*, ed. John W. O'Malley (Toronto: University of Toronto Press, 1998), 390.

18. David Atkinson quotes Erasmus as writing in the preface appearing in a 1538 English translation of *Preparing for Death* that he intended the book to "be made commun vnto many" for their edification and consolation. See David W. Atkinson, "Erasmus on Preparing to Die," 3.

19. John W. O'Malley, "Introduction [to Erasmus's Pastoral Works]," in *Spiritualia and Pastoralia*, vol. 66, *Collected Works of Erasmus*, ed. John W. O'Malley (Toronto: University of Toronto Press, 1988), xx. David Atkinson sees Erasmus's decision not to dwell on Roman Catholic sacramental rites in his work on dying as a means of emphasizing that all must prepare for a good death (i.e., this is a work intended for an ecumenical audience). See Atkinson, "Erasmus on Preparing to Die," 19.

20. Cited in Atkinson "Erasmus on Preparing to Die," 3. His citation again refers to the 1538 English translation of *Preparing for Death*.

21. Desiderius Erasmus, *Preparing for Death* (*De praeparatione ad mortem*), trans. John N. Grant, in *Spiritualia and Pastoralia*, vol. 70 of *Collected Works of Erasmus*, ed. John W. O'Malley (Toronto: University of Toronto Press, 1998), 400.

22. Erasmus, *Preparing for Death*, 393.

23. Erasmus, *Preparing for Death*, 393–94.

24. The fundamental assumption of eternal life (whether damned or saved) is most vivid in all four authors when they make appeals to repentance to their readers on the basis of reason. For example, Erasmus offers the argument that *given* that your eternal fate depends of your actions throughout life, it behooves you to live a life of holiness and piety and to endure whatever suffering may come your way. Whatever hardship this may entail is nothing compared to eternity in union with God. See Erasmus, *Preparing for Death*, 407–8. This theme is most prominent in the writing of Robert Bellarmine. The theme of 2 Corinthians 4:17 (enduring a short trial for an eternal reward) is the concluding theme of his *The Art of Dying Well*. See *Robert Bellarmine: Spiritual Writings*, ed. and trans. John Patrick Donnelly and Roland J. Teske (New York: Paulist Press, 1989), 372–75.

25. Philippe Ariès, *Western Attitudes*, 36.

26. Atkinson *English Ars Moriendi*, 3–9 (for the primary text on temptations). For a commentary on this aspect of the tract, see Nancy Lee Beaty, *The Craft of Dying: A Study in the Literary Tradition of the Ars Moriendi in England* (New Haven, Conn.: Yale University Press, 1970), 10–17.

27. Erasmus, *Preparing for Death*, 420–21. I maintain that this statement is indicative of Erasmus's view that how one responds to the difficulties of illness or deathbed temptations is of decidedly lesser importance than the manner in which one lived one's

life. However, it is also indicative of a belief among Roman Catholics at this time (one which persists still today) that one cannot know with any certainty the goodness or badness of any individual (even oneself!). To put the matter in contemporary theological terms, any one person's exercise of the fundamental option either in embrace of God's love or in rejection of it can never be known with certainty. Some evidence that Erasmus holds to this uncertainty can be found on page 428 where he writes, "I do not know if we can be certain whether the gift of faith is in us." For a good overview of the concept of the fundamental option that includes reference to some key primary sources see Richard M. Gula, *Reason Informed by Faith* (New York: Paulist, 1989), 78–81.

28. William Perkins, *A Salve for a Sicke Man*, in "The English *ars moriendi*," ed. David William Atkinson (New York: Peter Lang, 1992), 149.

29. Erasmus, *Preparing for Death*, 398. The close relationship among the theological virtues in this work (especially between faith and hope) will be explored below.

30. Erasmus, *Preparing for Death*, 398.

31. This view is in contrast with a modern liberationist view of eschatology, which focuses upon the Kingdom of God (conceived primarily as a new, more just social arrangement) emerging within history, although ultimately fulfilled only at the end of time. See Gustavo Gutiérrez, *A Theology of Liberation* (Maryknoll, N.Y.: Orbis, 1987), 92–97.

32. Erasmus, *Preparing for Death*, 434.

33. Erasmus, *Preparing for Death*, 398.

34. Erasmus, *Preparing for Death*, 399.

35. Erasmus, *Preparing for Death*, 402.

36. Erasmus, *Preparing for Death*, 397 and 400.

37. Erasmus, *Preparing for Death*, 440–46.

38. Erasmus, *Preparing for Death*, 441.

39. Erasmus, *Preparing for Death*, 441.

40. Erasmus, *Preparing for Death*, 442–43.

41. Erasmus's specific advice on the importance of prudence in this regard can be found on Erasmus, *Preparing for Death*, 446. He notes that the scriptures are filled with passages that can cause terror and those which can console the terrified. Each of these remedies has a use if applied judiciously and in the appropriate circumstances. His overall emphasis on the importance of consolation and attention to God's mercy is qualified here; Erasmus notes "it is one thing to console, another to flatter," arguing that one should not mislead even those in a state of agitation and fear as to the need for repentance in pursuit of God's mercy. I maintain my position that his emphasis is upon consolation, however—especially in light of the fact that while numerous passages are cited to provide consolation (ten on page 445 alone!), no citations are provided which call to mind God's vengeance or wrath.

42. Erasmus, *Preparing for Death*, 445.

43. Erasmus, *Preparing for Death*, 421.

44. Erasmus, *Preparing for Death*, 421.

45. Erasmus, *Preparing for Death*, 421.

46. Erasmus, *Preparing for Death*, 421. See also page 415 where Erasmus argues for the importance of preparing for death while you are well and strong. He asserts that the short period of time during which one is dying is insufficient to learn to do well the host of required activities (esp. how to deal with various types of temptation). Instead, he

proposes a military metaphor urging the reader throughout life to be like a soldier preparing for battle (i.e., one's final battle with Satan).

47. Erasmus, *Preparing for Death*, 421.

48. Erasmus, *Preparing for Death*, 422. For an excellent contemporary discussion of the importance of worship and religious practice for the development of character and identity, see William Spohn, *Go and Do Likewise: Jesus and Ethics* (New York: Continuum, 1999).

49. Erasmus, *Preparing for Death*, 433–34.

50. Erasmus, *Preparing for Death*, 416.

51. Erasmus, *Preparing for Death*, 447–48.

52. See Joseph J. Kotva, *Christian Case*, 6. See also Stanley Hauerwas and Charles Pinches, *Christians Among the Virtues: Theological Conversations with Ancient and Modern Ethics* (Notre Dame, Ind.: University of Notre Dame Press, 1997), 31–51.

53. William Spohn also explains how each virtue of the Christian moral life is shaped by the story of Jesus and preeminently by its conclusion, the cross and resurrection. See Spohn, *Go and Do Likewise*, 32. Edward Schillebeeckx provides an excellent, concise account of the importance of the imitation of Jesus for the Christian life. His description is particularly good in explaining how contemporary imitation or remembrance of Jesus is not a matter of recalling or mimicking what took place two thousand years ago, but rather a living imitation appropriate to our own situation and circumstances (i.e., he captures well the necessity of interpreting and appropriating the model of Jesus in one's own life). See Edward Schillebeeckx, *Interim Report on the Books Jesus and Christ* (New York: Crossroad, 1981), 50–62.

54. Erasmus, *Preparing for Death*, 448.

55. Erasmus, *Preparing for Death*, 434.

56. Erasmus, *Preparing for Death*, 402.

57. David W. Atkinson, "*A Salve For a Sicke Man*: William Perkins's Contribution to the *ars moriendi*." *Historical Magazine of the Protestant Episcopal Church* 46, no. 4 (December 1977): 409.

58. James F. Keenan, "William Perkins (1558–1602) and the Birth of British Casuistry," in *The Context of Casuistry*, ed. James F. Keenan and Thomas A. Shannon (Washington, D.C.: Georgetown, 1995), 114. Gordon Wakefield refers to Perkins as "the greatest Puritan theologian of all." See Gordon S. Wakefield, *Puritan Devotion: Its Place in the Development of Christian Piety* (London: Epworth Press, 1957), 3.

59. His emphasis of the duty of all Christians to play a part in giving comfort to the dying and being present at the bedside of the dying makes it particularly clear that this is not a book written for ministers in the pastoral care of the dying, but rather one written for pastors and lay people alike. The unity of moral, pastoral, and devotional theology in Perkins's work and in this genre as a whole is significant (especially as a contrast to most contemporary work in this area) and should be noted. Some attention to this quality of the *ars moriendi* literature as a whole will be taken up in the conclusion of this chapter.

60. For example, Perkins attacked the idea that auricular confession was necessary for the forgiveness of sins. He also questioned the validity of the sacrament of anointing the sick and the value of bringing the Eucharist to the homebound.

61. Gordon Wakefield has observed that for Puritans scripture had a self-evident and supreme authority. For his brief, but careful explanation of the Puritan approach to scrip-

tural authority, see Wakefield, *Puritan Devotion*, 12–27. James Keenan captures the essence of this approach well when he writes that Perkins understood the task of theology primarily as coming to know the art of living well (thus, fundamentally practical rather than speculative), an art to be discerned primarily through reflection on the word of God. See Keenan, "William Perkins," 114–15.

62. William Perkins, *A Salve for a Sicke Man*, in *The English ars moriendi*, ed. David W. Atkinson (New York: Peter Lang, 1992), 136.

63. Erasmus makes this move to a certain extent, but simultaneously addresses some of the specific temptations believed to be visited upon the dying by Satan (e.g., his somewhat lengthy treatment of the temptation to heresy). Perkins makes no mention of a diabolical visit to the deathbed, nor of the temptations traditionally held to be specific to that venue. Atkinson concurs with the view that Perkins's work marks a noticeable shift in this regard. See Atkinson, "William Perkins's Contribution," 415.

64. Perkins, *Salve*, 157.

65. Perkins, *Salve*, 157.

66. Richard C. Lovelace has argued that in the view of early-modern Protestants, a deep union with Christ in conversion is central to Christian faith. Any outward signs of faith or practices were seen as useless without giving one's whole self over to Christ in devotion. See Richard C. Lovelace, "The Anatomy of Puritan Piety: English Puritan Devotional Literature," in *Post-Reformation and Modern*, vol. 3, *Christian Spirituality*, ed. Louis Dupré and Don E. Saliers (New York: Crossroad, 1989), 302.

67. Perkins, *Salve*, 135.

68. Perkins, *Salve*, 157. Charles Lloyd Cohen argues that Puritans saw love of God as always calling Christians to devote all aspects of their lives toward God. See Charles Lloyd Cohen, *God's Caress: The Psychology of Puritan Religious Experience* (New York: Oxford University Press, 1986), 129.

69. One's mode of living was indeed essential, but must also always be connected to a more emotional level at which the believer had a deep sense of being loved by God and loving God in return. Activity and attachment are equally important. See Cohen, *God's Caress*, 122–24.

70. Perkins, *Salve*, 135–36.

71. Perkins, *Salve*, 139.

72. Perkins, *Salve*, 139.

73. Note even in his brief lament over the commonly uncatechized state of persons as they approach death that Perkins wonders how so many can live as upright Christians attending church and so forth, without regularly coming to renew "their faith *and repentance*" and wonders why people delay until their deathbed to "be catechized in the doctrine of faith *and repentance*" (*Salve*, 145). Faith and repentance are closely joined.

74. Perkins, *Salve*, 157.

75. Perkins, *Salve*, 141.

76. Perkins concurs with Erasmus on the point that being at the bedside of the dying can be morally educational, but places more emphasis in this regard on the preparation that one must undertake in order to be a useful helper to the dying. He admonishes those who make their visits to the sick and dying without the slightest notion of what it might be appropriate to say, or what prayers might be appropriate for such a circumstance. See *Salve*, 146.

77. This is also true in Erasmus, where the support of friends and a priest is assumed. Philippe Ariès provides a helpful discussion of the public nature of dying during this period. He observes that the bedchamber of the dying was considered a place to be entered freely. He writes that even as late as the early nineteenth century passers-by encountering the priest bearing the holy viaticum would form a small procession and accompany him to the sickroom. The presence of family, including children was also customary and expected. See Ariès, *Western Attitudes*, 11–13.

78. Perkins, *Salve*, 146.

79. Despite the fact that these two authors emphasize different aspects of this one practice, I see no reason why one purpose necessarily excludes the other. Rather, these two perspectives on the importance of visiting the sick should be combined.

80. Perkins, *Salve*, 149.

81. Perkins, *Salve*, 157. Perkins's work is divided into two major parts: a general instruction on how to prepare for death throughout the whole of life, and "particular instruction" as to dispositions, actions and behavior specific to the time when one is actually dying.

82. Perkins, *Salve*, 158.

83. Perkins, *Salve*, 159.

84. Perkins, *Salve*, 141.

85. Elsewhere on this same page Perkins uses this language himself, urging readers to endeavor "to bear [afflictions] patiently." Perkins, *Salve*, 141.

86. Stannard, *Puritan Way*, 63. Wakefield also holds that this was the Puritan understanding. See Wakefield, *Puritan Devotion*, 133. It should be added that death was not necessarily viewed as an entirely negative event (i.e., it was not always *punishment*). In fact, death had an ambiguous quality in the view of many people during this period; it was both a sweet release from sin and misery to God's glory, and a calamity which came as punishment for sins. The ambiguity of death is discussed in Stannard's book on pages 76–77. The ambiguous nature of death is also evident in Perkins's discussion of whether one can ever morally embrace death as escape from the world (*Salve*, 161–62). His introductory section on the issue of how it could be true that the day of death is better than the day of one's birth also illustrates this ambiguity.

87. Erasmus, *Preparing for Death*, 409–10.

88. Perkins, *Salve*, 140.

89. Over 130 books on preparation for death were published in France alone during the period 1625–1724. Fact cited in John Patrick Donnelly, "Introduction," in *Robert Bellarmine: Spiritual Writings*, ed. John Patrick Donnelly (New York: Paulist Press, 1988), 35.

90. Donnelly, "Introduction," 23. The first English translation was published in 1621. A "Protestant version" of Bellarmine's work was published in English in 1720. It was a popular practice among English Protestants to translate Roman Catholic devotional tracts, deleting passages perceived to be doctrinally erroneous.

91. Donnelly, "Introduction," 25.

92. Donnelly, "Introduction," 14.

93. For more of details of Bellarmine's biography, consult James Brodrick, *Robert Bellarmine Saint and Scholar* (London: Burns & Oates, 1961), which provides the most

comprehensive account of Bellarmine's life and work. A brief sketch is also included in Donnelly's introduction to Bellarmine's selected writings.

94. Brodrick, *Robert Bellarmine*, 218.

95. Donnelly, "Introduction," 25.

96. For Augustine on the centrality of love of God and the importance of the right ordering of loves see St. Augustine, "On the Morals of the Catholic Church" in *St. Augustine: The Writings Against the Manichaeans and Against the Donatists*, vol. 6, *A Select Library of the Nicene and Post-Nicene Fathers of the Christian Church*, ed. Philip Schaff (Grand Rapids, Mich.: Eerdmans, 1956).

97. See chapter two of book one, "The second rule of the art of dying well, which is to die to the world." Robert Bellarmine, *The Art of Dying Well*, in *Robert Bellarmine: Spiritual Writings*, trans. and ed. John Patrick Donnelly and Roland J. Teske (New York: Paulist Press, 1989), 241–45.

98. Bellarmine, *Art of Dying*, 245–48.

99. Bellarmine, *Art of Dying*, 246–47.

100. Hope is defined by Bellarmine elsewhere (page 264) as an action of the will by which we "cling firmly to the divine goodness and trust with certainty that God will indeed do what we ask," provided it is for our good.

101. Bellarmine, *Art of Dying*, 247–48.

102. Bellarmine, *Art of Dying*, 248.

103. Bellarmine, *Art of Dying*, 246–47.

104. Bellarmine, *Art of Dying*, 247.

105. Erasmus, *Preparing for Death*, 434, and Bellarmine, *Art of Dying*, 291–92.

106. Erasmus, *Preparing for Death*, 432–33, and Bellarmine, *Art of Dying*, 290–92.

107. Bellarmine, *Art of Dying*, 257.

108. Bellarmine, *Art of Dying*, 257.

109. Bellarmine, *Art of Dying*, 258.

110. Bellarmine, *Art of Dying*, 258.

111. Bellarmine, *Art of Dying*, 258–59.

112. Bellarmine, *Art of Dying*, 259.

113. Bellarmine, *Art of Dying*, 260.

114. Bellarmine, *Art of Dying*, 260.

115. The chapter on prayer discusses how various virtues are a precondition for true prayer and also are strengthened by its practice. In contrast, the chapters on fasting and almsgiving treat these practices more as techniques—discreet actions with specific consequences. For example, almsgiving is described as destroying sins' guilt and punishment (274), fasting prepares the soul for prayer and mortifies the flesh (272). The consequences discussed do not generally have a bearing on any change in the actor's character.

116. Bellarmine, *Art of Dying*, 263.

117. Bellarmine has a sense of the virtues as also infused as well as acquired. Thus, growth in virtue is not solely a matter of human exercise and endeavor, but also a matter of grace. For example, he terms piety "a gift of the Holy Spirit" (*Art*, 258) but also discusses how human activity can promote or hinder the development of this virtue.

118. Robert Nossen, *A Critical Study of the Holy Dying of Jeremy Taylor* (Ph.D. diss., Northwestern University, 1951), 206.

119. David Atkinson writes that "there is little question that Jeremy Taylor's [work] constitutes the artistic zenith of the *ars* tradition, despite its polemical overtones in criticizing Catholic 'how to die' books." See Atkinson, *English Ars Moriendi*, xxiii. Nancy Lee Beaty concurs, calling Taylor's *Holy Dying* "the artistic climax of the tradition." See Beaty, *Craft of Dying*, 197.

120. The Earl of Carbury was Taylor's benefactor and protector. Carbury permitted Taylor and his family to take refuge in seclusion on his estate when Oliver Cromwell's parliament abolished the Anglican episcopacy soon after defeating King Charles militarily in 1645 (Taylor himself was a bishop of the Church of England). For more on the relationship between Taylor and Carbury as well as additional biographical details on Taylor see Thomas K. Carroll's introduction in *Jeremy Taylor: Selected Works* (New York: Paulist Press, 1990), 15–85, especially 22.

121. Jeremy Taylor, *Holy Dying*, vol. 2, *Holy Living and Holy Dying,* ed. P. G. Stanwood (Oxford: Clarendon Press, 1989), 9.

122. Taylor, *Holy Dying*, 13.

123. Chapter 3 provides a good example of Taylor's organization. The overall theme of the chapter is "temptations incident to the state of sicknesse with their proper remedies." Section I contains general remarks on the state of sickness, Section II takes up the temptation of impatience, section three examines the integral parts of patience, and sections four and five provide remedies against impatience by way of consideration and exercise respectively. See Taylor, *Holy Dying*, 68–85.

124. Beaty describes well the power of Taylor's approach when she notes that through the use of practices and an Ignatian style of meditation, Taylor engages not only the intellect but also the will and the emotions. See Beaty, *Craft of Dying*, 232.

125. Taylor's work is the most explicit in articulating the fundamental insight of virtue ethics that one's actions throughout life shape one's character and thereby affect the scope of one's freedom to act later in life. As Taylor puts it, all a sick or dying person can do is exercise those virtues previously acquired and perfect the repentance that was begun long before (Taylor, *Holy Dying*, 6). Taylor never closes the door entirely on the possibility of deathbed conversion leading to salvation, but he is very skeptical regarding this possibility because he sees it as unlikely that one would have the skills or the character required to succeed at such an endeavor. Genuine deathbed conversion or repentance is unlikely because the choices one made earlier in life cut off the possibility of salvation. It is not that one's sins carry a mandatory death sentence, but rather that the choice to omit practices of faith and repentance so deeply informs how one ultimately lives through the process of dying.

126. Nancy Lee Beaty puts the matter well when she describes Taylor's work as a turn toward *sacrificial* virtues nurtured in the context of devotion to God; Taylor paints the Christian life as a perfection of repentance and the way of the cross as the route to salvation. See Beaty, *Craft of Dying*, 217.

127. Beaty, *Craft of Dying*, 222.

128. Taylor, *Holy Dying*, 52–53.

129. Six sections are devoted to patience, two times more than to any other virtue.

130. Taylor, *Holy Dying*, 74. Emphasis mine.

131. Taylor, *Holy Dying*, 132–33.

132. In Perkins, the focus is always upon the Christ of faith. Here, there is more emphasis on the human Jesus. See Beaty, *Craft of Dying*, 217.

133. Taylor, *Holy Dying*, 121.

134. Living through affliction properly not only promotes patience according to Taylor; he writes that faith, hope and mercy all arise from "fellowship of sufferings" (see *Holy Dying*, 131). Such heavy emphasis upon the free endurance of suffering is a potentially problematic aspect of Taylor's spirituality. The model of selfless suffering as the keystone of the Christian life has been heavily critiqued by feminist scholars, among others. However, I would prefer to forego discussion of the potential problems of appropriating the *ars moriendi* literature to the concluding chapter where I shall undertake to bring the historical tradition into productive dialogue with the contemporary theological and death and dying literature, and to move toward a synthesis of these together with my investigation of Biblical resources.

135. Taylor, *Holy Dying*, 122–23.

136. Taylor, *Holy Dying*, 124.

137. Taylor, *Holy Dying*, 51.

138. Taylor, *Holy Dying*, 155 and 210.

139. Taylor, *Holy Dying*, 156.

140. Taylor, *Holy Dying*, 133.

141. Taylor, *Holy Dying*, 156; Erasmus, *Preparing for Death*, 408; Perkins, *Salve*, 135; Bellarmine, *Art of Dying*, 346.

142. Ellen Carni suggests this understanding of hope as rooted in a faith in one's own sense of worth or in a life well lived. See "Issues of Hope and Faith in the Cancer Patient." *Journal of Religion and Health* 27, no. 4 (winter 1988): 285–90.

143. Erasmus, *Preparing for Death*, 416 and 433; Perkins, *Salve*, 154; Taylor, *Holy Dying*, 61.

144. Perkins, *Salve*, 141.

145. See especially Perkins, *Salve*, 137–41 and Jeremy Taylor, *Holy Dying*, 49–50.

146. Ariès, *Western Attitudes*, 106.

147. See especially Perkins, *Salve*, 146–49, and Taylor, *Holy Dying*, 236.

148. See especially Erasmus, *Preparing for Death*, 447–48.

149. Wendy Farley provides one compelling alternative that will be taken up in the next chapter. See Wendy Farley, *Tragic Vision and Divine Compassion: A Contemporary Theodicy* (Louisville, Ky.: Westminster John Knox Press, 1990).

Chapter 3

Competing Visions of Compassion:
How Should We Respond to Suffering?

The texts that were examined in the last chapter took the activity of dying persons themselves as their main focus. In contrast, most recent writing in ethics on the topic of dying has not focused upon how the terminally ill should respond to their affliction but rather upon how family, friends, and medical professionals should respond when someone else is dying. Whereas patience, faith, and hope were the dominant virtues in the tracts of four centuries ago, today the discussion has gravitated toward clarifying what it means to be compassionate toward someone who is dying. Compassion can be defined compactly as the capacity to be moved by another's misfortune in a way that leads us to act on their behalf.[1] As such, it is the virtue most appropriate for those who are bystanders at the bedside of the dying and thus for our consideration of what would constitute a morally exemplary response to suffering.

This chapter takes up two different understandings of compassion. One is drawn from the work of Timothy Quill, a medical doctor who works in end-of-life care and favors the legalization of physician-assisted suicide. The second is drawn from a variety of authors writing in the field of Christian ethics. Despite some similarities, a fundamental difference exists between these two visions of compassion. Quill suggests that the elimination of suffering and the maximization of patient autonomy should be at the heart of compassion. The alternative drawn from Christian ethics recognizes the importance of patient autonomy, but goes beyond its facilitation to foster patience and hope in the dying as well. Furthermore, this Christian notion of compassion recognizes that while *pain* should be minimized or eliminated for the dying, the causes of *suffering* in dying cannot be entirely eliminated; while physical pain might be overcome, one must still endure diminished physical capacities, parting from loved-ones, the loss of life itself and all the goods associated with it.[2] As such, the expression of compassion toward the dying must be an exercise that accompanies them in their suffering and helps them to resist the power of suffering to dominate them. To put the matter differently, Christian compassion toward the dying must entail helping them to be patient and hopeful even in the face of death. The connection of Christian compassion to patience and hope instead of to engineering death "on one's own terms" (to use Quill's words) will be the mark of its distinctiveness.

Contours of the Contemporary Experience of Dying

In his book, *The Puritan Way of Death,* John Stannard paints a bleak picture of the ravaging effects of disease on people living in England and New England during the seventeenth century. The life expectancy of an English nobleman toward the end of the seventeenth century was thirty-five years, and even lower for those of more humble birth.[3] The outbreak of plague was regular and expected in London and on the continent.[4] Waves of smallpox epidemics were similarly prevalent in New England. Medicine could do little to prevent or cure illness or extend life. As such, dying was not a medical event so much as a familial, communal, and religious one. People often acted almost as presiders over their own death, generally dying at home with friends and family close at hand.[5] One's dying often had a rapid onset and progressed to an equally rapid conclusion.[6] The process of dying rarely lasted longer than eight weeks.[7] It was this experience of death that the authors we examined in the last chapter had in mind when they wrote of dying well.

The experience of dying today in the United States is decidedly different. Death by communicable diseases such as influenza, tuberculosis, and diphtheria (the three leading causes of death as recently as a century ago) has become much more rare, with heart disease, cancer, and stroke now accounting for about two-thirds of all deaths.[8] Thus, death now comes principally from chronic diseases, with their corresponding long period of "dying" (e.g., the average length of time from the detected onset of terminal cancer to a patient's death is about three years).[9] The venue of dying also has changed. Recent mortality statistics show that about 60 percent of deaths occur in hospitals and about seventeen percent occur in nursing homes; thus, more than three of every four deaths take place in a medical, institutional setting.

What has changed perhaps most strikingly in the last century is the ability of medical personnel to profoundly impact the course of disease. Medical technology can often arrest infection, bypass blocked arteries, send cancer into remission, and so forth. It can extend life for even the most debilitated patients.[10] This technology should be regarded as a good. At the same time, technology has made the experience and process of dying much more complicated. The line between those who are dying and those who might recover has become increasingly thin and hard to discern.[11] With the availability of more treatments and technologies, it becomes more difficult to say that modern medicine has attempted "everything that can be done" and conclude that any further efforts would be futile. For example, is a man with kidney cancer and a poor prognosis (three weeks to live) still "dying" if there is a 1 in 100 chance that he might benefit from an experimental treatment that could extend his life to a year or two?[12] The experience of dying often involves calculating whether it is worth the chance to extend one's life (e.g. a 1 percent chance) at the risk of compromising one's quality of life (end-stage treatments often come with substantial side effects). These issues are difficult not only for the dying, but also for their loved ones who sometimes act as proxies in the determination of care (Did I give up on my mother too soon? Should I have tried that experimental therapy? What would she have wanted? Did I forego treatment and "let her go" just because I wanted to get it over with?).

Medicine and its technologies focus on the physical aspects of dying, but the experience entails far more than this. The mental or spiritual dimension of a person also comes under assault in the process of dying, and is often a source of much suffering.[13] The fact noted above that today most people die in an institutional setting rather than at home is experienced by many as a trauma.[14] Furthermore, the physical segregation of the process of dying from the sphere of everyday living sends a not-so-subtle message: where dying begins, living is seen to have already ended.[15] Cultural and medical practices place the dying in effect outside the sphere of the human by rendering them invisible.[16] Similarly, what it means to be a dignified human is strongly correlated in the popular culture with being a strong, autonomous, independent free actor. Those who fit this "healthy" description (consciously or otherwise) seek to place dependence and frailty outside of the sphere of our conception of human life.[17] The paradigm of the autonomous, independent, free actor dominates to such an extent that people who cannot conform to it are erased from public view.

Some would rather die than embrace a notion of human life that accommodates or even emphasizes the frailty, inter-personal nature and ultimate dependence of people. However, even those who take a less dogmatic view of the centrality of autonomy can find the dependency that comes with some forms of disease to be a cause of suffering. Many dying people fear that they are becoming a burden to their spouse or children.[18] Many also find their need for care (especially with bodily tasks such as bathing, using a commode, etc.) to be a sign of a loss of their dignity. Thus, the dying can experience feelings of isolation and even self-loathing at their sudden or growing dependency.

In a similar vein, many people who are dying experience their condition as an assault on their very identity or sense of who they are. This suffering derives largely from the fact that prior to terminal diagnosis their worldview or self-understanding did not include a place for death. Their sense of self was that of an immortal. As such, their self-understanding is shattered by the news that they are dying. Any sense of self-worth that depends exclusively upon one's autonomy ("I can take care of myself") or a notion of personal invincibility ("I'm a survivor") is compromised by the realization that in the end one will be unable to protect oneself from debility and disease. One's "personal narrative" cannot accommodate the news of one's own dying, making it difficult to retain a sense of personal integrity in the face of illness. The physical pain and debilitation which accompany serious illnesses are compounded by the fact that this debilitation compromises the patient's very sense of who they are.[19]

Dying is a process that can bring suffering on many levels. The complexities of treatment and the need to rely heavily upon medical personnel can make the terminally ill feel powerless. The physical venue for dying today, combined with persistent social practices that segregate the dying from the living can leave them feeling utterly alone. Suddenly, they find themselves no longer fitting their former definition of "dignified human life." Their identity and sense of self can be shattered. God's place in their lives can become uncertain ("Why have you abandoned me to die, Lord? Where are you in my suffering?"). These are the experiences of suffering that today's writers must address.

One Response to the Suffering of the Dying: The Compassion of Timothy Quill, MD

At this moment in history, any consideration of how we should respond compassionately to the dying tends to gravitate toward a debate over the legitimacy of physician-assisted suicide (PAS). The movement for PAS has captured the popular imagination around the question of compassion and dying to such an extent that the understanding of compassion in the context of this debate cannot be ignored. Furthermore, I want to take seriously the assertion by many in society and medicine that compassion for the dying does indeed demand endorsement of PAS. In light of these concerns, I have chosen to begin my own discussion of the virtue of compassion in this context. My purpose here is not to present a full discussion of whether PAS is legitimate or illicit and in what circumstances. Rather, I begin here in an attempt to analyze the use of compassion by proponents of PAS: what other virtues are linked to compassion here (if any)? What is it about their understanding of compassion that leads them to condone PAS while others employ the same virtue to condemn PAS as an illegitimate practice? Is there any common ground on the two sides of this debate around the proper shape of compassion?

To answer these questions, we will begin by focusing on the understanding of compassion that is operative in Dr. Timothy Quill's work. Quill is a practicing medical doctor who has written rather extensively on care for the dying in both medical journals and the mainstream media. I have chosen to focus on his

work because I believe that he presents the "best face" of the pro-PAS movement. He is firm in his advocacy of PAS, but a moderate voice who distances
himself from more extreme advocates of the practice in a number of ways, for
example by insisting that assisted death is only a last resort to be tried after the
repeated failure of comfort care measures.[20]

Quill's purpose in writing is not to develop a comprehensive or even a substantial account of compassion. As such, the shape of compassion in his writing
must be pieced together. Nevertheless, a relatively clear, but somewhat thin
view of Quill's understanding of compassion does emerge from a careful reading of his texts. He perceives the key components of compassion to include
maximizing patient autonomy or control over their bodies and their dying, facilitating the relief of suffering (both physical and existential), and promising never
to abandon a patient, no matter what challenges might arise, whether medical or
moral. Let me now turn to each of these components in turn.

Facilitation of Patient Autonomy

Quill states directly that one of his goals is to maximize his patients' control
over their own dying.[21] Toward this end, Quill advocates listening as the first
step for physicians in establishing a plan of care. He believes that the practice of
listening is important because it should lead to a recognition that everyone dies
in a unique way that cannot be predicted, and that should not be made to conform to any preconceived notion of a "good death."[22] A physician or other caregiver must listen to a patient in order to gain a sense of his or her values and
desires in order to tailor treatment options (or their withdrawal) to this unique
individual patient.

Interestingly, in Quill's writing, listening emerges not only as a practice
necessary for respecting patient autonomy, but also as a means for discovering
the importance of autonomy itself for patients. In his practice of listening to patients, Quill hears time and again that what they fear most about the process of
dying is losing control. Sometimes this fear is expressed as a fear or hatred of
"the prospect of being dependent."[23] At other times, patients are even more direct and state a desire "to die on [their] own terms" or at least at a time and in a
manner of their choosing.[24] Thus, Quill provides the testimony of his own patients as the primary warrant for the importance of facilitating autonomy as a
component of providing compassionate care.

Relief of Physical and Existential Suffering

The second component of Quill's understanding of how properly to be
compassionate toward the dying is endeavoring to do all one can to relieve pa-

tient *suffering*. It is important to be clear on the fact that Quill names his task as the relief of *suffering* and not merely pain. Pain is a much more straightforward matter; it is a physical sensation typically caused by the progression of disease and nearly always treatable through the use of drug therapies.[25] As Quill himself recognizes, suffering is much more complex. It can result from physical agony, but might just as often have a psychological, social, spiritual, or existential basis.[26] Indeed, in almost every case that Quill presents, the suffering he seeks to relieve in his patients does not arise from inadequate pain relief, but rather from what he terms "existential" sources. Most often, the chief cause of suffering is the diminishment of autonomy as the patient's disease progresses. Thus, a strong connection emerges between these first two components of Quill's compassion: facilitating autonomy and relieving patient suffering.

One case is particularly helpful for illuminating the way in which Quill sees the facilitation of patient autonomy to be a means of relieving suffering. In a chapter entitled "Friendship and Hemlock," Quill describes "Jane," a woman who develops the unfortunate combination of emphysema and a cancerous lump on her breast, requiring her hospitalization. Soon afterwards, Jane develops pulmonary hypertension and a feeling of constant exhaustion. These physical difficulties are not the root of her suffering as much as the fact that she "hated being in the hospital and depending upon others for her care."[27] In other words, it is her diminished autonomy that she finds most intolerable. Soon after her release from the hospital, Jane reports that "she could see no prospect for improvement" in her condition. At that time, she requests a DNR order and prepares a living will requesting comfort care only. At an appointment soon afterwards, Jane requests a prescription for barbiturates "for sleep." Quill has had a lengthy professional relationship with this patient and is aware that she is a supporter of the Hemlock Society, so he sees her request for barbiturates as a warning sign that she may be contemplating suicide.[28] After evaluating Jane for depression and concluding that she was "not happy, but not depressed either," Quill agrees to prescribe the barbiturates.

Quill sees Jane again soon after prescribing the barbiturates and finds that her mood has "brightened" to such an extent that she becomes even "optimistic."[29] This fact is quite significant. One of the main arguments Quill is making in *A Midwife Through the Dying Process* is that it is not so much suicide itself that his patients desire, but rather the *option* to end their life should they so desire.[30] Quill writes that it has been his experience that patients do not take a lethal dose of barbiturates immediately after he prescribes them, but rather that they then take the time to say goodbye to friends after they become more at peace, secure in the knowledge that they are in control of when and how they will die. Thus, it seems fair to say that in Quill's view, the main cause of suffering is a loss of control, and the remedy he sees himself as prescribing is a restoration of control. However, one should realize that the control that is given as a remedy is not the restoration of what has been lost, but rather the substitution of another kind of control. Jane wishes to control her body again in a way that would eliminate her dependency on others; Quill delivers instead the ability to control when to put an end to her life.

Although restoring a *sense* of control in patients by allowing them to have in their possession enough barbiturates to commit suicide is sometimes enough to ease a patient's suffering, this does not prove to be the case for Jane. After a number of weeks, Jane says goodbye to friends and brings all of her affairs in order. At this point she sees no point in waiting for death and decides to bring it about by taking the barbiturates prescribed by Quill. To protect himself legally, Quill chooses not to be at Jane's bedside when she takes the drugs; instead she does so in the presence of two good friends.[31] Sadly, something goes wrong in Jane's attempt at suicide and she remains alive, but in a coma five hours after medicating herself. At that point, her friends decide to follow the advice of the Hemlock Society and place a plastic bag over Jane's head in order to cause death by suffocation.

This is an action about which Quill feels morally ambivalent, but which he ultimately condones. He writes, "[Jane] was very fortunate to have friends who had the courage to listen and respond to her and did not turn their back when they faced a terrible challenge at the very end."[32] Thus, although Quill characterizes the whole process of Jane's death as "made unnecessarily harsh and isolating by current legal constraints," he approves the actions of her friends, plastic bag and all. What we must conclude from this is that Quill's notion of compassionate assistance at death includes within its scope not only the use of "peaceful" lethal means such as ingestion of a massive dose of barbiturates, but also the more physical or even violent measure of causing death by suffocation.[33] According to Quill's logic, the need to respect autonomy and facilitate the elimination of suffering sometimes necessitates the elimination of the sufferer if it is their will.

One should note that Quill's insistence on making the control or elimination of *suffering* the proper end of medical care is a somewhat novel expansion of the scope of the physician's role and plays no small part in his decision to condone PAS. Furthermore, many physicians regard such an expansion as problematic and controversial. As Ezekiel Emanuel has written,

> Suffering—like mental anguish—is a vague and controversial notion; there is no shared interpretation of what constitutes suffering. Consequently, there are no agreed upon and validated standards or measurement instruments for health care providers to assess suffering and to discriminate how much there is. Similarly, there are no clear interventions that should be instituted and no clear understanding of when adequate palliative measures for suffering have been tried and failed.[34]

Making suffering the ground for PAS rather than unremitting pain greatly expands the scope of candidates for the practice (the case of Jane being just one example of that expansion).

The Principle of Nonabandonment

The third and final component of Quill's understanding of compassion is what he terms "the principle of non-abandonment." In fact, for Quill non-abandonment is more than a discreet principle. It is a comprehensive approach to medicine and to the consideration of medical-ethical questions that emphasizes the personal commitment of physicians to their patients and "a relationship grounded in continuity, realistic expectations, and a shared understanding of goals and values."[35] The commitment of nonabandonment both assumes an ongoing caring relationship and a structure of shared decision making regarding care. He believes that this relationship is medically important because it facilitates discussion of difficult treatment options such as shifting to strictly palliative care. In the context of relationship, frank discussion becomes easier for physicians, and "taking the easy way out" becomes less likely.[36]

In the context of this special relationship, the importance of listening re-emerges. The practice of listening becomes important in itself because it can have beneficial therapeutic value. Quill notes that dying people often have a very specific fear or set of anxieties about their impending death that they feel they cannot discuss. The only means of relieving a patient's suffering resultant from such an anxiety is to foster a relationship of trust and active listening so that the patient can share their fear, which is the first and crucial step to dealing with it.[37] Thus, the listening relationship itself is an expression of compassion in that it serves as a means not only for coming to know the shape of a patient's suffering, but also as a means for relieving that suffering.[38]

The benefits and importance of an ongoing relationship between physician and patient seem clear enough, but the reason why Quill would use the framework of "nonabandonment" to describe such a relationship requires some more explanation. Obviously, a pledge not to abandon patients entails minimally that one should see to it that they do not die alone.[39] But Quill suggests that nonabandonment requires more than simply being with the dying. He writes that whenever the dying are suffering and medical professionals refuse to entertain "other options" to *eliminate* that suffering, these suffering patients have been abandoned. Thus, we find that the first two components of compassion (facilitating autonomy and eliminating suffering) provide additional content for this third aspect (nonabandonment). That is to say that what Quill is really pledging in his commitment to nonabandonment is not merely to be with someone in their suffering, but rather to act always in such a way so as never to leave patients in a situation in which their dying is not under their control nor where they must suffer (physically or "existentially"). The commitment to nonabandonment is to an "open ended" plan of care that can include extreme measures of treatment when a patient's dying goes radically wrong, or (as we saw in the case of "Jane") when death is the only logical means of escaping from one's suffering (in the patient's own view).[40]

An Alternative Response to Suffering:
Compassion from a Contemporary Christian Perspective

In the above discussion of compassion in the writing of Timothy Quill, it was necessary for me to piece together what I perceived to be his understanding of compassion. By sifting through his case studies and essays, I was able to discern some key components of what he would regard as compassionate care for the dying. However it was never really clear to me whether these components describe the shape of compassionate care or simply describe what Quill sees as *good* care, cloaked after the fact in the term "compassionate." Quill uses the terms "compassion" and "compassionate" very infrequently; it is only implied that the various dimensions of good care I have described are necessarily descriptive of *compassionate* care. The virtue of compassion is not used as a rich concept that serves as the guidepost for particular action in the specific context of care for the dying. Rather, what Quill perceives as the right thing to do is described and then later re-described as compassionate after the fact.[41] Thus, in Quill's work there is a very close proximity and attentiveness to the process of dying that is supported by a significant body of experience and expertise, but his approach is only loosely connected to a thinly constructed working understanding of compassion.

As we now turn to some writings on the virtue of compassion drawn from the contemporary literature in Christian ethics, we will find them to have qualities that contrast somewhat to the way I have just described Quill's work. The understanding of compassion is well developed, but its implications in the context of dying are sometimes left unconsidered and unsaid. It remains for me to make connections to the specific context of dying well after the main shape of compassion becomes clear.

One cannot say that there is a singular understanding of compassion among Christian ethicists today, but there are some consistencies of understanding. What follows is my own synthesis of contemporary Christian ethical understandings of compassion. In the context of dying, this virtue consists of four component parts. First, one undertakes to listen to the voice of the one suffering. Second, one seeks to enter into that suffering and to feel it as one's own. Third, Christian compassion calls for action on behalf of and in concert with the dying. Fourth, Christian compassion seeks to integrate and connect the dying to the Christian community and to its memory of the suffering and death of Jesus.

Listening to the Voices of the Suffering

The first component of a Christian understanding of compassion entails attempting to listen to the voice of the one who is suffering.[42] Although a somewhat obvious move, listening is not an easy task. It requires laying aside preconceptions we might have as to the cause of another's suffering as well as the shape of it.

James Keenan has noted that it is a common tendency—especially in the United States—to moralize the suffering of others. [43] We assume that we know the cause of another's suffering or death (he smoked too much, ate too much, etc.).[44] Satisfying our need to know or name the cause of this suffering can often also be a prelude to acquiring the (false) sense that we actually know their suffering. The scriptures challenge our ability to make such an assumption. The story of the man born blind (Jn 9:2ff) and of Job both point to the unknowability of the causes of another's suffering and of the distance between its cause and its significance. In the book of Job, the efforts of Job's friends to discern the cause of his plight prove fruitless, misguided, and actually compound his suffering. God's treatment of Job is less than exemplary in many ways but in the end does point toward the first dimension of compassion. God allows Job to speak of his suffering.[45] Thus this move toward listening as the first step of compassion has a theological as well as a practical basis.

How does one go about the act of compassionate listening? Warren Thomas Reich has argued that we should turn to an analysis of the experience of suffering for cues regarding how to respond compassionately to that suffering.[46] He sees suffering as a three-staged process in which the one suffering moves from silence and feelings of powerlessness through a stage of learning to verbalize and name the causes of suffering to a third stage of articulating a developed new sense of self or identity that accommodates the suffering one endured. In the structure of my discussion here (i.e., of listening as the first component of compassion), I will consider only Reich's first stage.

The first phase of suffering might be called the "mute" stage because during this initial time suffering typically reduces a person to silence.[47] In the case of a person facing a new terminal diagnosis, she may become preoccupied with this news; she can think of little else besides the suffering she is experiencing at the sudden loss of her previous sense of indomitable physical well-being, or of the impending loss of self in death and the separation from loved ones that entails or of the dependency upon medical professionals and others that terminal illness invariably requires. This preoccupation is likely experienced amorphously or as a confused question that the one suffering feels unable to answer and may even be unable to articulate: "What is the meaning of my life, of which suffering is now an inescapable part?"[48]

Reich argues that the proper response to mute suffering is what he terms "silent empathy."[49] This compassionate silence entails simply being with the patient while striving to put aside one's own expectations, wishes, advice, and interpretations.[50] In other words, silent empathy or compassion consists of openness to the otherness of the suffering—a recognition that the suffering is not one's own and that one cannot assume to know it already; it must come to be made known in this compassionate encounter. The initial moment of compassion is that of utter receptivity. This is not a matter of the person expressing compassion asking himself "what if I were in the other's place?" Compassionate listening is not the *projection* of one's own fears and suffering, but rather a *reception* of the suffering experienced by the one to whom one endeavors to show compassion.[51] One's own silence is a mark of receptivity and respect which has the further purpose of enabling the one suffering eventually to look within for their own voice—a voice which speaks to the uniqueness of their experience.[52]

The point here is to recognize unequivocally that the suffering one will seek to alleviate has its locus in the person in one's care. No matter how deeply or strongly one might share empathetically in that suffering, it remains that of the other. She is the one who must ultimately endure that suffering; she must ultimately die and do so in her own way. The death of another—even of one's dearest spouse or beloved parent or child—is not one's own. The uniqueness of each person's death must be respected and kept to whatever extent possible under their control. It is for this reason that this stage of silent listening is so important.

Experiencing the Sufferer's Pain as One's Own

The effort to know and understand the pain of another through the act of compassionate listening leads to the second component of Christian compassion in our discussion here: feeling the pain of the sufferer as one's own. What I stated immediately above remains true (i.e., it is still *the other's* suffering ultimately), but it is a suffering that affects me, or moves me and therefore is also in some sense shared.[53] This second aspect of compassion points to its emotional dimension. Compassion is more than the acquisition of knowledge *about* the suffering of another person. It involves experiencing that suffering emotionally. In the words of Diana Fritz Cates, this component of compassion is "to take in, or be taken in by, a friend's original physical sensation, her dislike of that sensation, her wanting that sensation to cease, and her accompanying agitation, such that we can be said to feel one and the same pain."[54] How is it possible to bridge the gap between persons and feel the pain of another? What specific actions or practices make such compassionate feeling possible?

One way in which this gap is bridged is through recognition of the power and importance of ongoing relationship. One should begin considering the question of how we can feel one another's pain with an assumption of deep connection among people.[55] This move is supported by the empirical consideration of who is actually involved in the care of the dying. Typically, dying people are cared for by members of their own family.[56] Thus, when we are asking how one is to practice compassion toward the dying, we are not asking how stranger is to minister to stranger, but rather how children, spouses, or significant others are to share in and seek to alleviate the suffering of someone whom they love.

The ethics of Aristotle and Thomas Aquinas can be a useful resource for explaining how being in a deep and ongoing relationship with someone facilitates one's ability to feel their suffering.[57] Thomas believed that one's friend stands in relationship to oneself as if the friend were oneself or at least a part of oneself.[58] There is a mutual indwelling of sorts between friends or lovers such that "the lover reckons what affects his friend as affecting himself."[59] Thomas believed this to be so in large measure because, like Aristotle, he believed that the best of friends and lovers are drawn together on the basis of each other's excellence of character and conception of the good.[60] That is, the deepest and truest loves and friendships take root among people who are already alike in many respects, particularly in their shared notion of the shape of good character and the good human life. The closeness between friends in terms of their conception of the good leads them each to see the other as "another oneself." My own pleasures and pains are in a sense extended to this "another myself" in a way that unites my desire for my own good to a desire for the good of my friend. The good of the other is so closely bound up with mine that I see hers as my own.[61]

What has been said about the special connection of friendship can be extended to familial relationships as well. Parents and their children as well as brothers and sisters are physically and genetically very much like "another myself." Furthermore, all families share a substantial history of common experience and of observing each other's patterns of perception and notion of the good. As Cates observes, siblings often interpret experiences together and come to know just what the other is noticing and thinking about a given situation even before any words about it have been spoken.[62] The same could be said about parents and children. Feelings, perceptions, and opinions are anticipated. There is a deep emotional connection that provides a window into what the other is feeling.[63]

The practices of sustaining a friendship or a close family provide one means of bridging the gap between sufferer and compassionate caregiver. An additional practice more specifically geared toward seeking to know and share another's pain involves focusing on the embodied nature of their suffering. It is sometimes not enough to desire intellectually to know the suffering of the person in one's care; one's imagination and physical presence must be engaged as well.

Again the work of Diana Fritz Cates is helpful here. She recounts the story of visiting a sick friend who is bed-bound and in pain. In addition to actively listening, she seeks to be physically near her suffering friend, curling up beside him in his bed. Next, she attempts to breath in unison with her friend, while imagining that this connection is uniting them. Cates has found that shared breathing can be a means of deeper insight into the other's experience of pain. She writes,

> I recall, for example, breathing in synchronicity with a friend while he was suffering acute abdominal pain and realizing only in our quick, shallow, irregular breathing that he was utterly terrified. I could see that he was in pain, and I suffered pain *at* his pain, but it was not until my body was caught up in his body's basic movement that I discerned the particular nature of his pain as terror and felt this terror *with* him.[64]

Thus, Christian compassion must draw upon the resources of attentive listening, a history of shared experience and perception, and practices that engage the imagination and physically focus our attention on the suffering of the other in order to understand, feel, and be moved by that suffering.

Acting to Ease or Eliminate Suffering

The third part of compassion is action on behalf of and in concert with the dying with the intention of easing or eliminating their suffering. I describe and analyze this third dimension of compassion as follows: First, I explain why compassionate activity should strive to be empowering and nonviolent rather than coercive (thus that it should respect the autonomy of the dying). Second, I offer a specific practice that exemplifies such a strategy of empowerment: restoring the voice of the dying. Finally, I explain briefly why I see the endorsement of legalized PAS as outside the sphere of Christian compassion.

The Importance of Empowerment; The Dangers of Coercion

In *Tragic Vision and Divine Compassion,* Wendy Farley explains the nature of compassionate empowerment by describing two contrasting types of power. One kind of power is coercive and dominating; this is the power characteristic of evil—marked by domination, violence, and terror.[65] This type of power always carries with it an irresistible temptation to dominate, and therefore it can never truly be used as a means to a good end. Even if coercive or violent power is used to throw off an oppressor, the mere exercise of power of this kind corrupts its users so thoroughly that they would be doomed to take the place of the specific oppressor rather than eliminate oppression. The would-be liberators would find themselves becoming instead the new oppressors.[66] Although she makes no mention of this tradition, Farley's argument resonates strongly with the pacifist tradition within Christianity, particularly the Anabaptists of the sixteenth century who held that any resort to "the sword" by Christians was an inherently corrupt move.[67]

In opposition to coercive, violent, dominating power, Farley proposes "power for preservation," which is the type of power characteristic of the good and of compassion. This power refuses to fight evil on its own terms, choosing instead to repudiate the desire for domination.[68] Farley explains the distinction between these two types of power as follows:

> Power as domination or even as benevolent coercion cannot redeem because it falsifies the nature of human being and it betrays the nature of love. To resist suffering demands strength and courage, hence power. This is the internal paradox of compassion: it is a power but it cannot coerce. It must resist in this uneasy tension, empowering others to resist suffering without becoming indifferent or overwhelming. Redemptive power gives power to someone else: it is empowering rather than controlling.[69]

Thus, it is important for Christian acts of compassion to be nonviolent and noncoercive both to avoid the corruption of the caregiver and to maximize the empowerment of the sufferer.

Farley's warning that controlling, coercive, or violent behavior should not be exercised in the name of compassion is consistent with similar concerns expressed by theologians in their analysis of other virtues that involve care. For example, Christine Pohl warns that the virtue of hospitality is sometimes practiced in such a way that the others are made to be the passive recipients of one's efforts. She writes, "Under the guise of acting generously, [some] avoid the questions of maldistribution of power and resources and reinforce existing patterns of status and wealth. They make others, especially poor people passive recipients in their own families, churches, or communities."[70] This is a warning that should also be applied to the practice of compassion. Compassion should not be practiced in such a way that it controls or disempowers the dying. One must not forget the lessons learned from silent, compassionate listening described above; the dying must be allowed to die in their own, unique way and empowered to face their own suffering.[71]

Farley's move to describe the end of compassionate action as alleviating the suffering of the dying by empowering them gains additional legitimacy from the fact that it is very consistent with the latest guidelines on patient care found in the *Ethical and Religious Directives for Catholic Healthcare Services*.[72] The 1995 revision of the *Directives* is distinguished by a shift from a largely paternalistic "best-interest" model of medical decision making (found in the previous version) toward a model that urges health care providers to endeavor to carry out the wishes of responsible patients within certain parameters.[73] Thus, these directives affirm that Christians should see their role as empowering the dying to exercise their freedom and to shape their plan of care. They are to be empowered to discern with God the meaning of this experience of suffering and dying, and also to discern how God is calling them to act in the face of it.[74]

The general nature of compassionate action as empowering and supportive of freedom is now clear, but its shape must be further specified. Recall that in our discussion of listening above only the first stage of suffering (mute) and its corresponding response were discussed. Let us now turn to another mode of compassionate activity that follows silent empathy: expressive compassion—the practice of restoring the voice of the dying.[75]

Restoring the Voice of the Dying

Warren Reich notes that there are many "languages" that can be offered to the suffering for use in finding their voice and verbalizing their suffering. For example, even the technical language of a medical diagnosis can serve this purpose. With a diagnosis, one is given the power to name one's affliction (naming can be a source of power) and the power of knowing what one can typically expect from the trajectory of that disease.[76] A different, and specifically religious form of "language" that Reich does not take up is the Psalm.[77] These traditional, poetic prayers of Judaism and Christianity have been used for centuries to describe the negative as well as the positive moments of human life—moments of praise for God, and moments of despair. Walter Brueggemann has argued that some of the Psalms—the Psalms of Lament—are particularly suited to reflect moments of tragedy and disorientation.[78] The dying often are experiencing just such a radical disorientation; their world is perceived to be falling apart as they face imminent separation from the people and places they have loved, their previous sense of self (as physically inviolable) is shattered, and so forth. Thus, the Psalms of Lament are written from the point of view of people in the same sort of situation as the dying.[79] They speak not only to the physical, but also to the psychological and social aspects of suffering.[80] As such, they are ideally suited to helping the dying to give voice to their specific suffering.[81]

Psalm 77 provides one example of a prayer that can give voice to some of the experiences of the dying.[82] This Psalm is from the point of view of one who is silenced by their suffering ("I am so troubled that I cannot speak," v. 4), and whose soul refuses to be comforted. The speaker feels abandoned by God, and wonders if that state of abandonment is permanent ("Has God's steadfast love forever ceased? Are God's promises at an end for all time?" v. 8). A Psalm of this kind "gives permission" to the one praying it to question God and ask the difficult question of where God is in one's suffering. It puts into words what the dying might have been feeling but was unable to express in the stunned silence that can follow terminal diagnosis.

Psalm 88 provides another example. Here, the Psalmist is again overtaken by desolation and hopelessness, focusing on the nearness of death and the isolation that it will bring. But, whereas the writer of Ps 77 could only turn to memories of better times, the Psalmist in Ps 88 is better able to express his or her despair and puts questions to God, demanding to know *why* they feel so alone, why they must suffer and die.[83] There is more of an expectation here of a response from God ("O Lord, my God, I call for help by day; . . . Let my prayer come before thee, incline thy ear to my cry!" v. 1-2), although the shape of God's response remains unclear. A more exhortative prayer is Psalm 143 where the writer expresses a deep longing for God and implores God to deliver him or her from affliction. Thus, we find even in these few short examples the expression of a wide range of emotions that the dying might be experiencing, but feel unable to express: isolation or abandonment, anger against God, questioning the reason for or meaning of their suffering, a longing for deliverance, a hope that God is present even in their moment of darkness.

The Incompatibility of Christian Compassion and PAS

Clearly, praying the Psalms with the dying is compatible with Christian compassion or even a necessary part of it, but what about other methods of acting to relieve suffering? More specifically, we must ask whether PAS is an empowerment of the dying that is compatible with Christian compassion. At first glance, the evidence here seems contradictory. On the one hand, the use of lethal means is an example of the use of dominating or coercive force. It is an act of control or the unilateral execution of one's own personal will. On the other hand, from the perspective of the physician or other caregiver who might facilitate suicide, it is the quintessential act of empowering one who is suffering—a facilitation of their freedom to find "death on their own terms."[84] How are we to resolve this question?

Let me begin by making some clarifications. First, this is a discussion of the *virtue* of compassion. I want to describe what should be a regular practice or a normal course of action, not what one should do in extreme circumstances. I am not ruling out that in some rare instances PAS might be justified, but I see those circumstances as extreme and extraordinary. Second, the argument against PAS included here is by no means comprehensive. I will not develop the question of how normalizing PAS might be a violation of justice, for example.[85] I only want to consider PAS in the context of our discussion of *compassion*. That being said, I will proceed by arguing briefly that legalizing PAS is contrary to a Christian notion of compassion because it is ultimately disempowering (when considered from a social perspective) and because it compromises other important goods, including the social goods necessary to sustain the practice of compassion for the dying.

On the face of it, it seems that providing the dying with an option that they can choose to exercise in their autonomy must be empowering. However, when the consequences of providing such a legally sanctioned option are considered, its status as empowering becomes more doubtful. As Allen Verhey has argued, seeking to maximize freedom by increasing options can often have the effect of eliminating other existing options or changing their character radically, with the ultimate result being a net loss in freedom.[86] In the specific context of dying, providing the option of legalized assisted suicide would effectively eliminate the "option" of staying alive without having to justify one's own existence; the sick, suffering, and potentially vulnerable become accountable for living, and he or she can be asked to justify that choice. The act of providing a choice can actually create some pressure to make a particular choice (i.e., those who see themselves to be "a burden" to their loved ones would be under more pressure to "choose" to have themselves euthanized).[87]

In a similar vein, Daniel Callahan has argued that the legalization and practice of PAS would change the social dynamics that support a patient's ability to choose not to take his or her own life. He writes:

> By assuming that the relief of suffering is a goal important enough to legitimate killing as a way of achieving it, we corrupt the idea of such relief as a social goal and duty. We cease helping to bear one another's suffering, but eliminate altogether the person who suffers. We thereby jeopardize both the future of self-determination and the kind of community that furthers its members' capacity to bear one another's suffering. Why bear what can be eliminated altogether? For the sake of controlling the conditions of death, we would introduce a fundamental change in the conditions of living a life. In the name of controlling our mortality, we would enter a claim to change the nature of human relationships.[88]

The regular practice of legalized PAS reduces freedom by changing the shape of our community and our relationships such that it compromises the network of compassion that makes the endurance of dying possible.

Diana Fritz Cates's work is helpful in summarizing why the legalization of PAS should not be included under the scope of Christian compassion. She writes that compassion seeks to promote the good on at least three levels: my own good, the good of the specific other in my care, and the common good.[89] Our desire to benefit the one in our care in a way that they want to be benefited (i.e., to promote their good as they see it) might pull us toward honoring their request for our help in committing suicide. However, Wendy Farley's discussion of power tells us that this move would not promote our own good (the use of violent or coercive power corrupts the one who uses it), and Callahan and Verhey (among others) tell us that the regularization or legalization of such a measure is disempowering in the long run and compromises the ability of one's community to sustain forms of compassion other than PAS. For these reasons, I would conclude that PAS as a regulated, legal practice runs contrary to Christian compassion.[90]

Connecting the Dying to the Christian Community

The fourth and final aspect of Christian compassion involves connecting the dying to the Christian community and their remembrance of the suffering and death of Jesus. One of the main concerns of the dying is a fear of abandonment or of dying alone. As indicated in the section on the experience of dying above, dying today can be an isolating experience that brings with it a debilitation and dependency that can make the dying see themselves as less than human.

Given these facts, an important part of sharing in the pain of the dying entails removing their sense of isolation and assuring them of their ongoing dignity, humanity, and place in the community. One should assure the dying and remind oneself that the eventual debilitation of our physical capacities, our aging and our dying are all part of the very meaning of being human, and therefore not a source of shame.[91] Such a move affirms a place in the human community for those facing imminent death and places caregivers in solidarity with them. This solidarity makes an affirmation of the dignity of the infirm "other," and also requires some introspection and the recognition of one's own vulnerability and mortality. Annette Geoffrion Brownlee captures this fact well:

> To tell someone yes, your life is over and you feel useless, but you are not an outcast and I will not shun you, requires that we look into the mirror and accept our own aging selves, accept the part of us that is infirm, incontinent, and unproductive. This acceptance, to be a source of hope, must go beyond recognition; it must be a deep form of acceptance.[92]

Thus, this aspect of compassion for the dying points to how its exercise is not merely for the benefit of the dying, but also for those who care for them. Seeing that one shares with the dying an ultimate future of infirmity and dependence not only serves to affirm the worth and dignity of the dying, it also assists the caregiver in coming to know the true nature of their humanity.

In addition to emphasizing a union between caregivers and the dying rooted in their common humanity, the exercise of Christian compassion breaks through the isolation that can engulf the dying by reminding them of their membership in the specifically Christian community and by linking them and their suffering to Jesus Christ. Every year, Catholic Christians, and others who follow a similar liturgical calendar and cycle of readings, recall the birth, life of ministry, and death of Jesus. In this way, even if at an unconscious level, a sense of the shape of life is proposed—one that includes suffering and sacrifice and death.[93] Similarly, in the regular celebration of the Eucharist, the community comes together to remember the death of Jesus and to celebrate his resurrection. These two aspects of liturgy (the narrative journey of life leading ultimately to Jerusalem and the cross in the Liturgy of the Word, and the remembrance of the death and resurrection of Jesus in the Liturgy of the Eucharist) together provide a framework in which suffering and death can be contextualized and seen to be meaningful and even redemptive.

These liturgical aspects of membership in the Christian community are important for at least two reasons. First, over one's lifetime prior to the stage of active dying, they provide time and quiet space for the contemplation of death— of its place within human life, its meaning, and how one might come to terms with it (e.g., with the aid of Christian hope). In a culture where death remains largely removed (at least at an existential level), this is a valuable resource.[94] Second, involvement in liturgy provides a narrative "vocabulary" for developing a vision of one's own life story that can accommodate suffering and death. In other words, being shaped by the narrative of the life of Jesus in which suffering and death play a significant part can make easier the task undertaken by the dying to find meaning and coherence in the story of their own lives and the course of their own suffering and dying. The ability to make suffering a purposeful activity and to construct a personal narrative that "gives coherence to the distinctive events of the long-term course of suffering" requires not only the physical and emotional support of a community, but also "narrative" support that aides the dying in their struggle to find meaning in suffering and death.[95]

The work of William Perkins, explored in the last chapter, further clarifies the sense in which nurturing someone's faith is an expression of *compassion*. Perkins concerned himself primarily with the suffering experienced by the dying that derives from fear of death (or damnation). He saw such suffering to be rooted in a lack of faith and hope and therefore believed that the appropriate response to this suffering was to nurture these two virtues.[96] In other words, one of the key things Perkins saw to be accomplished in attentiveness to scripture, participation in liturgy, and finding a connection between the life of Christ and one's own was the development of faith and hope.

The fruits of these virtues included a deep attachment to Christ and a life of right living and active service to Christ and neighbor. These obviously have an inherent value. However, in the context of dying, nurturing faith and hope can also be seen as an expression of compassion. This is so because the only true comfort to the dying is the hope of salvation, which in turn can only be derived from the assurance of true faith and repentance. Perkins writes, "Death joined with reformed life hath a promise of blessedness as adjoined unto it, and it alone will be sufficient means to stay the rage of our affections, and all inordinate fear of death."[97] It is for this reason that Perkins describes the duties of visitors to the dying as bolstering their faith through the use of appropriate prayers and reference to God's word. The exercise of compassion toward the dying thus not only requires the development of dispositions of concern and attachment toward the suffering, it also requires the very concrete preparation of nurturing one's own faith so that one is able to provide comfort through appropriate prayers and reference to scripture. This preparation is also essential for one to be able to communicate a deep personal sense of hope in God's mercy. Thus, integrating the dying into the community of faith is a key practice because it illustrates the deep interrelationship of faith, hope, and compassion, and because it points to the necessity of conscious, concrete activity to nurture those virtues and make them of value in the context of dying.

Linking Compassion and Patience

The shape of compassion as I have depicted it above is really incomplete until its place in a more comprehensive web of virtues has been described. It is a classic principle in virtue theory to say that the virtues are a unity and therefore can only be understood as part of a whole.[98] In Timothy Quill's understanding of compassion, for example, the exercise of compassion is linked to the promotion of individual autonomy and control in his patients; he believes compassionate medicine should maximize a patient's ability to control death "on their own terms."[99] I propose that a contrasting Christian understanding of compassion toward the dying should instead seek to nurture and support the exercise of patience by the dying. Thus, while both approaches will be the same in their attempt to relieve maximally the physical pain of the dying, and in their insistence on the importance of companionship or nonabandonment, they will differ in their response to the patients' "existential" suffering.[100]

There is little contemporary sense of the nature of patience and little regard for its importance. In a recent lecture on medical and theological perspectives on pain and pain relief, Dr. Arthur Kleinman noted that there are virtually no cultural resources for helping patients to endure in the face of suffering.[101] The single culturally reinforced response to pain and suffering is to strive for its eradication; in instances where this fails or is not entirely possible, patients and their caregivers are at a loss as to what to recommend, especially at a spiritual or psychological level. In his remarks, Kleinman indicated that he thought it would be valuable if scholars of religions as well as professionals in ministry could find some way of helping patients to tap into a religious or "spiritual" resource for building what he termed "endurance."

Unfortunately, contemporary theologians have not been prolific on the subject of building endurance, or what I would prefer to call, patience. This trend is not new. David Baily Harned has traced the obscurity of patience back to around the middle of the nineteenth century. This was a time of massive political upheaval and revolution in Europe, and when *The Communist Manifesto* was published. By the mid-century, patience had disappeared as an independent topic in Christian literature and had come "to be seen either as an anachronism or as a notion devised by oppressors to contain the restlessness and discontent of the oppressed."[102] Some years later, with the emergence of the modern sense of progress, patience fell into further disrepute as a sign of failure to imaginatively pursue the possibilities of radical social and personal transformation; in Harned's words, "Insofar as patience meant the uncomplaining endurance of adversity, it frequently seemed childlike in no very admirable sense."[103] Today, what is left culturally of a once rich concept is a mere caricature; it is a disposition that has come to be equated with passivity and submission that one might seek to impose on unruly children, but that one would not likely seek to embrace oneself.[104]

In this section, I will utilize David Baily Harned's insightful work on patience to help rehabilitate this virtue, indicating that a contemporary Christian notion of patience is properly conceived of as an active, social virtue rather than the isolated personal endurance of hardship. I will also examine the virtue of patience as it is to be practiced by the dying (as opposed to their caregivers). For them, Jesus serves as the primary role model of patience, and its practice primarily functions to foster their ability to embrace graciously the compassion of others, to see and accept the limitations of their autonomy, and to find meaning in the endurance of suffering. Finally, I take up patience as practiced by caregivers of the dying. For this group, God is the model of patience, and its practice fosters forbearance and persistent love toward the dying.

Distinguishing Christian Patience from Stoicism

One way to come to a better understanding of what patience is or should be is to get a clear sense of what patience is not. One understanding of patience that should be rejected from a Christian ethical perspective is a view of patience that derives primarily from Stoicism. The Stoic ideal of patience is one that advocates seeking to endure suffering primarily by avoiding the attachment to goods (wealth, power, fame, etc.) whose attainment can be beyond one's control, or to persons whose place in one's life can be fleeting. One seeks to quell the passions that draw one to these goods and to focus instead on eternal wisdom through contemplation.[105] The anthropological ideal operative here is that of the solitary, self-sufficient individual.

From a contemporary Christian ethical perspective, the Stoic ideal of patience is undesirable for a number of reasons. First, it is based on a radically individualistic understanding of human life. The fundamental unit of human existence is conceived in Stoic thought to be an individual in solitude; the good life is attained by the detached, passionless individual contemplating Wisdom alone. Any sense of the importance of dialogue or interdependence with others is lacking. Of equal importance, there is no sense here of patience as the exercise of forbearance toward someone genuinely different or other.[106] Both of these facts highlight the absence in Stoic thought of a sense of the importance of relationships. In contrast, one of the most fundamental insights of contemporary theological and ethical scholarship (especially in the Catholic tradition) has been to emphasize the interdependence of human beings. As we saw above, community and solidarity are crucial for Christian compassion. They are similarly crucial for Christian patience.

Patience as a Virtue for the Dying

For Christians facing their own death, Jesus provides the quintessential model of patience. In times of pain or suffering or trial, Christians have long been encouraged to join their suffering to the suffering of Jesus Christ and thereby to fortify their own patience. For example, the Roman Catholic Congregation for the Doctrine of the Faith writes in its *Declaration on Euthanasia*:

> Suffering during the last moments of life, has a special place in God's saving plan; it is in fact a sharing in Christ's Passion and a union with the redeeming sacrifice, which he offered in obedience to the father's will. Therefore one must not be surprised if some Christians prefer to moderate their use of painkillers, in order to accept voluntarily at least a part of their sufferings and thus associate themselves in a conscious way with the sufferings of Christ crucified.[107]

Although I can see the value of desiring to join one's own suffering with that of Jesus Christ, I am concerned that it can lead to the distorted view that pain and suffering is in itself a good thing. A somewhat simplistic logic can emerge: Jesus suffered, so we must suffer; we suffer now, but if we join our suffering to Christ we will be rewarded in the next life.

What I see as a better appropriation of the example of Jesus will be taken up in detail in the next chapter. For now, let me say simply that an integral part of patience from a Christian perspective is a willingness to endure pain and suffering, but not as intrinsic goods. Jesus models a patience that endures suffering only reluctantly and only when he must do so to remain faithful to God, and responsive to the needs of people around him.

Stanley Hauerwas and Charles Pinches see the patience of Jesus as illustrative of the ultimately social nature of the good human life. They conclude: "There is no question, then, but that Christians must enter into suffering for their friends. As [Jn 15:7–17] indicates, this is a sign of great love. But perhaps more importantly (and contra Aristotle), Christians must be those who are capable of sharing their suffering with others."[108] Thus, the example of Jesus here highlights the importance of compassion, and specifies the proper shape of patience (i.e., that part of being a patient Christian is to accept the compassion of others).

This understanding of patience helps us to understand the importance of mutuality and the limits of our own autonomy. The significance of mutuality can be derived from the scriptural example of the patience of Jesus Christ if the meaning of his suffering is considered more carefully and broadly. To be more precise, the meaning of suffering should be expanded beyond the limits of its association with pain or the feeling of sorrow. As I have used it above, we can also *suffer* the care of a parent or friend. Harned captures well this expanded notion of patience:

Suffering represents the way our opportunities and attitudes are shaped for better and for worse by the words and deeds of other people, whose initiatives are
so often necessary if we are to find our own. Responsible life is attentive suffering, because only by way of it are we truly set free. Irresponsible life is inattentive suffering. The universality of suffering, therefore, is not merely an acci-
dental truth of the human situation but its essence.[109]

Suffering, and therefore patience, entails coming to some awareness of the mutuality and interdependence of human life. There is still some dimension of pain
and suffering in this conception of patience in that one is willing to accept pain
and suffering for the sake of what God demands or for the sake of those with
whom one is in relationship.

Thus, Jesus Christ serves as a model for Christians in his exercise of patience not in the sense that he embraced suffering and pain and even death for its
own sake, but rather in his willingness to endure these things for the sake of love
of God and humanity (i.e., out of a recognition of himself as being in relationship with both). His example also, by contrast, illuminates the shape of impatience. Impatience is to regard suffering (whether understood in the sense of
interconnectedness or of the endurance of pain and sorrow) as a hindrance to
human flourishing and something to be avoided at all costs.[110]

In light of this understanding of the way in which Jesus models patience for
the dying, the suggestion from the CDF above that some Christians might "prefer to modify their use of painkillers" makes little sense. Jesus does not embrace
crucifixion to maximize pain; it arises as a consequence of his fidelity to the
marginalized and to God (and preaching God's Reign).[111] Similarly, the dying
patient should not endure physical agony for its own sake by refusing pain
medication. Instead, the proper expression of patience by the dying would be to
endure *unavoidable* suffering associated with dying in order to pursue other
goods that come in the midst of and sometimes as a result of that suffering, such
as coming to terms with one's own mortality and dependence, experiencing the
compassion of loved ones as expressed in physical care, and to be a role model
of hopeful, patient endurance (and thereby a sign of hope for those around the
deathbed).

Patience is also important because it helps us to recognize the limits of our
own autonomy. Just as patience can be misunderstood to mean the quiet acceptance of injustice or the passive, hopeless embrace of the status quo, it can also
easily be misunderstood to mean self-deprecation in the extreme.[112] Obviously,
that is not how I mean to use it here. Rather than seeing patience in opposition to
self-care or self-esteem, it should be understood as knowing one's relative place
in the universe and the limitations of one's own power. That is to say that it entails coming to know that I myself am not the center of the universe, that in
many ways I am incomplete and limited—dependent and needy and powerless.[113] From a Christian theological perspective, this is an achievement of extreme importance. Harned captures this well:

It is often difficult to be a patient and an object, hard to accept our dependence on others, and never easy to receive as gifts what we would much prefer to acquire for ourselves. But perhaps there is no better preparation for hearing the gospel, which is a story about gifts. The recognition of our need to rely on others can cure us of illusions of independence and of the satisfactions of self-reliance and other expressions of pride. Not always and not everywhere, of course, but at some times and in some places the status of patient can bring us the two great goods of sharpened attentiveness and heightened caring, along with the more discerning appreciation and release from selfishness they provide. In such cases the situation has been, at least for the eyes of faith, truly sanctified by God. Then the monologue that busyness encourages is transformed and existence becomes what it was intended to be: a conversation.[114]

The Christian tradition has often stressed the importance of emptying oneself in service to others; it is important to realize the value in receiving such gifts of care as well.

Patience as a Virtue for Caregivers

Patience is a virtue not only for the dying, but also for caregivers. Whereas the Jesus narratives are the primary source for understanding patience for the dying, narratives about God's forbearance are the chief resource for caregivers. Biblically, one of the primary ways in which humans experience God's own patience is as forbearance. In the Old Testament, God's exercise of patience as forbearance is particularly evident. One of the themes of the Hebrew scriptures is that Israel, despite its chosen status, is nevertheless a wayward people. Despite the sinfulness of Israel, God is shown to be as God was first known at Sinai: "a God merciful and gracious, slow to anger, and abounding in steadfast love and faithfulness" (Ex 34:6).[115] Israel suffers mightily across the history recorded in the Bible, but the emphasis in those accounts is not upon the faithfulness and patience of Israel despite those afflictions, but rather upon the patience of God toward an often impatient and faithless people.[116]

God's patience toward Israel and toward humanity more generally is an expression of a dynamic notion of God's creative activity and an expression of respect for the integrity of that creation. That is to say that God's patience communicates the unfinished nature of God's own creative act; creation is not the production of a finished, static masterpiece, but rather a matter of setting something in motion and continuing to call it forward toward the realization of its potentiality. God's patience is an expression of respect for the integrity of creation in the sense that God allows mortals the freedom to err or to turn away from God in sinfulness; God allows creation genuine responsibility.[117] Furthermore, God does not carry out this expression of patience with an air of indifference, but rather in the context of an abiding love.

This understanding of Divine patience has at least two important implications for the shape of Christian patience among those who care for the dying. First, one should patiently accept the otherness of the dying in one's care. Recall in the discussion above how listening is a crucial dimension of compassion. We can now name this aspect of compassion patience. It is the patient acceptance of the undeniable reality of the distance between the dying and their caregivers that makes understanding the suffering of "the other" a constant task. Each person suffers in a different way and must die in a different way. Christian compassion should accept this fact and be forbearing, not controlling in the context of care for the dying. Second, God's forbearance provides a model for how one should respond to a loved one who may very well try to push the caregiver away or resent dependency. Despite the repeated attempts by humanity to deny its dependence upon God and to push God away—in the Garden of Eden (Gen 3), during the wanderings in the desert (Exodus 32), in the unfaithfulness to the covenant as reported by the prophets (e.g., Ezek 5:5), and so forth—God remained a model of patient, abiding love.

Waiting is a final aspect of the practice of patience for both the dying and their caregivers. To be patient in a Christian manner is also to wait expectantly for God's activity in the world to be revealed. Christian patience includes the belief that God's patience cannot ultimately be thwarted. It includes an expectation that suffering, pain, and death are not the final words about life. In other words, a final crucial aspect of patience is hope. It is to this third virtue that we now turn.

A Hope Beyond Recovery:
Christian Hope for the Terminally Ill

The importance of some form of hope has long been recognized by those caring for the dying, but a good sense of the proper shape of hope and acceptable ways of nurturing hope in dying patients has been more elusive. To put the matter more strongly, hope has often been misunderstood and manipulated to such a degree that it has sometimes been invoked to support wrongful activity. One of the most alarming instances of this misunderstanding and misappropriation of hope can be found in efforts to conceal a terminal diagnosis from a dying patient. This deception can be undertaken by medical professionals or close family members; it can be done with good intentions (e.g., to "protect" the victim) or bad (e.g., to escape the difficult task of sharing bad news or probing the often uncharted terrain of one's own beliefs and feelings about death). In almost any case, the action is wrong and finds its basis in an inadequate understanding of hope.

Dr. Ira Byock recounts one such case of concealment in his book, *Dying Well*, where he tells of how his own father's physician refused to deliver an honest prognosis because he believed that "a doctor must not destroy hope."[118] Byock was stunned and shocked that a fellow physician would deceive a patient in the name of preserving "hope." Exasperated, he asked rhetorically, "Hope? Hope for what—to live forever?! What about truth?" In a very curt, rhetorical sort of way, Byock points to the weaknesses of this false hope: it is not rooted in truth. Rather, such hope is opposed to truth in the simple sense that medical personnel and family members must shield the dying from an accurate awareness of their condition, and need to suspend awareness of their mortality in order for this false hope to be sustained. It can be described as an erroneous attempt to "protect" people from knowledge of painful medical truth.[119]

Today, few medical doctors would advocate the paternalistic deception just described. However, the notion of hope that supports a decision not to disclose a terminal prognosis to a dying patient (i.e., a hope which allows no place whatsoever for death—one that simply leads a patient to believe "you will not die") is not far from what Daniel Callahan has described as the predominant notion of hope in the modern medical context: "You won't die *now* from *this*."[120] In both conceptions, the basis for hope is rooted in the possibility of recovery. Where there can be no recovery, there is "no hope" in the modern medical sense. Obviously, this understanding of hope is of no use to anyone whose prognosis is unquestionably poor or who has accepted the fact that they are dying and there is no chance of recovery.

As an alternative, I propose a Christian understanding of hope that is not opposed to death, but one that can endure even in the face of it. There is a fine line between a hope that can endure even through suffering and dying, and a hope that glosses over these realities in order to cope with them (e.g., by imagining death as a mere "portal" or "crossing over" that minimizes death's negativity). Nevertheless, this is a line that can and must be drawn.

Christian hope is rooted deeply in an abiding faithfulness in God. This faith steers the Christian away from despair by affirming that God's love is more powerful than death. This faith also moves the Christian away from a facile or "cheap" hope by linking God's promises of eternal life to a simultaneous challenge to conversion. Christian hope does not promise the continuation of the status quo after death, but rather offers a *new* life with God at its center.

A False Hope: Life Without Death

As with all virtues, hope is a mean between extremes. One extreme has been described above. It can be named as a cynicism or perhaps as vitalism: cynical because it sees no possibility for hope more powerful than death, and therefore, vitalistic (i.e., concerned with preserving physical life at all costs) because without physical life, there can be no hope. At the other extreme, is what might be called "easy" or facile hope. This is a hope that sees death as little more than a bump in the road to continued life in a world "beyond." Oddly, we can find an advocate for such an understanding of hope in Elisabeth Kübler-Ross, one of the leading figures in the early movement to remove the social taboo surrounding death.[121]

About ten years after her groundbreaking book, *On Death and Dying*, appeared, Elisabeth Kübler-Ross published a new volume entitled *To Live Until We Say Goodbye*, and about five years later wrote *Death: The Final Stage of Growth*.[122] In her first book the focus was upon a psychological examination of the experience of dying. Kübler-Ross famously broke down the process of facing death into a five-staged process in which patients move from denial through anger, bargaining, and depression ultimately to acceptance. Her approach was largely phenomenological, relying heavily upon clinical case studies in an attempt to find a common pattern in the process of dying.

In her later books, Kübler-Ross began to shift her focus toward investigating more deeply the significance of "near-death" experiences, and expectations of life-after-death upon the dying process. In this work, she concludes that physical death is not a real enemy of humankind because the soul or spirit will go on living as the body dies.[123] Death is portrayed in an unqualified, positive light as both natural and even a moment for personal enrichment—"the final stage of growth in this life."[124] An unmistakably dualistic understanding of body and spirit emerges in her writing and thought, as revealed most directly in an interview in *Time* magazine where Kübler-Ross is quoted as saying: "When people die, they very simply shed their body, much as a butterfly comes out of its cocoon."[125] Encouraging the acceptance of death as good and natural and as even a positive existential experience, is a line of thought that has persisted prominently in the death and dying literature.[126] A recent example can be found in the book *Final Gifts*, where two hospice nurses recount "nearing-death awareness" in patients as something which often gives assurance of the acceptability or even desirability of death. Dying is once described here as moving "into light, warmth, and peace."[127]

At first, this understanding of hope for the dying seems attractive: it combines an effort at coming to accept the inevitable end of one's life (described by Kübler-Ross as a process of psychological development) with the pleasant discovery that death is not so bad after all. Furthermore, it provides a very coherent agenda of tasks for the dying (moving through anger, fear, etc. to acceptance) and appears to be in harmony with a Christian theological perspective in its affirmation that death is not the final word about human life. However, upon more careful consideration, this form of hope should be seen as inadequate at both an existential and theological level. Furthermore, the promise of eternal life here is markedly different from an understanding rooted more deeply in Christianity.

Denial is a powerful and sometimes a necessary psychological defense mechanism, but it should not be the basis for Christian hope. And yet, the vision of hope proposed by Kübler-Ross and others today is heavily dependent upon the *denial* of the negativity of death. Even at an experiential or existential level, denial cannot be ultimately satisfying. Kübler-Ross and others do not offer a way of enduring the emotionally painful experience of being separated from friends and loved ones by dying, nor of coping with the horror of the failure of one's own body (which sometimes includes physical pain). Rather, the experience itself is recast as warmth and light in a manner that is arguably contrary to fact. James Gustafson has written that for something to be a hope and not a mere wish or desire, it must have a plausible or believable basis.[128] The "hope" of a warm, blissful death does not account for the enduring negativity of the experience. The possibility of life beyond death should not be ruled out as a basis for hope, but it should not be used in such a way that the difficulty of the real experience of dying is discounted or ignored.

Beyond Optimism: The Shape of Christian Hope

Christian hope distinguishes itself from a sort of naïve optimism in at least three ways. First, it takes a more cautious view of what can be known about the possibility of life after death, and adopts a corresponding modesty of interpretation regarding symbolic language about that life. Second, the promise that is the basis of Christian hope is that of a life transformed in union with God, as opposed to a continuation of life as we have known it. Another way to describe this distinction theologically would be to say that Christian hope includes a call to conversion, and additionally that the promise of Christian hope is not a *resuscitation* of the dead, but their *resurrection*. Third, Christian hope necessarily includes a social component, both in terms of how it is supported, and how it is expressed.

A Modest Hope: Interpreting Christian Language About Life After Death
Monika Hellwig has noted that an empiricist mindset dominates the consideration of death and life after death in contemporary American society.[129] This empiricist perspective seeks out proof of life after death and evidence of the nature of such a life by appeals to near-death experience. The empiricist way of thinking also leads to a mode of biblical interpretation in which eschatological images are taken to be literally true, and perceived as windows into another realm to which we do not have ready, regular access.[130] Both of these trends run counter to the understanding of Christian hope that I would propose.

In place of an empiricist understanding of biblical eschatology, I propose an interpretation that takes a more modest view of what these symbols (and indeed this whole literary genre) can tell us. To start, symbolic language about resurrection and eternal life in the Kingdom of God is a very different kind of language than an historical, eyewitness account of events.[131] This is a language that seeks to speak about that which is beyond history—about a future that cannot be known in any usual sense.[132] As such, it is a language that is often expressed in terms of negation: for example, "Death will be no more; mourning and crying and pain will be no more, for the first things have passed away" (Rev 21:4).[133]

Given its eschatological nature, Christian hope is not entirely baseless, but its assurances always entail an act of faith.[134] The truth-claims made by the symbols of Christian hope rest upon faith, even if that experience of faith has a historical component rooted in the experience of Christ as risen by the apostles.[135] This is one tension inherent in the understanding of Christian hope I am proposing: a balance or a mean must be found between taking the promises of Christian hope to be verifiably true and taking them to be the product of the imagination; if one moves too far toward either of these poles, the credibility of Christian hope begins to falter.[136]

Resurrection versus Resuscitation

A second important distinguishing characteristic of Christian hope is that it does not promise an unending continuation of one's life in the status quo, but rather is an invitation to a life of conversion leading ultimately to charity and union with God. "Eternal life" is not an unchanged continuation of this life, but a life radically transformed.[137] This is true in the sense that life after death must be conceived as radically unlike the life we have known (see Mk 12:18-27), and this is true also in the sense that with the promise of eternal life comes a call to conversion—to a life transformed here and now.

Many popular images that provide assurances about life after death tend to evoke an understanding of afterlife as the indefinite continuation of this life. People remain physically recognizable as the same, and their behavior is often largely unchanged. Of equal importance, God remains distant and removed from the popular conception of life after death. There are few if any images of a divine power of resurrection; instead one moves from this plane of experience to the next in a natural or automatic sort of way, as if passing through a portal. Furthermore, those "above" do not typically spend their "time" captivated by the delight of the beatific vision, but rather tend to remain obsessed with what is happening in the life they have left behind.[138]

In contrast to the contemporary, empiricist foundation of hope, which seeks an extrinsic proof or a scientific guarantee that death is not the final word about life, Christian hope begins first with relationship. Robin Wakely has argued that even in the Old Testament, where one finds the predominant belief that there was no life beyond the grave, there are at once signs of hope for such a life. In those sections of the Old Testament that begin with a consideration of God's love and fidelity for Israel or of the possibility of human fellowship with God (e.g., Ps 49 or Ps 16), these themes eclipse the terror of death. Even in the depths of despair, even in the face of death, there is a sense that communion with God is ultimately indestructible. Since nothing can shatter that fellowship with God, death loses its terror.[139]

This understanding of hope does not eliminate the possibility of suffering or death, but rather places it within the context of a relationship with God, thereby removing some of its sting and power. Allen Verhey quite eloquently describes the shape of such hope:

> Jesus has been raised, the "first fruits of those who have fallen asleep" (1 Corinthians 15:20), but we live under the sign of the cross, and the good future of God is not yet fully come. Yet, to those who suffer, although the story of Jesus is a glad story indeed, it does not deny the sad truth about our world. It does not announce here and now an end to our pains or an avoidance of our death, but it does provide an unshakable assurance that we do not suffer alone, that we are not and will not be abandoned, that Jesus suffers with us, that God cares. The glad story of Jesus is indeed a hard reminder that in a world like this one, however righteous or repentant we are, we cannot expect to be spared pain, sorrow, or death.[140]

The shape of Christian hope just described is significant because it is successful in finding a mean between the extremes of despair and incredulity. It neither says that where there is suffering and death, there can be no hope (despair) nor that one must never suffer or die (incredulity).

From a practical, ethical point of view, this approach to hope is important because it avoids a tendency toward triumphalistic hope within the church and among "the hopeful." In other words, it guards against a self-deceptive kind of hope that ignores sad truths about the world and sometimes a dying patient.[141] At the same time, as a mean, it guards against the other extreme more typical of the medical-scientific community, which can exhibit a tendency to lead us to believe that with the next technological advance suffering and even death might be defeated enemies. To quote Verhey again, "Apart from eschatological realism our culture is at risk of extravagant (and idolatrous) expectations of medicine, tempted to regard the physician as a medical wizard whose magic will deliver us from death and suffering."[142]

From Fellowship to Action

The Christian understanding of hope I am proposing does not rest by connecting Christian hope to the comfort found in deep fellowship with God. This fellowship not only provides comfort, it also has an exhortative dimension. That is to say that Christian hope, through its connection to faith in God, demands conversion of heart, and vigorous service directed to neighbor. Interestingly, this understanding stretches back at least to the *ars moriendi* tradition. Recall from the last chapter that William Perkins proposed that the best general preparation for death was to pursue the life of a repentant sinner.[143] To put the matter differently, he held that the best way to preserve Christian hope in the face of death is to strive to nurture one's Christian faith, which entails reconciling oneself to God, attaching oneself to Christ, and striving to live rightly.[144]

For Perkins, a key means of nurturing Christian faith and ultimately Christian hope is to enter into a mode of living that he names "the first degree of eternal life." Living under "the first degree of eternal life" entails allowing Christ to guide one's thoughts, affections, and will so that one's heart and indeed one's entire life becomes ordered according to the will of God.[145] According to Perkins, this mode of living can be recognized by at least three signature characteristics. Those who have begun to live in this way have a profound personal piety marked primarily by reverence for God and a very humble sense of one's own importance; this disposition of humility has an introspective function that constantly calls the Christian to an ever deeper state of conversion and repentance. Second, this "eternal life" is marked by vigorous service to the community and the commonwealth.[146] Thus, ordering one's affections, thoughts, and will with those of Christ brings about not only introspection and prayer, but also active service. Finally, ordering one's life in this way leads to peace of conscience—to a hopefulness that one is among God's elect (the third distinguishing characteristic of "eternal life" begun here and now).

Contemporary authors agree that attaching oneself to God through Christ necessarily entails attaching oneself to the cause of Jesus Christ. As we move from the sixteenth century and William Perkins to the twentieth century, there is a shift in the fundamental question surrounding Christian hope. For Perkins, the question was essentially "what must I do to be saved?" For contemporary theologians such as Jürgen Moltmann, the question has become "is life meaningful?"[147] Whereas despair arose in Perkins's time as a result of a profound awareness of one's own personal sinfulness and from fear at the prospect of eternal damnation, for Moltmann despair arises from an acute awareness of the depth and strength of social sin and evil in the world. For Moltmann, the question is whether there is reason to believe that the future will hold anything but more of the same legacy of evil and human misery. To put the matter in terms of an existential choice, the question is whether one should commit oneself to the cause of justice and building a better future, or if such an act would be foolish and futile. This shift in the fundamental question thus points to the importance of social activity and service as a means of nurturing Christian hope. For Moltmann, the key to nurturing Christian hope is the development of a willingness to give one's whole self to the Kingdom of God as revealed in Jesus Christ.[148]

The development of Christian hope thus points one back in the direction of Christian compassion. It is a proactive virtue that not only provides comfort and assurance, but also demands that one *become* an instrument of comfort, assurance, love, justice, and so forth. This is what is meant by the demand that one give oneself to the Kingdom of God. Given this fact, the hope of the Christian cannot be a hope that promises an escape from pain and vulnerability. Indeed, it is in this dialectic of deep investment in precious, but ultimately fragile goods, that the meaning of a Christian hope in the resurrection becomes clear.

The author of John's gospel writes, "Unless a grain of wheat falls into the earth and dies, it remains alone; but if it dies, it bears much fruit" (Jn 12:24). For the Christian, hope is not the wish that they might never experience pain or death. If we love deeply and strive earnestly to witness to and serve God's Reign, pain and disappointment are inevitable. Thus, the hope of the Christian is rather that in their living for the Kingdom and in their dying some good might come. For a Christian, hope is rooted in the faith that after we experience the real negativity that is a part of living in a finite, fallen world, there is still God who is eternal, and who has promised eternal fellowship to us. God, who "is" after we are all no more, shall heal the brokenness of our botched attempts to establish justice, practice compassion, and love. God will mend the separation from loved ones that is the most painful part of death. In the words of Jürgen Moltmann: "All the moments of time will be gathered together in an eternal present. A broken form of life will be healed and the broken off story of our lives will be taken up and completed. Eternal life is the final salvation of these mortal lives for the fulfilled wholeness for which it was created."[149]

Christian Care for the Dying:
The Strength of a Web of Virtues

I began this chapter with the examination of two contrasting notions of compassion. Let me conclude by highlighting the similarities and differences that have emerged between my interpretation of the compassion of Timothy Quill and the Christian conception of compassion I have developed. For ease of description, I will refer to these two as "Quill" or "Quill's compassion" and "contemporary Christians" or "Christian compassion" even though I recognize the latter two designations are a bit too sweeping.

Quill and contemporary Christians find a substantial amount of common ground in their agreement on the need to begin compassionate care with the practice of listening. Both see the need to recognize the uniqueness of the situation and suffering of each individual who is dying, and to respect that person's need to exercise responsible freedom in the face of that experience. Both Quill and contemporary Christians also recognize the need for deep relationship in the practice of compassion, and the need for caregivers to pledge not to abandon the dying.

The main difference between Quill's compassion and Christian compassion is that the former exists in rough isolation—cut off from any connection to other virtues or to the support of goods other than the maximization of patient autonomy and the elimination of suffering. Quill is very attentive to the "existential" suffering of his patients, but comes to the table with little he can offer that might ease that type of suffering. His patients speak often of a sense of futility, meaninglessness, and utter hopelessness. Quill can do little other than offer to help

them to put an end to it all, because he and his patients share the same underde-
veloped understanding of hope. Theirs is the hope of the clinician described by
Daniel Callahan that I mentioned above: "You won't die *now* from *this*."[150] It is
a hope that can exist only where there is the possibility for recovery, or we
might add, where there is the possibility of the elimination of suffering by any
means necessary.

The distinctiveness and strength of Christian compassion lies in its location
within a web of other virtues, especially patience and hope. The ability of Christian compassion to ease much of the existential suffering that Quill encounters
derives from the fact that it can rely upon these other virtues. For those who feel
ashamed and undignified at the prospect of dependence, Christian compassion
can seek to instill patience and a sense of the dignity of interrelatedness and receiving the love and care of others. For those in despair who are enveloped by
their suffering, Christian compassion can bring hope by putting that suffering
into a broader context—into a context where suffering can be understood sometimes to be redemptive or at least meaningful, and where that suffering is not the
final word about one's life.

The resources necessary to ease the existential suffering of patients are not
medical resources, but communal and religious. Of course, Christian compassion with its nurture of patience and hope will not eliminate all suffering. It does
not provide a life or a death free of pain and suffering. However, Christian compassion at least responds to "existential" crises with "existential" resources—to
despair with resources of hope, to impatience with patience, to isolation with
community, to meaninglessness with meaning. The fullness of this response
should make clear the inadequacy of responding only with drugs—or even with
drugs and a heart filled with sincerity, profound concern and love.

Notes

1. Paul Wadell, "Compassion," in *Collegeville Pastoral Dictionary of Biblical Theology*, ed. Carroll Stuhlmueller (Collegeville, Minn.: Liturgical Press, 1996), 157.

2. The distinction between pain and suffering is an important one. Since this section
is a summary of my argument, the distinction is merely referenced here and not explained. I shall take up this distinction below.

3. David E. Stannard, *The Puritan Way of Death: A Study in Religion, Culture, and
Social Change* (New York: Oxford University Press, 1977), 38.

4. Stannard writes that "for a century and a half, from the early sixteenth to the mid-
seventeenth century, London was free of the bubonic plague for barely a decade." See
Stannard, *Puritan Way*, 37. John Hale concurs by observing that it was considered a curi-
osity that during the period between 1616 and 1624 there was no evidence of plague in
London. See John Hale, *The Civilization of Europe in the Renaissance* (New York:
Simon and Schuster, 1993), 551.

5. Philippe Ariès, *Western Attitudes Toward Death: From the Middle Ages to the Present* (Baltimore: Johns Hopkins University Press, 1974), 7.

6. Infectious disease was more typically the cause of death than chronic maladies such as Congestive Heart Failure or cancer that often cause death today. The former usually had a rapid onset and progressed quickly, serving to shorten the dying process and also affording the dying the opportunity to be lucid and alert even to the very end stages of dying. See Daniel Callahan, *The Troubled Dream of Life: In Search of a Peaceful Death* (New York: Simon & Schuster, 1993), 28–29. In addition see Arthur E. Imhof, "From the Old Mortality Pattern to the New; Implications of a Radical Change from the Sixteenth to the Twentieth Century," *Bulletin of the History of Medicine* 59, no. 1 (spring 1985): 1–29.

7. Callahan, *Troubled Dream*, 42.

8. Committee on Care at the End of Life, *Approaching Death: Improving Care at the End of Life*, ed. Marilyn J. Field and Christine K. Cassel (Washington, D.C.: National Academy Press, 1997), 37.

9. Callahan, *Troubled Dream*, 43.

10. For a very readable set of case studies of patients facing serious illness and a description of some of the technological medical options at the disposal of their care providers, see Jerome Groopman, *The Measure of Our Days: New Beginnings at Life's End* (New York: Penguin Books, 1997). A similar account of the progress of various diseases and chronic conditions (e.g., congestive heart failure) can be found in Sherwin Nuland, *How We Die: Reflections on Life's Final Chapter* (New York: Alfred A. Knopf, 1994).

11. Callahan, *Troubled Dream*, 42–48.

12. See the case of "Kirk" in Groopman, *Measure of Our Days*, 7–38.

13. John T. Carmody and Denise L. Carmody, "The Body Suffering: Illness and Disability," in *Embodiment, Morality and Medicine*, ed. Lisa Sowle Cahill and Margaret A. Farley (Dordrecht: Kluwer Academic Publishers, 1995), 186. They cite two autobiographical works that explore deeply the many facets of suffering encountered when one experiences debilitating illness. See Arthur Frank, *At the Will of the Body: Reflections on Illness* (Boston: Houghton Mifflin Company, 1991) and Robert F. Murphy, *The Body Silent* (New York: Henry Holt and Company, 1987). Frank's book treats the author's experience of suffering a heart attack and later being diagnosed with testicular cancer. Murphy's work recounts his paralysis resulting from a tumor exerting pressure on his spinal cord.

14. Two studies (one in 1992 and one in 1996) found that at least 90% of people would prefer to be cared for at home if they were diagnosed with a terminal illness and had only six months to live. Committee on Care at the End of Life, *Approaching Death*, 45–46.

15. Arthur C. McGill provides a very interesting analysis of efforts in American culture to isolate death from the rest of life. He opposes two notions of death: one is a "medical" view in which death can be empirically determined and observed. Under the medical view, death is something known by "other people," not the dying themselves. Opposed to "medical" death, is a sense of dying as a lifelong experience of loss and deterioration that foreshadow our final end. Here, death is a constant wearing away of life of which the dying themselves become increasingly conscious in every sickness, farewell, going to sleep, and in major life changes such as the movement from adolescence to adulthood. McGill argues that American culture is entirely dominated by a medical no-

tion of death, which permits death to be wholly the concern of "others" (i.e., the dying who are seen to be a group apart from the living). McGill sees American journalistic preoccupation with disaster, murder, and violence as a means of culturally reinforcing the alien nature of death; it is a force that intrudes upon life, which otherwise would go on indefinitely. See Arthur C. McGill, *Death and Life: An American Theology* (Philadelphia: Fortress Press, 1987), especially chapters 1 and 2.

16. William F. Lynch, *Images of Hope: Imagination as Healer of the Hopeless* (Notre Dame, Ind.: University of Notre Dame Press, 1965), 222–23.

17. McGill makes the analogy that just as the poor must be hidden away in order to mask the suffering that is a part of the success of others in the American economy, so must the aging and the dying be hidden away in order to maintain the illusion of a life of pure happiness, untainted by suffering, deterioration, or dependency. See McGill, *Death and Life*, 19–22.

18. Ira Byock, *Dying Well: Peace and Possibilities at the End of Life* (New York: Riverhead Books, 1997), 97–98. Byock notes in the case cited here and in others that aversion to accepting care from family members is quite common, but a repugnance that often can be overcome.

19. Eric Cassel notes that people often experience pain and disease as a threat not only to the continuation of their lives, but also to their integrity as persons. Thus, the suffering that can derive from pain comes not from the physical agony, but from the threat of this pain to one's sense of self. See Eric J. Cassel, "The Nature of Suffering and the Goals of Medicine," *New England Journal of Medicine* 306, no. 11 (March 18, 1982): 639–45.

20. The best summary by Quill himself of how he distinguishes himself from others advocating PAS can be found in chapter 6 of his book, *Death and Dignity: Making Choices and Taking Charge* (New York: W. W. Norton, 1993), 121–32, especially pages 124–28.

21. Quill, *Death and Dignity*, 20. See also Timothy E. Quill, *A Midwife through the Dying Process: Stories of Healing and Hard Choices at the End of Life* (Baltimore: Johns Hopkins University Press, 1996), 199, where Quill argues that part of the reason patients should be given maximum control over their dying is that it should be a moment for self expression; dying is a deeply personal activity unique to each individual.

22. Quill, *A Midwife*, 2. Dr. Sherwin Nuland concurs that the recognition that each patient's death is unique is an important insight. See Nuland, *How We Die*, xv.

23. Quill, *A Midwife*, 107 and 157. See also Quill, *Death and Dignity*, 36 where the patient is described as "terrified at losing independence" and for whom "illness and dependency would have been humiliating," and page 105 where he describes being "out of control" as a "fate worse than death" for some patients.

24. Quill, *A Midwife*, 165. See also the case of "Diane" in Quill, *Death and Dignity*, 12 where Quill writes that "it was extraordinarily important to Diane to maintain control of herself and her own dignity during the time remaining to her."

25. It is estimated that good palliative care can relieve pain in all but about 5% of patients in the months immediately preceding death. See K. M. Foley, "The Treatment of Pain," *New England Journal of Medicine* 313 (1985): 84–95. On the distinction between suffering and pain, see Eric Cassel, "Nature of Suffering," 639ff.

26. Quill, *A Midwife*, 3. See also Quill, *Death and Dignity*, 104 where he states that control of physical symptoms alone is not sufficient care and argues that physicians must also attend to the remedy of "emotional and existential suffering."

27. Quill, *A Midwife*, 157.

28. Quill, *A Midwife*, 164. The Hemlock society provides literature describing how patients can legally obtain the barbiturates needed to "peacefully" commit suicide by complaining to their physician of ongoing sleeplessness. See Quill, *Death and Dignity*, 126.

29. Quill, *A Midwife*, 166. It is not clear exactly what Jane is "optimistic" about. Optimism or hopefulness is typically used by Quill (and many others in the medical field) to refer to hope *for recovery*. However, that is not possible in this case. A fuller discussion of hope and optimism shall take place below in my consideration of the virtue of hope.

30. Quill makes this point repeatedly. Some patients never actually use the drugs, but having them in their possession throughout their illness made them feel at ease and in control. In my view this points to the centrality of the restoration of control as being the key element of Quill's action rather than the escape from physical pain such a prescription might offer.

31. Quill finds it very troubling that he must choose between protecting himself and ensuring that Jane and his other patients do not die alone or suffer as a result of inept attempts to take their own lives. Quill uses this conflict to indict the current legal status quo prohibiting PAS as a violation of both humane care for the dying and his own principle of nonabandonment. See Quill, *A Midwife*, 167. See also Quill's comments on the same point in his most famous case of "Diane," where he writes that it "violates every principle of humane care of the dying if she felt she had to be alone because of our laws." See Quill, *Death and Dignity*, 22.

32. Quill, *A Midwife*, 170.

33. The use of the plastic bag placed over a dying patient's head (advocated by the Hemlock Society) recurs in Quill's work. Quill has a clear discomfort with the practice, but never really articulates why. He seems to sense that its use is traumatic for the family of the dying patient and finds its use almost obscene in itself. An interesting question to pursue is what moral difference there is between the use of a massive dose of barbiturates and the use of the plastic bag. Does taking moral offense at suffocation but virtually none at the use of drugs point to a lack of awareness of the full shape of the act of prescribing barbiturates that are used for the purpose of suicide? Or on the other hand is there a real moral difference between these means?

34. Ezekiel Emanuel, "What Is the Benefit of Legalizing Assisted Suicide?" *Ethics* 109 (April 1999): 632.

35. Timothy E. Quill and Christine K. Cassel, "Nonabandonment: A Central Obligation for Physicians," *Annals of Internal Medicine* 122, no. 5 (1 March 1995): 368–74. The quotation is from page 368 where he also contrasts the approach he favors for medical ethics—one that is rooted deeply in the circumstances of the individual patient's situation and where decisions are evaluated in the context of a longstanding relationship—to what he characterizes as an "episodic" approach to ethical questions, that is, one that resembles a series of decisions about particular therapeutic options.

36. The claim here makes sense intuitively, but it should be noted that Quill does not cite evidence to support it.

37. Quill, *Death and Dignity*, 82.

38. Recall the definition of compassion given at the start of this chapter; compassion minimally includes the capacity to be moved by another's misfortune, and (where possible) acts of care on behalf of those who suffer.

39. Quill, *Death and Dignity*, 16.

40. On the importance of the open-ended nature of the commitment to nonabandonment see Quill and Cassel, "Nonabandonment," 370.

41. In fact, Quill's argument does not always make any reference to compassion. "Humane care" or even simply "proper care" for the dying seems to be interchangeable in his view with "compassionate care." Even so, I maintain that my analysis of Quill's notion of "compassionate care" under the heading of the notion of compassion is valid. Quill's understanding of what constitutes good care is quite consistent, and he has applied the term "compassionate" to it. The fact that he has conflated the notions of good care and compassionate care for the dying does not negate the fact that his understanding of compassionate care is as I have described it.

42. Recall Paul J. Wadell's definition of compassion that was given on page 53: compassion first entails the ability to know the suffering of another as well as the capacity to be moved by another's misfortune because we see it as our own. See Wadell, "Compassion," 157. I have separated this first dimension of Wadell's definition into two parts here. Diana Fritz Cates agrees with Wadell's definition. See *Choosing to Feel: Virtue, Friendship and Compassion for Friends* (Notre Dame, Ind.: University of Notre Dame Press, 1997), 236.

43. James F. Keenan, "Listening to the Voice of Suffering," *Church* 12 (autumn 1996): 41–42. For a more elaborate treatment of this same theme see James F. Keenan, "The Meaning of Suffering," in *Jewish and Catholic Bioethics: An Ecumenical Dialogue,* ed. Edmund D. Pellegrino and Alan I. Faden (Washington, D.C.: Georgetown University Press, 1999), 83–95.

44. Richard Gunderman offers a similar perspective that focuses on such a tendency in clinical staff in particular. See "Illness as Failure: Blaming Patients," *Hastings Center Report* 30, no. 4 (July-August 2000): 7–11.

45. Keenan, "Listening," 42. Elaine Scarry provides a very helpful discussion of the importance of "voice" and how the inability to express oneself can be personally destructive. Scarry's discussion focuses on the dynamics of torture and how the silencing of victims by the torturer combined with forcing one to involuntarily give voice to one's secrets (to be "forced to talk") are at the heart of its destructiveness. This philosophical analysis supports Quill's clinical findings as to the importance of allowing patients to verbalize their fears and suffering, and conversely of the potentially damaging effects of not permitting them to do so. See Elaine Scarry, *The Body in Pain* (New York: Oxford University Press, 1985). Keenan provides a good summary of her work and how it pertains to this discussion on pages 41–42.

46. Warren Thomas Reich, "Speaking of Suffering: A Moral Account of Compassion," *Soundings* 72 (spring 1989): 83–108.

47. Dorothy Sölle uses this term "mute suffering" to describe the type of suffering that afflicted people in German concentration camps where the extreme conditions they endured rendered them essentially incapable of learning from their experience or even speaking words that could describe what was happening to them. Sölle argues further that a similar stage of silence characterizes the first stage of less severe experiences of suffering as well. See Dorothy Sölle, *Suffering* (Philadelphia: Fortress Press, 1975), 68–74.

48. Viktor Frankl, *Man's Search for Meaning: An Introduction to Logotherapy* (New York: Pocket Books, 1963), 154. Cited in Reich, "Speaking of Suffering," 86.

49. Reich, "Speaking of Suffering," 93.

50. Reich, "Speaking of Suffering," 93. Arthur Becker agrees with Reich on this point, advocating that anyone striving to be compassionate in such a situation should strive to be with the one suffering in a manner similar to the silent presence of God-with-us. See Arthur Becker, "Compassion: A Foundation for Pastoral Care," *Religion in Life* 48 (June 1979): 147.

51. Karen Lebacqz offers a helpful discussion of the distinction of receptivity versus projection, explaining well how compassion must be an expression of the former. See Karen Lebacqz, "The Weeping Womb: Why Beneficence Needs the Still Small Voice of Compassion," in *Secular Bioethics in Theological Perspective*, ed. E. E. Shelp (Dordrecht: Kluwer Academic Publishers, 1996), 91.

52. Reich, "Speaking of Suffering," 93.

53. Wendy Farley describes this sharing of the suffering of another as "neither direct experience nor guesswork." Since the suffering is not directly experienced, it remains that of the other, but one nevertheless comes to know the nature and shape of that suffering and to be moved by it in such a way that it is experienced and shared. The nature of this sharing shall be explained further immediately below. For Farley's treatment of this question see her chapter on the phenomenology of compassion (chapter 3) in Wendy Farley, *Tragic Vision and Divine Compassion: A Contemporary Theodicy* (Louisville, Ky.: Westminster John Knox Press, 1990), especially 71–73.

54. Cates, *Choosing to Feel*, 139–40.

55. Lebacqz, "Weeping Womb," 93. Here Lebacqz is arguing for an anthropology rooted in a feminist perspective, which highlights the situated, relational identity of persons. That is to say that our basic image of person should not be the autonomous man of classical liberalism (completely detached, self-sufficient, and faceless) but rather that of a person with entrenched relationships (with parents, friends, loves, perhaps children, etc.). The moral importance of relationships among persons is a key insight of feminist scholarship. See Mary C. Segers, "Feminism, Liberalism, and Catholicism," in *Feminist Ethics and the Catholic Moral Tradition*, ed. Charles E. Curran, Margaret A. Farley, and Richard McCormick (New York: Paulist Press, 1996), 586–615 (especially 591 on the critique of liberal anthropology). See also Susan Frank Parsons, *Feminism and Christian Ethics* (Cambridge: Cambridge University Press, 1996), especially 39–65.

56. More specifically, it is usually adult daughters or female spouses who care for the dying. See Ada C. Mui, "Caring For Frail Elderly Parents: A Comparison of Adult Sons and Daughters," *The Gerontologist* 35, no. 1 (1995): 86–93. J. W. Dwyer and R. T. Coward, "A Multivariate Comparison of the Involvement of Adult Sons vs. Daughters in the Care of Impaired Parents," *Journal of Gerontology: Social Sciences* 46 (1991): S259–69. Of course I am not advocating the perpetuation of the stereotypical role of female as "natural" caregiver. It is my hope that male spouses and adult children can learn to be compassionate caregivers as well. Even so, the fact would remain that likely caregivers would be those already in (probably familial) relationship with the dying and not a stranger, which is my point here. Paul Lauritzen provides an interesting commentary on how the moral formation of men and the social practices in which they are expected to engage should be critically examined as a cause of their failure to be as compassionate as their sisters and mothers. That is to say that the failure of men to feel empathy and to

express compassion is rooted in the fact that they do not typically participate in practices such as childrearing, nurturing, and so forth that sustain compassion. See Paul Lauritzen, "Reflections on the Nether World: Some Problems for a Feminist Ethic of Care and Compassion," *Soundings* 75, no. 2-3 (summer/fall 1992): 383–401.

57. For an additional treatment of friendship and Thomistic ethics, see Paul Wadell, *Friendship and the Moral Life* (Notre Dame, Ind.: University of Notre Dame Press, 1989). Wadell is less concerned with the question of whether friendship enables shared emotional experience, but his book deals quite effectively with the importance of social factors and significant relationships for the development of virtues. See also Gilbert C. Meilander, *Friendship: A Study in Theological Ethics* (Notre Dame, Ind.: University of Notre Dame Press, 1981).

58. Cates, *Choosing to Feel*, 92. Citing ST I-II 28.1 ad 2 and 26.2.

59. Cates, *Choosing to Feel*, 92. Here, Cates is citing ST I-II 28.2.

60. Cates, *Choosing to Feel*, 50–51.

61. Cates, *Choosing to Feel*, 94.

62. Cates, *Choosing to Feel*, 60.

63. It must be said that Cates's discussion of the ways in which the connection of family and friendship enable a shared experience of pain does not eliminate the need for receptivity and true listening. Friendship demands more than seeing the world similarly; it demands the actual sharing of pleasure and pains. Friendship brings comfort not because we know that we have a friend who would be pleased and pained by the same thing, but because our friend is there to recognize *our pain* and is moved by it; we are comforted by the knowledge that someone knows *our* pain and acknowledges that it matters to them that we are suffering. Thus, what friendship and a shared life bring to the table here is a deepened sense of our own ability to know and understand when the dying before us seek to express in their suffering. It is not a substitute for listening and receptivity. On this point, see Cates, *Choosing to Feel*, 61.

64. Cates, *Choosing to Feel*, 186. For more on the importance of embodiment as a resource for perception in Cates, see her discussion of "bodily commotion" as a source of knowledge on pp. 25ff.

65. Farley, *Tragic Vision*, 90.

66. Farley, *Tragic Vision*, 90.

67. Although Farley does not make reference to earlier works on this question, the argument that dominating or coercive power is inherently evil is not a new one in Christian ethics. A pacifist line of thought on power and the use of force is well represented throughout the history of the Christian moral tradition. One of the most prominent documents in this tradition is the Schleitheim Confession of 1527. A good secondary source on this subject is Lisa Sowle Cahill's *Love Your Enemies: Discipleship, Pacifism and Just War Theory* (Minneapolis, Minn.: Fortress Press, 1994) where many of the crucial authorities in the tradition are discussed.

68. Farley, *Tragic Vision*, 91–92.

69. Farley, *Tragic Vision*, 93–94.

70. Christine D. Pohl, "Hospitality From the Edge: The Significance of Marginality in the Practice of Welcome," *Annual of the Society of Christian Ethics* (1995): 121–36. Pohl makes this point most forcefully on page 135.

71. Karen Lebacqz believes that it is the first two aspects of compassion discussed above (receiving the suffering of the other and being moved by it) that shields compas-

sion from the tendency toward paternalism found in the exercise of the principle of beneficence. In the practice of the latter, the experience of the one suffering is not received, but rather eclipsed by the *projection* of one's own expectations about suffering, allowing for the projection of my own values and will upon the dying. See Lebacqz, "Weeping Womb," 93.

72. National Conference of Catholic Bishops, *Ethical and Religious Directives for Catholic Health Care Services* (Washington, D.C.: USCC, 1995). Also found in *Origins* 24, no. 27 (Dec. 15, 1995).

73. James F. Keenan, "What's New in the Ethical and Religious Directives?" *Linacre Quarterly* 65, no. 1 (Feb 1998): 36–38. The parameters mentioned here are designed to make it clear that personnel in Catholic hospitals are not required to provide services that conflict directly with Catholic moral principles (e.g., sterilization, abortion, PAS, etc.). See the *Directives*, 28. Keenan argues (rightly) that within these parameters there remains great latitude for patients to exercise responsibility for making decisions concerning their care (e.g., it is up to the patient to determine what constitutes extraordinary vs. ordinary means).

74. Keenan brings out the fact the respect shown in the *Ethical and Religious Directives* for the patient's autonomy and freedom is not rooted in an American notion of freedom (which might more properly be called license or the freedom to do whatever one wants) but rather in the Christian notion of freedom of conscience. This freedom entails duty as well, namely an obligation in conscience "to determine what God wants from [the patient]" and to strive to carry out that calling. See Keenan, "What's New," 38.

75. Reich, "Speaking of Suffering," 94.

76. Reich, "Speaking of Suffering," 94.

77. Barbara A. Bozak, CSJ, "Suffering and the Psalms of Lament: Speech for the Speechless, Power for the Powerless," *Eglise et Théologie* 23 (1992): 325–38. Bozak's work is especially relevant to our discussion here because she focuses on the Psalms of Lament as a resource for people living with HIV/AIDS.

78. Walter Brueggemann, *The Message of the Psalms: A Theological Commentary* (Minneapolis, Minn.: Augsburg, 1984).

79. One must note these Psalms were not written by people in the *same* situation as the dying, but rather from a similar point of view. The fact that they were written at all implies that those who wrote them did not die, but lived and went on to reflect poetically on the experience after the fact. The narrative point of view in these Psalms resembles the point of view of the dying even though their authors may not have been in an analogous situation when they were writing.

80. Bozak, "Suffering and the Psalms," 330.

81. Jeremy Taylor recognized the usefulness of the Psalms for the dying. They figure prominently in his work, *Holy Dying*, in sections where he offers suggested prayers to be prayed by the dying with those who visited them. See Jeremy Taylor, *Holy Dying*, vol. 2, *Holy Living and Holy Dying*, ed. P. G. Stanwood (Oxford: Clarendon Press, 1989).

82. This example and the one that follows (Psalm 88) are both given by Barbara Bozak. See Bozak, "Suffering and the Psalms," 330–34.

83. Bozak, "Suffering and the Psalms," 333.

84. One avenue to explore on this question that I will not develop further would be to examine critically the notion of freedom assumed here by Quill, and to contrast it to

the notion of freedom (alluded to on page 29 above) developed in *Veritatis Splendor* and elsewhere.

85. This line of argument is particularly compelling in my view. In short and in part, PAS is seen to violate justice because it puts the most vulnerable of our society at risk; there is an inequitable distribution of the benefits and harms of legalization. In the words of Ezekiel J. Emanuel, "the advocates [of PAS] are likely to reap the benefits [of legalization] while avoiding most of the harms. . . . the harms of legalization are likely to fall on the vulnerable members of our population . . . financially less well-off and comparatively powerless patients who may not be insured or may be underinsured." See Ezekiel J. Emanuel, "What Is the Benefit?" 629–42. A similar argument appears in Susan Wolf, "Gender, Feminism, and Death: Physician-Assisted Suicide and Euthanasia," in *Feminism and Bioethics: Beyond Reproduction*, ed. Susan M. Wolf (New York: Oxford University Press, 1996), 282–317.

86. Allen Verhey, "Assisted Suicide and Euthanasia: A Biblical and Reformed Perspective," in *Must We Suffer our Way to Death*, ed. Ronald P. Hamel and Edwin R. DuBose (Dallas, Tex.: Southern Methodist University Press, 1996), 258.

87. Verhey, "Assisted Suicide," 259.

88. Daniel Callahan, *Troubled Dream*, 115–16.

89. Cates, *Choosing to Feel*, 157. Common good here is understood specifically as the promotion of the kind of human community where flourishing is possible, and which supports the ongoing expression of compassion.

90. William F. May summarizes my own position well: "I can, to be sure, imagine rare circumstances in which I hope I would have the courage to kill for mercy—when the patient is terminally ill, utterly beyond human care, and in excruciating pain. . . . But hard cases do not always make good laws or wise social policies. Regularized mercy killings would too quickly relieve the community of its obligation to provide good care. Further, we should not always expect the law to provide us with full protection and coverage for what, in rare circumstances, we may need morally to do. Sometimes, the moral life calls us out into a no-man's-land where we cannot expect total security and protection under the law. But who ever said that the moral life was easy?" William F. May, "Moral and Religious Reservations about Euthanasia," in *Must We Suffer Our Way to Death*, ed. Ronald P. Hamel & Edwin R. DuBose (Dallas, Tex.: Southern Methodist University Press, 1996), 118.

91. M. Therese Lysaught (drawing upon the work of John Dominic Crossan) has argued that the healing ministry or "miracles" that figure so prominently into the life of Jesus of Nazareth serve primarily to break down notions of untouchability that was practiced culturally and codified into Jewish law. That is, in his healing, Jesus challenged the notion that bodies that were sick or dying or dead were "unclean." Thereby, he expanded the boundaries denoting who was human and who was untouchable. See M. Therese Lysaught, "Patient Suffering and the Anointing of the Sick," in *On Moral Medicine: Theological Perspectives in Medical Ethics*, 2nd ed., ed. Stephen E. Lammers and Allen Verhey (Grand Rapids, Mich.: Eerdmans, 1998), 360–61. For a more comprehensive treatment of this issue, see John Dominic Crossan, *The Historical Jesus: The Life of a Mediterranean Jewish Peasant* (San Francisco: HarperSanFrancisco, 1991). For a more concise treatment, see John Dominic Crossan, "The Life of a Mediterranean Jewish Peasant," *The Christian Century* 108 (1991): 1194–1200.

92. Annette Geoffrion Brownlee, "The Dark Night of Hope," *Journal of Religion and Aging* 1, no. 2 (winter 1984): 20.

93. Amy Plantinga Pauw, "Dying Well," in *Practicing Our Faith*, ed. Dorothy C. Bass (San Francisco: Jossey-Bass, 1997), 164.

94. Alois Müller provides a helpful discussion of ways in which weekly liturgy could be used more effectively by pastoral staff as a context for moving a congregation to consider the place of death within life and to integrate consideration of suffering and death into their spiritual lives. See Alois Müller, "Care of the Dying as a Task of the Church," in *The Experience of Dying*, ed. Norbert Greinacher and Alois Müller (New York: Herder and Herder, 1974), 126–28.

95. Lysaught, "Patient Suffering," 360.

96. There is a fuller explanation of Perkins's approach to the development of hope as an act of compassion later on in this chapter. See the section on hope. William Perkins, *A Salve for a Sicke Man*, in *The English Ars Moriendi*, ed. David William Atkinson (New York: Lang, 1992), 59ff.

97. Perkins, *Salve*, 149.

98. David Baily Harned provides a helpful discussion of this point within the specific context of the virtue of patience. See the final chapter on "The Unity of Virtue" in his book, *Patience: How We Wait Upon the World* (Cambridge, Mass.: Cowley, 1997), 155–78.

99. For example, in the case of "Jane," Quill sympathized with her desire to die "at a time of [her] own choosing." See Quill, *A Midwife*, 165. The connection between compassion and fostering autonomy is also apparent in Quill's stated goal to provide "dignity, *control*, and comfort" to the dying (emphasis mine). See Quill, *Death and Dignity*, 20.

100. By "existential suffering" I mean sadness at loss of ability, fading away of life, and so forth rather than the physical pain of infirmity.

101. Harvard Divinity School, annual Alumni/ae day lecture, June 6, 2000.

102. Harned, *Patience*, 2.

103. Harned, *Patience*, 3.

104. Harned, *Patience*, 19.

105. Harned, *Patience*, 42–43.

106. Harned, *Patience*, 109.

107. Congregation for the Doctrine of the Faith, *Declaration on Euthanasia* (Washington, D.C.: United States Catholic Conference, 1980), 2.

108. Stanley Hauerwas and Charles Pinches, *Christians Among the Virtues: Theological Conversations with Ancient and Modern Ethics* (Notre Dame, Ind.: University of Notre Dame Press, 1997), 48.

109. Harned, *Patience*, 37.

110. Harned, *Patience*, 138.

111. There is no unanimous agreement among Biblical scholars, theologians, and others who have sought to give an explanation for the cause of the persecution of Jesus or the meaning of the crucifixion in the context of his life of ministry. However, a significant number of scholars in this area are of the opinion that the crucifixion should be interpreted as a sign that Jesus was persecuted for his advocacy for the poor and others living on the margins of the society in which he lived (e.g., prostitutes, tax collectors, etc.). For two prominent examples, see Jon Sobrino, *Jesus Christ the Liberator: An Historical-Theological Reading of Jesus of Nazareth* (Maryknoll, N.Y.: Orbis, 1993), espe-

cially 195–232, 254–71, 294–302. See also Elisabeth Schüssler Fiorenza, *Miriam's Child, Sophia's Prophet* (New York: Continuum, 1994). For a critique of Sobrino's position from the perspective of historical-critical biblical scholarship, see John P. Meier, "The Bible as a Source for Theology," *Proceedings of the CTSA* 43 (1988): 1–14.

112. Karen Lebacqz and Shirley Macemon suggest that patience is a virtue that should be paired with justice so as to avoid its abuse or its devolution into a vice. See "Vicious Virtue? Patience, Justice, and Salaries in the Church," in *Practice What You Preach*, ed. James F. Keenan and Joseph Kotva (Franklin, Wis.: Sheed & Ward, 1999).

113. Harned, *Patience*, 129.

114. Harned, *Patience*, 131–32.

115. Harned, *Patience*, 25.

116. Harned, *Patience*, 32.

117. Harned, *Patience*, 28–29.

118. Byock, *Dying Well*, 10.

119. This is the way in which Dr. Sherwin Nuland describes "medical hope." See Nuland, *How We Die*, 244.

120. Daniel Callahan, *Troubled Dream*, 128.

121. I am relying upon George Kuykendall's of Kübler-Ross's concept of hope. See George Kuykendall, "Care for the Dying: A Kübler-Ross Critique." *Theology Today* 38 (1981): 37–48.

122. Elisabeth Kübler-Ross, *Death: The Final Stage of Growth* (New York: Simon & Schuster, 1986). Elisabeth Kübler-Ross, *On Death and Dying* (New York: Macmillan, 1969).

123. Kübler-Ross, *Final Stage*, 164, 166.

124. Kübler-Ross, *Final Stage*, 166.

125. "The Conversion of Kübler-Ross," *Time*, Nov. 12, 1979, 81. Cited in Kuykendall, "Care for the Dying," 43.

126. Lucy Bregman, "Current Perspectives on Death, Dying, and Mourning," *Religious Studies Review* 25, no. 1 (January 1999): 30.

127. Maggie Callanan and Patricia Kelley, *Final Gifts: Understanding the Special Awareness, Needs, and Communications of the Dying* (New York: Poseidon Press, 1992), 80. For another more recent example, see Daniel R. Tobin, *Peaceful Dying* (Reading, Mass.: Perseus, 1999), especially 13–15 where death is described as a "benevolent teacher" and 29–33 where Tobin adheres to the notion of stages of dying through which patients ultimately move toward "serenity" and acceptance of death; such serenity is described as a readiness "to embark on a new journey" (32).

128. James M. Gustafson, "The Conditions for Hope: Reflections on Human Experience," *Continuum* 7 (1970): 538.

129. Monika Hellwig, *What Are They Saying about Death and Christian Hope?* (New York: Paulist Press, 1978), 21.

130. Hellwig, *What Are They Saying*, 21.

131. Obviously, the issue of the nature of symbolic language is a major topic that cannot be discussed in any sort of fullness here. A good, concise, general discussion of hermeneutical problems as they relate to symbols of hope and eschatology can be found in Monika K. Hellwig, "Eschatology" in *Systematic Theology: Roman Catholic Perspectives* vol. 2 (Minneapolis, Minn.: Augsburg Fortress Press, 1991), 347–72.

132. Hellwig, *What Are They Saying*, 18.

133. All biblical quotations are taken from the NRSV. Wayne A. Meeks, ed., *The HarperCollins Study Bible* (New York: HarperCollins, 1993).

134. Hellwig, *What Are They Saying*, 51.

135. Francis Schüssler Fiorenza provides an excellent discussion of why efforts to "prove" the truth of Christianity (and Christian hope) historically are misguided. See Francis Schüssler Fiorenza, *Foundational Theology: Jesus and the Church* (New York: Crossroad, 1992).

136. Douglas J. Hall proposes two similar extremes, naming them cynicism and credulity. See Douglas J. Hall, "Beyond Cynicism and Credulity: On the Meaning of Christian Hope," *Princeton Seminary Bulletin* 6, no. 3 (1985): 201–10.

137. Hellwig, *What Are They Saying*, 59.

138. James Carse offers an interesting discussion of a group of people he encountered who had sought to maintain contact with loved ones after death via a medium. He found that these people held to a static vision of their beloved. For example, a couple that had lost their adult son twenty-nine years previous still imagined him as exactly the same person he had been when he was killed. Here the dead are allowed no room for growth, development or transformation. The operative dynamic is certainly not that of radical conversion. See James P. Carse, *The Silence of God: Meditations on Prayer* (New York: Macmillan, 1985), 87–93.

139. Robin Wakely, "From Fear to Hope: The Riddle of Death and the Hope of Eternal Life." *Journal of Theology for Southern Africa* 59 (July 1987): 75–78.

140. Verhey, "Assisted Suicide," 247.

141. Verhey, "Assisted Suicide," 247.

142. Verhey, "Assisted Suicide," 247. See a similar warning about the susceptibility of contemporary medicine to an overblown sense of its own abilities and importance in Nuland, *How We Die*, 259. He calls for "medical humility" to replace what he terms "medical hubris," which sees no limit to the potential power of medical technology or to what should be attempted to save any patient from death.

143. Perkins, *Salve*, 136ff.

144. As I shall discuss below, the assurance of a life rightly lived is not the *only* basis for Christian hope in Perkins's view (and mine). The assurances of a life well lived must always be coupled with a reliance upon God's mercy "alone." Thus, in some ways, Christian hope sometimes does not emerge as the fruit of way of life, but despite it. See Perkins, *Salve*, 158.

145. Perkins, *Salve*, 140.

146. Perkins, *Salve*, 142.

147. Monica Hellwig has observed this shift in the fundamental question surrounding hope. See Hellwig, *What Are They Saying*, 9–12.

148. Moltmann, "Resurrection as Hope," *Harvard Theological Review* 61 (1968): 143.

149. Jürgen Moltmann, *Is There Life After Death?* (Milwaukee, Wis.: Marquette University Press, 1998), 18–19.

150. Daniel Callahan, *Troubled Dream*, 128.

Chapter 4

A Biblical *Ars Moriendi*:
Dying Well According to Luke

In the room where my grandmother died, a crucifix hung on the wall. It was her own crucifix, one that had been in her bedroom for many years, and that she had taken with her to an extended care facility as she neared the end of her life. A crucifix hangs on the wall of my own bedroom too and, from what I have seen, on the bedroom wall of many Catholics. Typically this is true in Catholic hospitals and nursing homes as well; where you find a bed, you find a crucifix. It was only when I began to think about the task of dying well that I realized that these devotional symbols are near not only to where Catholics begin and end each day, not only to where we lie sick and recover, but also near to where we are most likely to spend our final days and hours. There is a good chance that where we Catholics will die, there will be an image of Jesus dying close at hand.

More than a physical proximity connects the cross (and the whole narrative of the passion of Jesus that it represents) to the dying of contemporary Christians. It is a part of ordinary Catholic pastoral practice to urge those approaching death to make a conscious connection between their own dying and that of Jesus Christ. The introduction to the rites of pastoral care for the dying reads, "These texts are intended to help the dying person, if still conscious, to face the natural human anxiety about death by imitating Christ in his patient suffering and dying."[1] Such a turn to the contemplation of the death of Jesus not only comes from the pastoral directives of the church, but seems to arise spontaneously from a lifetime of participation in Christian liturgy and devotion to Jesus as well.[2] I think that a noted theologian spoke for many when he wrote that he found the crucifix to be a powerful focus for prayer and reflection during the time he spent at his mother's bedside when she lay dying.[3] Indeed, there is a long history of making this connection. All of the authors examined in chapter 2 of this work urged their readers to link their own dying to that of Jesus.[4]

The fact that many Christians turn to focus on the death of Jesus as they approach their own dying raises some important issues. What questions should we properly put to this image of Jesus on the cross? Is this symbol a reminder only of our death with Christ in baptism (which serves as a foundation of our hope for resurrection with Christ), or are the stories of the specific death it represents meant to guide us in some way along the path of our own dying? Can we find in these stories a biblical *ars moriendi*? If so, what exactly is it about Jesus' way of dying that is to be imitated?

A number of factors make developing a straightforward or comprehensive answer to those questions difficult or problematic. Most significantly, one is faced with the question of which passion narrative to focus upon. As Raymond Brown made clear in his monumental work, *The Death of the Messiah*, important textual and theological differences exist among the four canonical accounts of the passion of Jesus. For example, in John's gospel Jesus is portrayed primarily as the Son of Man come down from heaven. John's Jesus is utterly in control of his destiny and someone before whom even the power of Rome is ultimately impotent (e.g., in Jn 10:17-18 Jesus says, "I lay down my life in order to take it up again. No one takes it from me, but I lay it down of my own accord").[5] This triumphant Jesus of John's gospel is in stark contrast to the portrayal of Jesus in the passion narratives of Matthew and Mark where we find him deeply troubled by the abandonment of his friends and the prospect of death by crucifixion (Mk 14:32-38; Mt 26:36-46). Rather than in total control, he is portrayed as apparently abandoned even by God (see Ps 22:1) in the final moments before his death (Mk 15:34; Mt 27:26).

Thus, the issue of whether or to what degree Jesus might be a model for Christians as they face their own death is decided to a large extent by the specific text under consideration. I will not attempt an all-inclusive answer to the question of how each of the four gospels might provide a basis for a biblical *ars moriendi*. Instead I will show that the passion narrative *of Luke's gospel* can serve as a biblical *ars moriendi* and that what Luke would have us imitate is Jesus' practice of the virtues of patience, compassion, and hope.

Did Luke Intend to Present Jesus as a Model for Dying Well?

A contemporary reader might legitimately derive some meaning from a biblical text that differs from the meaning the passage had at the time of its composition.[6] At the same time, while the meaning and relevance of a biblical passage is not limited to that which its author(s) intended, an attempt to discern that intention is important nonetheless.[7] If scripture is to be a useful source for theology, it must provide more than a mirror for the reflection and affirmation of one's own pre-understandings. One of the reasons a theologian turns to scripture is in order to investigate whether his or her own thought is in continuity with the Christian tradition and its canonical literature.[8] Thus, it is important not only to show that Luke's passion narrative can be read in such a way that we see Jesus as a model for our own dying, but also that the early Christians (especially Luke) would have supported such an interpretation. It must be shown that seeing Jesus as a model for Christian dying is not an instance of imposing an alien meaning upon the biblical text.

There are many layers of meaning in the passion narrative. What is at stake for Christians as they read and reflect upon the death of Jesus is not merely how they themselves should approach dying. Here too is a tale of epic struggle between good and evil, between God and Satan.[9] Here too is an answer to the question of how God brings about the salvation of humankind.[10] To say that the passion narrative of Luke's gospel provides a model of dying for Christians is not to say that it does not simultaneously communicate many other important ideas.

Three facts point toward the legitimacy of interpreting Luke's narrative as a model for Christian dying. First, there is a noticeable literary similarity between the Lucan passion narrative and the *exitus clarorum virorum*, a Greek literary genre in which the noble deaths of heroes are retold. Second, there is a similar affinity between the Lucan passion narrative and the Hebrew martyrology tradition. Both of these types of literature were written with the direct intention of providing a model of dying that was to be imitated. Thus, the similarities between these texts and Luke's passion narrative are significant. Finally, the parallels between the description of Jesus' death in Luke's gospel and the account of the deaths of early Christian martyrs in Acts indicate that the author had in mind a connection between Jesus' death and the way a Christian should approach dying. Let me take up each of these points briefly.

Luke was a gifted writer, who demonstrates both a mastery of the Greek language and a deep familiarity with a variety of its literary forms.[11] John Kloppenborg has argued that Luke's passion narrative betrays a deep knowledge of the way in which the death of a Greek hero was typically recounted in the *exitus clarorum virorum*, or heroic death stories.[12] Kloppenborg points out that there are a number of similarities between the passion narrative and the *Phaedo*, Plato's account of the death of Socrates (among the most noted and famous works in this genre). Both are structured to begin with a farewell discourse or symposium, both emphasize the presence of friends or disciples at the hour of the hero's death, and both stress the untroubled manner with which the protagonist approached death.

In the *Phaedo*, the bulk of the text is devoted to Socrates' final discourse on the immortality of the soul, which serves both as a summary of one of his key teachings and as a source of comfort for his followers.[13] The *Phaedo* is exemplary of many other works that follow this paradigm by including a symposium in their account of the death of other heroes. For example, in the death of Cato, he summons his friends for a meal, discourses on Stoic philosophy, and then

offers consolation to his friends and followers.[14] Luke structures the beginning
of his passion narrative similarly. He expands the scene of the last supper into a
symposium (a meal followed by a series of discourses):

> Meal and words of institution (22:14-20)
> I: Prediction of Betrayal (22:21-23)
> II: Discipleship and Table Service (22:24-27)
> III: Promise of the Kingdom to Jesus' followers (22:28-30)
> IV: Prediction of Peter's Denial; Words of Comfort and Exhortation (22:31-34)[15]

Thus, just as in the *Phaedo*, in Luke we find the protagonist discoursing on key
aspects of his teaching, exhorting followers, and offering words of comfort and
consolation.[16]

Similarities in form are complemented by attention to comparable themes as
well. Both the *Phaedo* (and other accounts of the death of heroes) and Luke's
passion narrative stress the fact that the hero died in the company of friends and
conducted himself in noble fashion during his final hours, with a disposition that
seemed entirely untroubled.[17] A careful reading of Luke's passion narrative
alongside those of Matthew and Mark reveals that Luke has edited and reworked
the story to bring out these same facts. For example, whereas Matthew and Mark
make it unmistakably clear that the disciples abandoned Jesus during his crucifixion, Luke downplays this fact (the disciples' absence is only implied by the
fact that their presence is not noted).[18] Luke also removes almost all indications
of despair or emotional anguish from his account of Jesus' final hours. In the
Garden of Gethsemane, rather than "falling on his face" in prayer after saying "I
am deeply grieved, even to death" (Mt 26:38-39), Luke says only that Jesus
knelt in prayer (Lk 22:41-42).[19] Finally, just as Socrates dies with composure, so
too does Jesus in Luke. In contrast to the anguished "My God, My God, why
have you forsaken me?" (Mk 15:34, Mt 27:46), the death cry of Jesus in Luke is
"Father, into your hands I place my spirit" (Lk 23:46).

Unlike Kloppenborg, my primary concern is not to unravel the literary in-
fluences upon Luke. Rather, I raise this connection between genres only to make
the point that given the structural and thematic similarity between these works, it
is reasonable to suppose that they both served a similar purpose for their authors.
That is to say that they both seek to give witness to the innocence of their pro-
tagonists, offer consolation for his friends and followers, and provide a pattern
for them to imitate.[20] Similarities of structure and theme indicate that Luke may
have been writing with the intention of providing a Christian model of dying to
fit alongside (or take the place of) the many Greek tales with which he was familiar.

The Greek tradition of depicting the death of heroes is not the only genre to
which the Lucan passion narrative bears a resemblance. Many interpreters also
read it as an attempt to locate Jesus within the Israelite tradition of the martyr—

one who suffers innocently for his or her religious convictions and who dies a model of patience and forgiveness.[21]

Parallels between Luke's passion narrative and writings about the martyrs of Israel exist at both a linguistic and a thematic level. In terms of language, there is a striking similarity between the description of the sufferings of the martyr Eleazar in IV Maccabees and the description of Jesus' agony in the garden of Gethsemane. Eleazar is described as "bathed in sweat" and "flowing with blood" (4 Mc 6:11; 6:6) while Luke writes that while Jesus was praying "his sweat became like great drops of blood falling down on the ground" (Lk 22:44).[22] This specific connection is reinforced by the fact that Luke uses the term "*agonia*" to describe Jesus' disposition in the garden (Lk 22:44). This word and *agon*, a related term, find frequent use in accounts of the martyrs in Maccabees (2 Mc 3:14, 16; 15:19; 4 Mc 13:15; 16:16; 17:11-16).[23]

In terms of thematic and narrative similarity, the appearance of an "assisting angel" is found in both Luke's passion narrative and martyrological writings. For example, in the story of Daniel, an angel of the Lord is sent by God to give aid to Daniel and his two friends when they are thrown into a "fiery furnace" for refusing to engage in idolatry (Dan 3:28). Later, Daniel is visited again by an angel ("one in human form") to give him strength when he is suffering anguish at the prospect of God's coming wrath (Dan 10:18).[24] Similarly, Jesus is visited by a strengthening angel when grappling with his anguish over his impending suffering and death (Lk 22:43). Brian Beck has noted further that Luke's depiction of Jesus' death follows the thematic pattern of martyrology in the following ways: Jesus is portrayed as pitted against powers of darkness, he relies upon prayer as the crucial preparation for facing his ordeal, his innocence is emphasized (e.g., by Pilate and Herod in Lk 23:4, and 23:14-15, and by the centurion at the cross in Lk 23:47), and he is often mocked by bystanders.[25] Thus, in terms of language and theme, there exist substantial parallels between Luke's passion narrative and the martyrological literature, suggesting that Luke would have wanted his depiction of Jesus' death to be read in the same light (i.e., as a model to be imitated).

The issue of whether Luke's description of Jesus' death fits *exactly* within the martyrology tradition is a technical question in Biblical Studies that is somewhat beside the point here.[26] The relevant conclusion is this: the accounts of the deaths of martyrs (especially 2 Maccabees and Daniel) present a model for how believers should behave in the face of death. By drawing parallels between Jesus' death and this tradition, Luke implies that Jesus is to be imitated just as the martyrs were to be imitated.

The third and perhaps the most convincing evidence of the fact that Luke intended for Jesus to be a model for Christians as they faced death comes from the parallels between his passion narrative and his account of the deaths of the early Christian martyrs in Acts. The connections between the death of Jesus and that of Stephen are particularly pronounced. Two details of the death of Jesus that are uniquely reported in Luke also appear in his account of the death of Stephen. Compare the following:

"Father, into your hands, I commend   "Lord Jesus, receive my spirit."
my spirit." (Lk 23:46)   (Acts 7:59)

"Father, forgive them; for they do not   "Lord, do not hold this sin against
know what they are doing." (Lk 23:34)   them." (Acts 7:60)

In their final acts, both Jesus and Stephen express forgiveness of those who were doing them an injustice, and express hope or trust in God. Thus from these two accounts we can discern that Luke's image of a good Christian death includes forgiving others and being at peace with oneself and with God in the same way that Jesus and Stephen exemplified.[27] Furthermore, these parallels make it clear that Stephen provides a model of the good Christian death because of his conscious imitation of Jesus. He bears witness to Jesus' way of dying by imitation and thereby becomes a role model himself.

It should be noted that the very same evidence that provides support for my view that Luke's passion narrative can be read as a biblical *ars moriendi* calls into question the historical accuracy of the text. However, it already should be clear that my purpose here is not the reconstruction of historical fact so much as an analysis of how this narrative as rendered by Luke can prove life-giving for Christians today as they approach death. One must realize from the start that *all* renderings of the passion of Jesus are dramatic and written at some distance from the event itself.[28] The purpose of the narrative is primarily interpretive rather than historical. In Raymond Brown's words, the gospels were written "in order to communicate to their audiences an interpretation of Jesus that would nourish faith and life." [29] Thus, what is at issue here is not whether Luke's passion narrative corresponds exactly with the actual history of the death of Jesus, but rather whether mine is a faithful interpretation of Luke and whether my interpretation can enrich the contemporary Christian understanding of how one should approach dying.[30] With this purpose in mind, let us now turn to the narrative itself and the ways in which it illuminates the proper shape of Christian patience, hope, and compassion in the face of death.

Jesus' Practice of Patience, Compassion, and Hope in Dying

The purpose of this chapter is not to develop a sense of the meaning and shape of patience, compassion, and hope from scratch. Instead, we will examine in detail the instances of Jesus' expression of patience, compassion, and hope with the aim of enhancing the understandings of those virtues that have already been developed in the last two chapters. Our reading of this text will also serve simply to confirm the importance of patience, compassion, and hope for Christians as they approach death; to the historical and contemporary sources of the previous two chapters that make this affirmation we add a biblical witness.

What Must We Endure? The Patience of Jesus

One could argue that the whole passion narrative could be seen as demonstrative of the patience of Jesus. But rather than pursue this line of thought, I will focus on one key scene in which Jesus' patience is most clearly expressed: when he prays in the Garden of Gethsemane (Lk 22:39-45). It is there that we glimpse Jesus' anxiety concerning the death about to befall him, and witness his decision to accept it nevertheless.[31] This compact passage reveals Jesus' patience to have four qualities. First, we observe in Jesus the *reluctant* endurance of suffering; patience seeks to avoid suffering if possible, but to endure it if necessary. Second, the patience of Jesus rests upon a profound sense of Providence, or of divine purpose in the events that are about to unfold. Jesus chooses to face suffering and death patiently because he believes that God has placed him in this circumstance and has called him to respond in this way. Third, Jesus' patience can be interpreted as demonstrative of a particular understanding of autonomy; one of the things Christians must specifically be prepared to endure is some limitation on their exercise of autonomy. Fourth, Jesus shows a connection between patience and love for his disciples and many others. In this way, patience is an unmistakably social virtue. Let me now sketch briefly the scene in which these qualities of Jesus' patience are to be found.

After instructing his disciples to pray that they "may not come into the time of trial" (Lk 22:40), Jesus himself kneels and prays, "Father, if you are willing, remove this cup from me; yet, not my will but yours be done" (Lk 22:42).[32] Before turning to the issue of Jesus' patience, it is important first to be clear on the meaning of this passage. We must ask, to what does "this cup" refer?

By describing the decision facing Jesus as one of choosing whether to accept a cup, Luke provides the reader with many layers of possible meaning. "The cup" is a symbol used frequently and in reference to a variety of things in the ancient Near East, making an exact specification of its meaning here elusive.[33] Two connotations should be highlighted in preparation for the analysis of Jesus' patience that follows.

First, "the cup" refers to that which comes from God as one's portion or destiny. For example, in Ps 116:12-13, one's cup refers to bounty and salvation given by God. This allotted portion sometimes brings woe rather than blessing (for example, the cup can refer to divine retribution or punishment for sins as in Ps 75:8 or Jer 25:15-16).[34] Thus, in being offered a cup, Jesus is offered a destiny from God that will entail suffering and death. This use of language connects his impending suffering with a sense of Providence or divine planning.

Second, the language of the "cup" suggests that a connection must be drawn between Jesus' agony in the garden and the last supper he ate with his disciples. At that meal, Jesus expresses his loving offer of himself to his disciples via the symbolic gesture of giving them a cup of wine.[35] There he offers the cup to his disciples ("Take this . . ." Lk 22:17) and goes on to explain that "this cup that is poured out for you is the new covenant in my blood" (Lk 22:20). The similarity between Lk 22:17 where Jesus invites the disciples to "take this cup" and Lk 22:42 where Jesus pleads before God to "take away this cup" connects his decision here with the saving activity of God in the new covenant. These two connotations come together to offer a rich sense of the choice facing Jesus. He must choose to accept or to push away a portion from God that includes not only a taste of death, but potential blessing as well (at least a potential blessing for others in the form of a new covenant). What we have here is Jesus expressing some anxiety or a desire to avoid his "portion" and the impending suffering and death that he foresees it entails; he pleads (in the softest of terms possible, "*If* you are willing . . .") that he might not have to endure it.

To properly understand his patience, one must note here that Jesus does not embrace suffering gladly or as a means of moral development. Thus, we could say that the first significant characteristic of Jesus' patience is that it takes a negative view of suffering. We do not find here a role model for masochism. There is neither an enthusiasm about the trial that is to come (i.e., no sign that Jesus *wishes* to be tested as a means of proving his fidelity to God) nor any sense that the endurance of suffering to come is *in se* a good or a means to virtue. Jesus' first preference is not to endure suffering well or patiently but rather to avoid suffering if possible; this is the purpose of his prayer: "Remove this cup from me!"

Despite his aversion to the suffering that he foresaw, Jesus chose to endure it; balancing his sense that suffering was not a good to be pursued for its own sake was an equally compelling sense that some suffering is a necessary part of faithfulness to God. This brings us to the second important characteristic of the patience of Jesus: it manifests a profound sense of Providence or divine planning behind events, and also a desire to be obedient to God's wishes. It is noteworthy that in his prayer, Jesus refers twice to God's will ("If you are willing . . ." and "Not my will but yours be done"). Raymond Brown observes that *boulesthai*, the Greek verb Luke selects for "if you are *willing*" (also: "if you *desire*"), is one most often used by Luke when God is the subject and when a tone of a pre-ordained divine decision is desired.[36] The precise language Luke employs here indicates "Jesus is first of all concerned with the direction of divine planning."[37] Balancing Jesus' aversion to the experience of crucifixion that was before him is a sense that some suffering must be endured; faithfulness to God sometimes entails suffering.

Patience is typically understood today as a capacity to wait or to endure.[38] Exactly why one should be willing to wait is not generally obvious. Jesus' concern with God's planning and his desire to be obedient to God's will explains why such a capacity is virtuous from a Christian perspective. As David Baily Harned has noted, Christian patience entails a sense of "undying expectancy" regarding the unfolding of history because Christians believe that God is making God's will known in history.[39] This requires the development of patience in the sense of waiting; we must wait for events to unfold for God's will or purposes to be made known to us. Jesus' wait is not long lived in the garden, but waiting is part of the narrative; Jesus does not make a decision in favor of obedience to God and then run to the authorities to precipitate his death, but waits for them to come and arrest him.[40]

An inseparable part of the importance of waiting and discerning the meaning of events and history is a willingness to acknowledge that God has placed us where we are; we too are part of the unfolding of history *as participants*.[41] Thus, Christian patience requires not only a capacity for discernment or reading the sign of the times, but also some degree of endurance or a willingness to suffer through circumstances in which we believe that God will reveal Godself to us. When Jesus prays "not my will, but yours be done," he is expressing both of these aspects of patience that together might be called a sense of Providence. God has called him to this task or placed him in this circumstance. God's revelation of Godself is to be made known to the world in the events of his suffering and death, and therefore his willing participation is required.

One question that emerges from the first two qualities of the patience of Jesus I have described is: "What model of moral agency does Jesus exemplify here?" or "How does the patience of Jesus affect our self-understanding, especially our understanding of autonomy?" The concept of autonomy is very modern (but see Phil 4:11-12), and so we cannot properly ask what model of autonomy Jesus manifests by his actions. However, we can say that in his practice of patience, Jesus presents a model of acting that differs from the image of the autonomous actor one might typically find today. It is in this model of acting that the third dimension of patience in Jesus is revealed: a willingness to endure the difficulties entailed in sharing control of one's own destiny with others (most importantly, with God).

In his decision not to flee the difficult end he foresaw for himself, Jesus chooses to endure not only physical suffering, but perhaps more importantly to endure what we today might call the loss of absolute autonomy. He hands himself over. He makes an active choice to be one who is acted upon—handing over his will to God in the garden ("Not my will but yours be done") and immediately afterward allowing himself to be handed over quite literally into the control of the Roman and Jewish authorities. What is instructive about his patience is not only that he was willing to suffer pain, but more fundamentally that he was willing to endure the relinquishment of unfettered personal freedom. Harned writes:

Certainly the redemptive significance of the passion of Jesus is bound up with his whole life of obedience to the Father. Yet the ultimate instance of his power is the relinquishing of power, the consummate expression of his activity is his patience, and the greatest use of his initiative lies in waiting and endurance. So the obedience of the Son to the Father culminates in his submission to the hands of men, when the world's redemption is achieved.[42]

The example of Jesus makes clear that the expression of patience entails relinquishing the exercise of absolute or total control over one's own fate.

How might one today imitate this aspect of the patience of Jesus analogously? Traditionally there has been a tendency to focus on the physical suffering of Jesus as crucial for Christian efforts at discipleship.[43] I am proposing a different aspect of his dying as the most important thing for Christians to imitate today. We should not seek to imitate Jesus' fate of enduring the pain of lashings, or nails piercing one's body; Jesus' own prayer in the garden indicates that these should be avoided if possible. Rather, we should imitate the patience of Jesus in his acceptance of some limits to his own freedom; we should imitate Jesus in the sense of handing ourselves over.

Recall from the last chapter that for Dr. Timothy Quill's patients, the most difficult form of suffering was not caused by pain, but rather by their transformation from totally autonomous agents to something approaching the status of an object—that of persons utterly dependent upon others for life and care. In Jesus' example it is implied that sometimes allowing ourselves to be acted upon can be beneficial. As Harned observes: "Nevertheless, it is absolutely essential for us to affirm this dependence, helplessness, and need to wait upon the initiative of others, for these have all been sanctified by God in Jesus Christ."[44]

The assertion that, in their own dying, contemporary Christians are to imitate Jesus' decision to "hand himself over" is one that will undoubtedly raise many concerns. A great deal of serious theological scholarship over the last few decades, particularly by feminist theologians, has pointed in what seems initially to be the opposite direction. Drawing on the work of the psychologist Carol Gilligan and others, many have made clear that the piety of self-effacement and submission of one's own will to that of others is unsuitable for many women who are already socialized by our culture to be self-effacing servants to the people in their lives. [45] The concerns of these scholars must be addressed and taken seriously. Anyone who would recommend a model of "handing oneself over" must explain how this does not compromise the moral agency of vulnerable people, including some women.

I am in sympathy and agreement with the view that it is potentially damaging to advise some Christians to surrender their autonomy or to sacrifice their own self-interest for the benefit of others. However, the model of patience I am recommending here is distinct from that sort of damaging counsel in important ways.

Typically, feminist theologians and others are concerned about women who disregard their own welfare and personal development in favor of rendering services to their loved ones. They are suspicious of a piety that would encourage people to look at the suffering of Christ on the cross so as to become more willing to suffer in service to others. I am proposing a very different use of the model of Jesus' behavior—one in keeping with Luke's gospel. If one focuses on Jesus' willingness to recognize and endure some limits on his personal freedom—to curb efforts at absolutely controlling his own fate, to hand himself over to God and others—the possible analogies for oneself are expanded. For example, one should be willing to give up those same things (absolute control, etc.) in imitation of Jesus, but to *receive* care. The point is not self sacrifice, but a modified sense of self that can simultaneously accommodate dependence and dignity.

The relinquishment of some autonomy and the practice of patience actually offer more protection for vulnerable women than would the intensification of their right to absolute autonomy or independence. A helpful analogy to consider would be a woman's choice to enter a shelter to escape abuse. By this act, she relinquishes some degree of freedom and hands herself over to others to receive their care and protection. She surrenders absolute control over herself in order to receive care and protection she could not provide for herself. Throughout this process of giving herself over she remains a dignified human subject.

For those facing a debilitating or fatal disease, the alternative to allowing oneself willingly to become dependent is to eliminate oneself altogether. Recall, for example, the story discussed in chapter 3 of Timothy Quill's patient who was not suffering physically, but due to compromised cardio-pulmonary function found herself increasingly dependent.[46] Rather than cope with this dependence, the patient decides to attempt to end her life by overdosing on barbiturates. She said, "I cannot stand the way I am living right now, waiting for the end. I would rather die . . . at a time of my own choosing."[47] Rather than hand herself over to the care of others, this woman chose to kill herself.

The example of Jesus suggests that this woman's choice was a mistake; it is better to hand oneself over to others than to cling to a notion of absolute self-direction and independence. I would add that realizing that the main alternative to the practice of patience is suicide clarifies why the patience I advocate should not be looked upon with fear or suspicion by feminists. Susan Wolf, James F. Keenan, and others have highlighted the fact that the magnification of autonomy at the end of life has the undesirable effect of feeding the very kind of self-sacrifice feminists have criticized. Vulnerable old women, afraid of being a burden if they require care from their children are prone to choosing the self-sacrificial alternative of suicide. [48] A model of the patient Jesus as one who is vulnerable and acted upon—enduring patiently—would encourage these women to endure dependence and accept care rather than eliminate themselves to avoid "being a burden" to others. The focus of what is to be imitated must properly shift from self-sacrifice to the sacrifice of absolute autonomy and independence.

To recapitulate what has been said of the patience of Jesus so far: it relates to suffering as something to be avoided or endured only reluctantly; and it includes a sense of Providence and a willingness to be acted upon. Let me conclude this treatment of patience by turning to a final quality: it is practiced out of love. Jesus makes himself vulnerable and endures suffering not as an act of masochism, but out of love for God, friends, and the world. Jesus does not act out of blind obedience, but with the sense that some good is to come from his crucifixion. Narrative evidence of this fact can be found in the scene immediately before the start of his passion: at the last supper.

The scene in which Jesus shares a last meal with his friends and bids them farewell is very rich, as evidenced by the volume of articles and books written on this topic.[49] I refer the reader to other works for the full theological import of these texts. I intend simply to take the narrative at face value in order to make the point that along with whatever additional theological meaning might be derived from the last supper, it communicates a deep affection by Jesus for the disciples and connects his suffering to that love.

The affection Jesus had for his disciples is evident in the first words he speaks after all have gathered at table: "I have eagerly desired to eat this Passover with you before I suffer; for I tell you, I will not eat it until it is fulfilled in the kingdom of God" (Lk 22:15-16). Jesus knows he is about to suffer, and he longs to be with his friends once more before his suffering begins. In addition to this expression of longing for companionship, Jesus' love for his disciples is clear in the meaning he attaches to the events that are about to unfold. In what is traditionally called the institution of the Eucharist, Jesus depicts his death as endured for friends:

> Then he took a loaf of bread, and when he had given thanks, he broke it and gave it to them, saying, "This is my body, which is given for you. Do this in remembrance of me." And he did the same with the cup after supper saying, "This cup that is poured out for you is the new covenant in my blood" (Lk 22:19-20).

These words offer some insight into the meaning of what is to come from Jesus' perspective (at least his perspective as portrayed in this narrative): he is to suffer—he is to give himself over and allow himself to be acted upon—"for you." His *soma*—his entire life or whole human being—is given over for his followers.[50] As the author of John's gospel recognized, there is no greater love than this (Jn 15:13).

Here we also see a reprise of the importance of a sense of Providence in Jesus' practice of patience. This gift is portrayed as having salvific significance: "This cup that is poured out for you is the new covenant in my blood" (Lk 22:20). The bond created between God and humanity in Jesus' life is now to be sealed mysteriously in his suffering and death.[51] His death is not to be in vain, but (mysteriously) for the benefit of those he loves and all the world. His patient suffering and death are an expression of his own love and a sacramental expression of God's love for the world.

It is here that we glimpse the difficulty of modeling our own death on that of Jesus Christ. For what analogy can be drawn between our very ordinary dying and the death of the savior of the world? It is the very fact that one's own suffering and dying seems to be devoid of salvific purpose or meaning that makes dying so difficult for many people today. Finding an analogy between our own dying and this salvific death of Jesus presents a real challenge, but not an insurmountable one; however, I will leave that question for the conclusion of this chapter. For now, let me conclude simply by noting that Jesus' own patience was clearly an expression of love. More specifically, it was an expression of compassion—a love that sought to suffer with and for sinful human beings. Yet again, the connection among the virtues proves itself to be very deep.

Hope: The Power of God's Presence and Promise

Two scenes from Luke's text are particularly important for understanding how Jesus practiced hopefulness at the end of his life: Jesus at prayer in the garden of Gethsemane (Lk 22:39-44) and Jesus' last words before he died (Lk 23:46). These passages reveal that Jesus' hope has three fundamental qualities. First, it relies for comfort on the assurance of God's constant presence in the midst of suffering. Second, it moves Jesus to continued action as God's witness (thereby functioning as a support for the virtue of patience). Third, it includes an eschatological dimension or an expectation that God's presence is more powerful than death and endures beyond it.

We have already examined how the scene in which Jesus prays in the Garden of Gethsemane illustrates his practice of patience. Now we must return to this same passage in order to understand how Jesus practiced hope at the end of his life. Recall that here Jesus pleads with God on his knees that the cup placed before him might be removed (Lk 22:42). What was not discussed above was the response that comes from God. Despite the plea of Jesus, the cup is not removed; however Luke writes that "an angel from heaven appeared to [Jesus] and gave him strength" (Lk 22:43). Sensing God's response, Jesus in turn responds by "praying more earnestly, and his sweat became like great drops of blood falling down on the ground" (Lk 22:44).

Before attending to the issue of how this passage is instructive of the nature of Christian hope, it is important first to deal with some of the historical-critical issues that surround the text. Most importantly, we must address the issue of whether this passage should be regarded as a legitimate part of Luke's gospel. As Fitzmyer notes in his commentary on Luke, Greek manuscripts and other ancient versions of the text are almost equally divided on whether to include these verses (Lk 22:43-44) or omit them, as are contemporary textual commentators.[52] I do not wish to devote too much space to discuss the details of this controversy.[53] However, since this is one of only two biblical passages on which I will rely to describe how Jesus exemplified Christian hope in his dying, I think it is necessary to state briefly the reasons why I, along with many biblical scholars, accept these verses as Lucan.

Linguistic and stylistic evidence can be marshaled to support Lucan authorship of 22:43-44. [54] Most significantly, the first four words of verse 43 are identical to those in Luke 1:11, and appear nowhere else in the New Testament.[55] The verb used, *ophthe* ("appeared"), is also typically Lucan, occurring twelve times in Luke-Acts and only once each in Matthew and Mark.[56] Furthermore, the scene as a whole bears a resemblance to Acts 12:5 in which the church prays "earnestly" (*ektenesteron*, the same verb used in verse 22:43) for Peter, who is subsequently visited by a strengthening angel.[57] Thus, the language and style used here seem to be that of Luke.

A literary analysis of this scene, or an analysis of its structure also supports Lucan authorship. Some commentators have argued that the appearance of the angel interrupts the flow of the scene's description; they favor the omission of the angel so that there is a direct parallel in structure between verses 40-41 and 45-46.[58] However, Jerome Neyrey contends that the strengthening angel provides a logical centerpiece to the entire scene, rather than a misplaced interruption within it.[59] Neyrey interprets the scene as presenting a contrast between Jesus and the disciples. Jesus accepts the will of God that he must "enter the trial," prays to God to assist him in this endeavor, and receives an answer in the form of a strengthening angel; in contrast, the disciples fall asleep, fail to pray, and fail to become strengthened.[60] Thus, in Neyrey's reading the angel is pivotal to the import of the entire scene. To conclude this brief defense of the authenticity of Lk 22:43-44 by way of summary, we could say that the language used is characteristically Lucan and the appearance of the angel itself fits in well enough with the structure of the scene that we need not question the verse's authenticity.

Granted now that these verses are authentic, we must ask what they convey about the nature of Christian hope in the face of death. Recall that in the last chapter, I developed an understanding of Christian hope that was not opposed to death, but that could endure even in the face of it; Christian hope does not eliminate the possibility of suffering or death, but rather places it within the context of a relationship with God, thereby removing some of its sting and power. Hope functions to assuage the fears of Christians by shifting the focus of meaning in the events that are about to unfold. It is not a distraction from what is to take place, nor an empty promise that no harm will ever come; rather, it is a reorganization of the significance of the facts at hand: you will suffer, you will die, *but I will be with you.* Christian hope elevates the importance of this last fact to such a degree that it *outweighs* (but does not eliminate) the negativity of the other facts of the situation. This view is captured well by the spirit of Romans

8:31-39, where Paul writes that all hardship loses its *ultimate* power when we realize that it cannot separate us from the love of God in Christ. It is this same understanding of hope that is evident here in Jesus.[61] He must still enter into this trial, but now with the assurance that God is with him.

The second important quality of hope that Jesus exemplifies in his dying is that it moved him to continued action as God's witness; that is to say it fortified his patience. Some commentators have found it curious that after Jesus is visited by the strengthening angel, he prays more earnestly and he sweats profusely (Lk 22:44); they ask why a strengthening angel that communicates God's enduring presence would cause Jesus to be in agony. Jerome Neyrey and others have provided a helpful explanation that centers upon the Greek term, *agonia.* Neyrey notes that the meaning of agony can often derive from the kind of pain or struggle experienced in the context of athletics or physical struggle.[62] Thus, Jesus is in agony after the visit by the strengthening angel, not in the sense that he is pained by fear, but rather in anticipation of the struggle in which he has dedicated himself to engage. His agony and profuse sweat are analogous to those of a runner who is tensed up and prepared for the start of a race.[63] Hope—an assurance of God's presence in the face of severe struggle and grim circumstances—functions not only to reassure, but also to move one to action. Assured of God's presence communicated by the strengthening angel, Jesus finds the strength to engage in the difficult activity that he discerns he is being called to undertake. His hope in God's presence and care through the impending adversity fortifies his patience.

Let us now turn to the scene of the crucifixion itself for additional insight into the shape of Jesus' hope. There, its third fundamental quality—its eschatological dimension—becomes clear. In Luke's gospel, Jesus' last act before dying is to cry out, "Father, into your hands I commend my spirit" (Lk 23:46). His words are part of a verse of the thirty-first Psalm, which reads, "Into your hand I commit my spirit; you have redeemed me, O Lord, faithful God" (Ps 31:5). When spoken in the context of the scene at the cross, these words are unmistakably an expression of eschatological hope.[64] As in the garden of Gethsemane, hope here relies upon a connection between Jesus and God—a relationship that has been able to withstand the darkest of hours.[65] However, whereas Jesus' awareness of God's presence in the garden served as a source of strength and patience—as a force that moved him to continued action in service to God—here, only an eschatological interpretation is possible. To imply "you have redeemed me" and to convey directly the trust of one's soul to God at the moment of one's death at the conclusion of a period of horrible suffering only make sense if the surrounding darkness is not the final word on things. It only makes sense with an expectation of being saved or redeemed by God *after* death.

Thus we find in the hope expressed by Jesus in his passion a considerable similarity with the shape of contemporary Christian hope described in chapter 3 and also with the hope of the historical *ars moriendi* tradition discussed in chapter 2. In chapter 3, I concluded that contemporary Christian hope was a hope that could endure in the face of death (rather than standing in opposition to it), that required a commitment to be a witness to God's kingdom, and that held out the expectation that even death could not bring an end to one's relationship with God. These qualities are amply found in Jesus' expression of hope on the cross and in his prayer in the garden.

Compassion Even in Dying

In the last two chapters, compassion was explored as a virtue that was to be nurtured by those who would be caregivers to the dying. As I said in the introduction to chapter 3, compassion is the virtue that would guide the moral response of family, friends, and medical professionals to the suffering experienced by those who are dying. Examining the virtue of compassion in the context of Luke's passion narrative will take us on a different course. Although in Luke we do not find Jesus to be utterly abandoned by his friends as we do in the gospels of Matthew and Mark, the Lucan story nevertheless provides few role models of compassionate care for the dying Jesus.[66] Instead, what is remarkable is Jesus' own expression of compassion during his trial, suffering, and death. Thus, what this biblical material adds to our discussion is the suggestion that not only the reception but also the *expression* of compassion by the dying is a key component of dying well.

Three scenes from Luke's passion highlight Jesus' expression of compassion in his dying. First, at the scene of his arrest, Jesus takes a moment to heal the high priest's servant whose ear is cut off in a brief skirmish with the disciples (Lk 22:49-51). A second compassionate moment comes immediately after Jesus is betrayed by Peter (Lk 22:54-62). There, in a knowing glance, Jesus conveys forgiveness and concern for his disciple. Finally, after Jesus is lifted up onto the cross, he expresses compassion yet again by offering his forgiveness of those responsible for his death, and by assuring one of the men condemned to die with him that ultimately they would both be saved by God from the evil they were enduring together (Lk 23:33-34, and 23:39-43).

The shape of compassion that Jesus exemplifies in these passages differs noticeably from the description of Christian compassion that was developed at length in the last chapter. There, the focus was upon how one could share in the suffering of one's beloved. It involved listening, empathetic feeling, and action on behalf of the one suffering. Here, the circumstances under which Jesus practices compassion do not permit any elaborate effort to know deeply the suffering of those around him. Instead, his activity fits almost entirely within the third aspect of compassion as I have defined it—that of acting on behalf of and in concert with those suffering. To be more specific, Jesus expresses concern for the overall well-being of those around him and shows them mercy and forgiveness. The key point I wish to make in this section is that when compassion is expressed by the dying it has a different character from compassion as expressed by those who would care for them. Jesus' example reveals the importance of expressing care for one's caregivers, and expressing mercy and forgiveness even as one is suffering and dying. With the overall direction of this section now made clear, let us turn to the specific texts that exemplify Jesus' compassion.

When Judas comes with a number of other men who intend to arrest Jesus, the disciples initially contemplate resisting them violently. One of the disciples strikes the high priest's servant, cutting off his right ear (Lk 22:50). Jesus halts the disciples' attempts at resistance and proceeds immediately to heal the servant's ear. In his commentary on this passage, Robert Karris declares that this incident reveals the nature of "the compassionate God proclaimed by Jesus," a God who even heals an enemy.[67] Jesus' action of healing the servant's ear is one of *compassion* because he acts to relieve someone else's suffering. When entering into his own agony, Jesus nevertheless takes the time to relieve the pain of another. One could say that Jesus' compassion here is expressed as an ongoing sensitivity to the suffering of those around him and as a willingness to act to diminish their suffering and to preserve their well-being.

To gain a full appreciation of the way in which this instance of healing expresses Jesus' concern for the full well-being of others, this isolated act must be put into the context of Jesus' life of ministry. Jesus' life of preaching and healing focused primarily upon clarifying the shape of the Kingdom of God, not upon himself or his identity nor about God *in se*.[68] Jesus points to God's liberating love for human beings, and historicizes that love via concrete acts that both offer hope for the eschatological fulfillment of God's Reign and announce its immediate advent. An important way in which Jesus manifests God's liberating love is in the many miracles he performs. The miracle stories are not to function as supernatural proofs of Jesus' divinity. Rather, they indicate that for Christians the Kingdom of God dawns in the words and actions of Jesus. He not only models an authentic mode of human living via his actions (by having mercy on those who are suffering), but also mediates the very presence of God in them, making possible a profound level of human wholeness and healing.[69] The miracle of healing is thus a very significant act theologically.[70] It communicates his own concern and God's concern for the overall, embodied wellness of human beings.

Expressing concern for the well-being of those around him is the first mark of Jesus' compassion in dying. The second mark is his concern to relieve the suffering of others through mercy and forgiveness. One of the more poignant scenes in the passion narrative is the denial of Peter (Lk 22:54-62). It contains considerable dramatic narrative detail (e.g., Peter is accused once on the basis of having the accent of a Galilean; the cock crows at the moment Peter denies Jesus for the third time in verse 60) in order to maximize its impact. The scene serves primarily as a locus for contrasts. The calm of Jesus at the table with his disciples (less than thirty verses ago!) is contrasted with the action and hostility of the trial. The infidelity of Peter as he renounces any association with Jesus is contrasted to the fidelity of Jesus to God as he refuses to provide false testimony in order to save himself.[71] In addition to these contrasts, Peter's denial in Luke is also an occasion for the expression of compassionate forgiveness by Jesus.

In contrast to the way it is described in Matthew and Mark (where Jesus is inside on trial while Peter remains outdoors), Luke locates Peter and Jesus together in this scene. It is likely that he does so in order to show Jesus' enduring care for his follower at this moment when Satan has tempted him and he has failed.[72] Locating Jesus and Peter together allows Luke to add the following line (not found in Matthew or Mark) immediately after Peter denies Jesus for the third time: "The Lord turned and looked at Peter" (Lk 22:61a). It is this connection or "look" that causes Peter to remember "the word of the Lord, how he had said to him, 'Before the cock crows today you will deny me three times.' And he went out and wept bitterly" (Lk 22:61-62).

The "look" or turning of Jesus toward Peter seemingly could have any number of meanings—reprimand, dismay, anger, and so forth—because no more is said other than that Jesus looked at Peter. However, a number of noted commentators have concluded that this look was an expression of compassion.[73] This conclusion is based largely upon an examination of the full scene that Peter recollects when his eyes meet those of Jesus.

Jesus' prediction of Peter's denial takes place in verse 34. The prediction was not made with finger wagging, but rather in a spirit of concern. The following text precedes both Peter's pledge of fidelity and the prediction of his denials: "Simon, Simon, listen! Satan has demanded to sift all of you like wheat, but I have prayed for you that your own faith may not fail; and you, when once you have turned back, strengthen your brothers" (Lk 22:31-32). Jesus predicts not simply Peter's failure, but a subsequent ability to turn back again and strengthen the other followers. As Brown writes of this sequence: "Luke wants us to know how amid his sufferings Jesus was thoughtful of others."[74] Thus, Jesus' gaze does not communicate admonishment so much as it recalls his prayer and concern for Peter, as well as his hope that Peter will repent ("turn back") and return to strengthen the others.

In this scene we find compassion expressed both as empathy, and as mercy or forgiveness. Clearly, there is nothing here like the elaborate process of empathetic understanding in the service of compassion developed in the last chapter. However, if we take Jesus' prediction of Peter's denial not as an instance of fortune telling but rather as communicating the sense that Jesus knows that it is difficult to be faithful to him—an awareness that he would have developed by being attentive to the experiences of his disciples over time—then this entire sequence of events can be understood also as an example of empathetic compassion. He predicts that Peter will deny him because he knows how difficult it is to be his disciple. Such an interpretation gains strength when we recall that the scene is designed to draw both parallels and contrasts between Jesus and Peter.

Peter fails where Jesus succeeds under the pressure of antagonistic questions and accusations (the contrast), but both share a similar experience (the parallel). Jesus knows what Peter has experienced analogously by his own experience. So in this sense, Jesus' action here has a dimension of empathy—of knowing what the other is going through or at the very least having some degree of sensitivity to it.

The theme of mercy and forgiveness persists as we turn to the scene at the cross itself as the place where Jesus models compassion in dying for the last time.[75] There, Jesus demonstrates compassion first by expressing his forgiveness of his persecutors and then by showing mercy toward one of the wrongdoers with whom he died.

Immediately after he had been placed upon the cross, Luke depicts Jesus as saying, "Father, forgive them; for they do not know what they are doing" (Lk 23:34). This passage has been the focus of some debate among biblical scholars, both in terms of its meaning and authenticity. The chief uncertainties are to whom exactly Jesus is referring (is it merely the Romans who are physically carrying out the crucifixion, or the Jewish authorities as well?), and how he can meaningfully say that "they do not know what they are doing" when his execution has come about as a result of such a purposeful set of proceedings. An exact answer to these queries is somewhat beside the point for our purposes.[76] What is significant for my argument is that Jesus is portrayed as prepared to show understanding and forgiveness toward the people to whom he has chosen to allow himself to be handed over.

After a short time during which Jesus was mocked by "the leaders" and the soldiers standing nearby (Lk 23:35-37), Luke provides narrative details that are unique to his gospel. The other three canonical gospels each report the presence of two wrongdoers who are crucified alongside Jesus; Luke elaborates on that detail, providing an exchange among the three condemned (Lk 23:39-43). One of those crucified joins with those below in deriding Jesus: "Are you not the Messiah? Save yourself and us!" (Lk 23:40). A second criminal rebukes the first, proclaiming the innocence of Jesus. He goes on to express this request: "Jesus, remember me when you come into your kingdom" (Lk 23:42). Jesus replies, "Truly I tell you, today you will be with me in Paradise" (Lk 23:43).

In many ways, the meaning of this passage is strictly theological, or christological. Its focus is not upon the expression of human compassion by Jesus but upon his innocence, and his status as a king who (upon his death, or in the time of his kingdom) is empowered to dispense mercy and salvation; the "good" criminal does not plead for Jesus to be with him now in his pain and death, but rather to *remember* him afterwards, when their agony has ceased and Jesus has come into his glory.[77] The criminal's plea is for an eschatological expression of mercy.[78] At the same time, in addition to its richness as a source of reflection on eschatology, soteriology, and more, this passage is demonstrative of Jesus' compassion in dying. The scene depicts a very intimate encounter in which Jesus yet again offers mercy to someone in an unenviable position, providing him with comfort and hope.[79]

There is very little to go on here in terms of discovering the shape of Jesus' compassion. He offers only a one-line response to the request of the condemned, "Truly I tell you, today you will be with me in paradise" (Lk 23:43). The response does not give us a strong image of the shape of compassion; it merely reveals the bare fact that here compassion entails offering forgiveness and hope.

The repentant criminal is to be seen as another in the series of people who turn to Jesus throughout his ministry for forgiveness and salvation (e.g., the sinful woman in Lk 7:37-50, Zacchaeus in Lk 19:9-10, etc.).[80] However, here even more than for the others, the *graciousness* of Jesus' compassionate response of forgiveness is remarkable. This criminal did not seek Jesus out, but came upon him by chance when they were condemned to die together. There is no evidence of radical conversion or metanoia here or of the man's innocence ("we are receiving what is worthy of what we did," Lk 23:41). He merely states what he believes to be transparently true, namely that "this man has done nothing wrong" (Lk 23:41).[81] He follows up this modest defense of Jesus with an equally modest plea: to be *remembered*. Jesus offers much more—the assurance of salvation or accompaniment with him to "paradise." Implicit in this promise is the forgiveness of the man's sins, for it would not make sense for anyone in an unforgiven state to receive such an invitation. Thus, Jesus' response is exceptionally merciful in that it offers forgiveness without repentance or conversion, and in that it is much more than the forgiven man had dared to ask for.[82]

This graciousness of Jesus, this way in which he offers mercy without regard to the merits or accomplishments of the convicted man at his side, points to the distinctiveness of Jesus' practice and of a Christian virtue ethic.[83] We saw in chapter 2 that there was a recurring tension in the writing of Erasmus, Perkins, and Taylor: all of them called upon Christians to prepare diligently for dying by living well and pursuing virtue, and all of them simultaneously called upon Christians to rely upon the mercy of God. For example, William Perkins argued both that "a reformed life" was alone the way to prepare for death and a few pages later that a Christian must "rely . . . wholly on God's special love and favor and mercy in Christ."[84] In Jesus' forgiveness of the criminal condemned to die with him we see one of the sources of this "both . . . and" of Christian virtue ethics. For Christians, there is always the traditional Aristotelian sense of the importance of the pursuit of virtue and its development through conscious practice, but in addition there is always God who can generously and mercifully make up for what we lack. If a condemned criminal can be compassionately forgiven and invited to accompany Jesus to paradise, it is not too much to hope that we too might be forgiven for our own inadequacies.

Finally, this scene is significant because it highlights the connection of compassion to faith and hope. Jesus eases the suffering of the man beside him by providing hope for him, a hope rooted in faith in the power of God to save.

We read of no sign that comes from above or from within Jesus after making his promise that offers "proof" that both he and his new friend were bound for paradise. Instead, what follows is Jesus' prayer of hope in God ("Into your hands, I commend my spirit"), and then the death of both men. In the end, their comfort and their hope depend upon faith in the power of God to save them.[85] Thus, in this final act of compassion—of offering forgiveness and hope—Jesus is a worthy and fitting model for contemporary Christians.

Jesus as a Model of Dying Well Today: Problems and Possibilities

Unresolved Difficulties

The main problem in presenting Jesus as a model of dying well for contemporary Christians lies in the gap between the meaning and significance of the death of Jesus and the seeming meaninglessness and insignificance of our own dying. The reason this gap is such a crucial problem lies in the fact that it is the sense of meaninglessness that most urgently needs to be remedied. I have not found a comprehensive sociological survey that seeks to pinpoint what aspect of dying presents itself as most troubling for men and women today. However, if the anecdotal evidence presented by Timothy Quill in his books on dying is any indication, what people find most troubling and difficult to deal with is the fact that they see suffering as pointless and living through the experience of dying as yielding no benefit to themselves, their loved ones, or the world. For those thoroughly located in today's secular culture, suffering is perceived to be without purpose or benefit; it is always to be avoided. I would add that for many Christians, although there may be a lingering sense that suffering is not entirely bad, it remains difficult to draw inspiration from the example of Jesus in this regard. It is difficult for contemporary Christians to find an analogy between what confronted Jesus and what confronts us today; Jesus had to pray for patience and hope to go through with the experience of dying a death that was to be the sign of a "new covenant" (Lk 22:14-18); we must pray for patience and hope to go through with the experience of dying a death that will undoubtedly be hard, but offers little hint (much less an assurance) that the experience will be redemptive for anyone.

This difference between Jesus' death and our own is not just a matter of failing to see a connection between our own situation and the situation we are called to imitate; the lack of a sense of meaning and significance in our dying undermines our ability to develop the virtue of hope in the way that Jesus did. As I have noted, one of the chief sources of Jesus' hope was a belief in Provi-

dence—a belief in the fact that God had called him to this fate, and his affirma-
tive response to God's invitation would be of great benefit.

The failure of many Christians to see any redemptive purpose in their dying
points to a more fundamental issue: a crisis of belief in God's Providence. I
would not assert that Christians have ceased to believe in Providence. In my
own very limited pastoral experience I found that two of the most common theological statements made to me by parishioners were: "Everything happens for a
reason" and "God has a plan for my life." However, I do maintain that for many
Christians today, when the time comes for them to die or for their loved ones to
die, their belief in Providence or divine planning is eclipsed by something more
powerful. Few seem willing to embrace the sense that God may have called
them to their dying—to live out the last of their days vulnerable and in the care
of family. Some do not hold to any sense of Providence at all, and those of us
who do might still wonder whether there is anything redemptive that might result from our dying. Rather than a locus of our living and calling, dying and suffering present themselves as things always to be avoided. Christians seem un-
willing to see the experience of dying as something to be mined for insight into
what God has called us to in life, or as a part of our lives that might present an
opportunity to serve God.

A closely related issue lies in the quandary of discerning what suffering in
our dying might be "necessary." Jesus had a deep sense that the suffering he was
to endure—*his particular way of dying*—was somehow called for by God in
God's wisdom. I do not want to wade into the waters of theological reflection on
atonement here more than to say that this way of suffering and dying was for
some redemptive purpose. As I explained above in the section on patience, the
passion narrative holds together both the view that suffering which can be
avoided should be avoided, and the view that this particular suffering needed to
be endured in faithfulness to God. Unfortunately, the valid insight that only necessary, redemptive suffering should be patiently endured (and all other suffering
avoided entirely if possible) does not help us to discern what suffering today is
necessary and what is to be avoided. For example, if I have but a month or so to
live and I would prefer not to live any longer, is that month of living leading up
to a "natural" death a necessary suffering or not? If we, like Jesus, plead before
God to take this time of suffering away from us, how are we to know God's "answer"? We are always called to be partners with God in setting the direction of
our lives. Jesus' example that indicates some suffering is necessary does not
resolve the contemporary question of what exactly we should endure and why.

The Promise of This Approach

Read as a model for our own dying, the story of the passion of Jesus does
not solve every riddle, but it does yield some fruit in terms of making it clearer

what it would look like for a Christian to die well today. The way in which Jesus practices the virtues of patience, compassion, and hope are in fact suggestive of how we today should practice those same virtues in dying.

Reflection on the portrait of Jesus' death in Luke's gospel enhances our understanding of the shape of Christian patience by revealing that it necessarily entails enduring the loss of absolute, autonomous self-control. This model of patience runs counter to two currents that are prevalent in contemporary American culture and Catholic Christianity as it is sometimes expressed in the United States. Patience in imitation of Jesus is countercultural in the sense that it calls into question the contemporary emphasis on independence and self-reliance as a source of dignity and worth. It points to the possibility of value in allowing oneself to be acted upon—to putting one's own destiny and care into the hands of others.

The patience of Jesus as I have explained it also runs counter to some traditional Christian notions of what is to be imitated in Jesus' death. As I pointed out, there has been a longstanding emphasis on Jesus' endurance of pain and his willingness to sacrifice himself for others. It is not my purpose to argue for the elimination of this traditional interpretation, but rather to expand it. Alongside the traditional image of a Christian making the ultimate sacrifice of self (which has such rich support in the stories of the Christian martyrs as well) there should be an additional model of patience—that of one who is willing to be "handed over" in a very different sense, one who is willing to be cared for by loved ones.

In both images (that of the martyrs and the way of imitating Jesus that I have proposed here) we glimpse the reality of the limits of our power and autonomy. In both cases we are called to place ourselves in circumstances where control of our bodies and our fate slips away. Thus, there is continuity with the traditional understanding of patience, but it takes on a new richness that expands the Christian model of dying beyond the paradigm of martyr. This expansion of the notion of what constitutes patience speaks more directly to the context in which most North American Christians die today. They do not go to their deaths in a struggle against grave injustice or evil (a context in which God might call forth martyrs), but in the midst of a much more inward, personal struggle to come to terms with their own finitude and helplessness—a struggle to realize their ultimate dependence upon the love of God, and the care of family and friends. In this struggle, the model of choosing to be the patient subject of the care of others is more helpful than the model of the self-sacrificial martyr.

The reflection on the model of Jesus in the passion narrative that I have undertaken in this chapter also enriches our notion of the shape of Christian compassion in the context of death and dying. Most importantly, Jesus makes clear the need for the dying to express as well as receive compassion. Alongside a willingness to be patiently acted upon is an imperative to act—to express compassion. The example of Jesus provided by Luke makes especially clear his concern for well-being (healing the slave), and offering forgiveness for those who are close to us but let us down (Peter). Compassion complements patience in the sense that it calls to mind the ongoing importance of other-directed activity by the dying while existing simultaneously as a recipient of care or as one acted upon.

Finally, in Jesus we find a good model for contemporary Christian hope. The hope of Jesus is portrayed in Luke as connected to faith in God; Jesus, while unquestionably a savior, is simultaneously portrayed as one who finds himself powerless. Jesus does not boldly claim heaven at the end of his struggle, but rather dies with words of faith and hope on his lips. In this way, Luke emphasizes the more "human" aspect of a savior both human and divine, and provides a role model with whom contemporary Christians should readily relate.

Patience, compassion, and hope are shown by Luke to be a web of interdependent virtues that together proved valuable for Jesus in his approach to dying. Jesus was only able to patiently endure his final moments on the cross because of his hope that God would ultimately deliver him; his last expression of patience was at once one of hope: "Into your hands, I commend my spirit." Patience and hope, in turn, were nourished and deeply informed by compassion. As Jesus made clear at the last supper, his patient acceptance of his fate was a decision made out of love and with the hope that his suffering would be the foundation of a new covenant. It is in this interpenetration of the virtues that the Lucan Jesus demonstrates them to be a unity.

The virtues of patience, compassion, and hope find further unification in the prayerful manner in which Jesus practices each. Prayer serves as a common thread among the virtues and reshapes them. Jesus' patience is not achieved by the sheer force of his own exertion but is fortified by his prayerful intimacy with God (and by God's "strengthening angel"). The full force of his compassion can only be felt with reference to God; it is only by God's power that he can offer himself and his blood as the sign of a new covenant; it is only by God's power that he can offer mercy to the condemned man at his side. Similarly, hope is shown to be a virtue achieved and expressed through prayer. Jesus demonstrates that each of these virtues is incomplete when separated from prayer. His pursuit of patience, compassion, and hope is carried out with a sense of God's providential presence and guidance; his expression of these virtues must be seen as a prayerful response to God and to his discernment of God's calling in the specific circumstances of his life.

Let me conclude by suggesting that perhaps it is in the simple, yet difficult prayerful practice of patience, compassion, and hope on the path to our own dying that we might find a way forward in the face of the great problems of meaninglessness that many people confront today. Many have been frustrated by the apparent pointlessness of their own journey to death; the story of the death of Jesus Christ, through whom Christians believe God brought about the redemption of the world, seems an unlikely place to turn for an antidote for this sense of anticlimax. And yet as I hope this study of the Lucan passion narrative has made clear, it was not only Jesus' death itself that was salvific, but his manner of dying that had exemplary and saving significance as well. In his willingness to be patient, in the compassion he showed to the chief priest's servant, to Peter, and to others, in his unwavering hope in God, in all of these ways Jesus was indicating how to draw oneself prayerfully near to God while dying. In these much more modest ways, the Lucan Jesus provides a realistic, helpful example.

In following Jesus along this more modest path, perhaps Christians can find some purpose in their dying. Perhaps they can find purpose in learning patience (and the deep sense of human interdependence that it entails), in practicing compassion by forgiving others and showing love to their family and friends surrounding them, and in holding fast to faith and hope by which we are reminded of our ultimate dependence upon God's mercy and love.

Notes

1. National Conference of Catholic Bishops (USA), Bishops Committee on the Liturgy, *A Ritual for Laypersons: Rites for Holy Communion and the Pastoral Care of the Sick and Dying* (Collegeville, Minn.: Liturgical Press, 1993), 89.

2. What exactly moves Christians to connect the death of Jesus to their own dying or that of a loved one is hard to pinpoint, but regular participation in the liturgy is a likely source. William Spohn argues that liturgical practice and attention to biblical narrative have the greatest potential to impact Christian religious identity; it is from this deep level of character that spontaneous responses arise. See William Spohn, *Go And Do Likewise: Jesus and Ethics* (New York: Continuum, 1999), especially 9–74 and 163–84.

3. Daniel Harrington, *Why Do We Suffer? A Scriptural Approach to the Human Condition* (Franklin, Wis.: Sheed & Ward, 2000), 107.

4. This was especially true of Erasmus, who called the death of Jesus "our perfect example" and Jeremy Taylor who urged readers to try to conform themselves in patience to Christ's suffering. See Desiderius Erasmus, *Preparing for Death* (*De praeparatione ad mortem*), trans. John N. Grant, in *Spiritualia and Pastoralia*, vol. 70, *Collected Works of Erasmus*, ed. John W. O'Malley (Toronto: University of Toronto Press, 1998), 448. Jeremy Taylor, *Holy Dying*, vol. 2, *Holy Living and Holy Dying*, ed. P. G. Stanwood (Oxford: Clarendon Press, 1989), 120.

5. Brown sees Jesus' defiance of Pilate in Jn 18 as evidence of this theme ("You have no power over me at all"). See Raymond E. Brown, *The Death of the Messiah: From Gethsemane to the Grave* (New York: Doubleday, 1994), 34. For a summary of the contrast in theological perspective among the gospel writers, see 26–35. For a more complete account, see Frank J. Matera, *Passion Narratives and Gospel Theologies* (New York: Paulist Press, 1986).

6. This assertion rests on the hermeneutical theory of Paul Ricoeur, among others. Ricoeur argues that discourse has a revelatory power that can exceed the meaning intended by its author. Once written, a text takes on somewhat of an independent status; its meaning is not controlled by what the author had in mind when writing. See Paul Ricoeur, *Hermeneutics and the Human Sciences: Essays on Language, Action and Interpretation*, trans. and ed. John B. Thompson (Cambridge: Cambridge University Press, 1981),

especially 131–44 and 182–93. For a contrasting view, consult Eric D. Hirsch, *Validity in Interpretation* (New Haven, Conn.: Yale University Press, 1967), especially Appendix I: Objective Interpretation (209–44).

7. The very point of the historical-critical interpretive method that dominates contemporary biblical scholarship is to discern the author's intended meaning and the meanings received by the audience to which a text was initially addressed.

8. As Richard B. Hays writes: "Extrabiblical sources for theological insight stand in a hermeneutical relation to the New Testament; they are not independent counterbalancing sources of authority. The Bible's perspective is privileged, not ours. However tricky it may be in practice to apply this guideline, it is in fact a meaningful rule of thumb that discriminates significantly between different approaches to New Testament ethics. Scripture is not just one among several classics, not just one source of moral wisdom competing in a marketplace of ideas, experiences, and feelings. Scripture is the wellspring of life, the fundamental source for the identity of the Church." See Richard B. Hays, "The Church as a Scripture-Shaped Community: The Problem of Method in New Testament Ethics," *Interpretation* 44, no. 1 (1990): 42–55.

9. Jerome Neyrey brings out this motif. He notes that there are significant similarities between the scenes of Lk 4:1-13 where Satan tempts Jesus in the desert and Lk 22:40-46 where Jesus is again tempted in the Garden of Gethsemane. See *The Passion According to Luke: A Redaction Study of Luke's Soteriology* (New York: Paulist Press, 1985), especially 171 where he asserts this interpretation directly. Donald Senior agrees, arguing that the events at the cross should be interpreted (at least in part) as a *cosmic* struggle between good and evil. See Donald Senior, *The Passion of Jesus in the Gospel of Luke* (Wilmington, Del.: Glazier, 1989), 32.

10. Many commentators have suggested that Luke's passion narrative lacks a well-developed soteriology. They assert that the classic soteriological theme of atonement is missing from Luke, leaving open the question of how Jesus saves. For example, see Hans Conzelmann, *The Theology of Saint Luke*, trans. Geoffrey Buswell (London: Faber & Faber, 1960), esp. 201ff. Other commentators disagree, most notably Raymond E. Brown, who writes that Luke's gospel does include or assume the notion of Jesus' death as having saving significance via its atonement for the sins of humanity; Brown believes that the theme of atonement is not absent in Luke but merely different from how contemporary Christians are accustomed to reading and understanding it (i.e., via Paul's writings). Others see a well-developed soteriology, but simply one that does not rely upon the notion of atonement. See Neyrey, *Passion According to Luke*, especially 129–92. See also Richard Zehnle, "The Salvific Character of Jesus' Death in Lucan Soteriology," *Theological Studies* 30 (1969): 430–44.

11. Robert J. Karris, "The Gospel According to Luke," in *The New Jerome Biblical Commentary*, ed. Raymond E. Brown, Joseph A. Fitzmyer, and Roland E. Murphy (Englewood Cliffs, N.J.: Prentice Hall: 1990), 676.

12. John S. Kloppenborg, "*Exitus clari viri:* The Death of Jesus in Luke," *Toronto Journal of Theology* 8, no. 1 (1992): 108. Karris does not cite the *Phaedo* specifically, but agrees that Lk 22:14-38 shows a familiarity with the genre of "farewell discourse," which is one aspect of the literature to which Kloppenborg refers.

13. Kloppenborg, "*Exitus clari viri,*" 108.

14. Kloppenborg, "*Exitus clari viri,*" 110.

15. Kloppenborg, "*Exitus clari viri,*" 109.

16. For an alternate viewpoint, see William S. Kurz, "Luke 22:14-38 and Greco-Roman Biblical Farewell Addresses," *Journal of Biblical Literature* 104 (1985): 251–68. Kurz holds that Jesus' farewell speech in Luke is rooted more deeply in biblical examples, such as I, II, and IV Maccabees.

17. Kloppenborg, "*Exitus clari viri,*" 108 and 112.

18. Brown, *Death of the Messiah*, 984 and 990. Luke also portrays the crowds present at the crucifixion as mixed rather than unequivocally hostile. For example, Luke includes an exchange between Jesus and some weeping women (Lk 23:27).

19. Brown notes that the position of kneeling in prayer indicates that Luke intends Jesus as a model here. Such a position is the mark of distinctively Christian prayer in Acts. See Brown, *Death of the Messiah*, 165.

20. Kloppenborg, "*Exitus clari viri,*" 111.

21. Brian E. Beck, "*Imitatio Christi* and the Lucan Passion Narrative," in *Suffering and Martyrdom in the New Testament*, ed. William Horbury and Brian McNeil (Cambridge: Cambridge University Press, 1981), 28. Beck cites Martin Dibelius as one of the founding thinkers of this line of thought. See Martin Dibelius, *From Tradition to Gospel* (New York: Scribner, 1965). Raymond E. Brown highlights the comparison between Jesus and the martyrs repeatedly in his treatment of the passion narratives. His extensive bibliography is also helpful on this point. See Brown, *Death of the Messiah*, especially 187 and 625–26. See also Daniel Harrington, *Why Do We Suffer?*, 111–12.

22. Brown describes this similarity. See Brown, *Death of the Messiah*, 187.

23. Brown, *Death of the Messiah*, 187.

24. Brown, *Death of the Messiah*, 188.

25. Beck, "*Imitatio Christi,*" 28–33.

26. For a detailed treatment of the connections between Luke's passion narrative and the tradition of martyrdom, see P. E. Davies, "Did Jesus Die as a Martyr Prophet?" *Biblical Research* 19 (1974): 34–47, and J. Downing, "Jesus and Martyrdom," *Journal of Theological Studies* n.s. 14 (1963): 279–93.

27. Brown, *Death of the Messiah*, 31.

28. Brown, *Death of the Messiah*, 11.

29. Brown, *Death of the Messiah*, 13.

30. William Spohn takes a similar view of the way in which narrative supports Christian spirituality and moral practice. Historical scholarship plays a valuable role in unmasking certain distorted portraits of Jesus. However, Christians must go beyond what can be known historically to undertake a personal engagement of the text in which one reexamines how one should live in the midst of the living God. Speaking of scripture, Spohn writes: "That story becomes our story as we appropriate it progressively through imagination, emotions, convictions and actions." See Spohn, *Go and Do Likewise*, 12. In this sort of engagement, historicity takes on a secondary importance. For example, Spohn describes various ways in which John's story of Jesus washing the feet of his disciples might shape Christian identity and the Christian moral imagination (51–54). The legitimacy of such a reflection is not undermined by the fact that the foot-washing scene is unique to John and therefore unlikely to be true in a strictly historical sense.

31. Again, in Luke we see only a glimpse of Jesus' anxiety. His grief is much more pronounced in Matthew and Mark.

32. Here and throughout (unless otherwise noted), the scripture translation comes from the NRSV. Wayne A. Meeks, ed., *HarperCollins Study Bible: New Revised Standard Version* (New York: HarperCollins, 1993).

33. Brown notes that the cup as "cup of wrath" is very ancient and widespread in the ancient Near East. See Brown, *Death of the Messiah*, 168 and his reference to A. T. Hanson, *The Wrath of the Lamb* (London: SPCK, 1957). Taking a cup is also widely used to convey the plainer meaning of tasting death or severe suffering. Brown suggests that this is likely the meaning in yet another instance of "the cup" in Mk 10:38-39 where Jesus asks the disciples, "Are you able to drink the cup which I drink. . ." This scene is not examined here because no direct parallel exists in Luke's gospel. Throckmorton suggests that Luke 12:50 may be an equivalent, but the image of cup does not appear there. See Burton H. Throckmorton, ed., *Gospel Parallels: A Synopsis of the First Three Gospels*, 4th Ed. (Nashville, Tenn.: Thomas Nelson Publishers, 1979), 133.

34. Brown provides these two examples along with some others (Is 51:17, Ez 23:33). See Brown, *Death of the Messiah*, 169.

35. Brown, *Death of the Messiah*, 170.

36. Brown, *Death of the Messiah*, 171.

37. Brown, *Death of the Messiah*, 171.

38. A modern dictionary points in this direction: the ability to endure or remain composed in the face of delay or suffering. See *Random House Dictionary of the English Language, Second Edition, unabridged* (New York: Random House, 1987).

39. David Baily Harned, *Patience: How We Wait Upon the World* (Cambridge, Mass.: Cowley, 1997), 118.

40. The motif of waiting in the garden is much more pronounced in other versions of the passion narrative. For example, in Matthew, the disciples fall asleep three times while Jesus waits anxiously ("my soul is sorrowful to the point of death"–Mt 26:38; scene: Mt 26:36-46). Luke has omitted the repetition of Jesus' pleading to his disciples to stay awake with him while he waits. Commentators speculate that this move was to cast the disciples in a better light; thus, the omission of waiting is a side effect of Luke's desire to exonerate the disciples.

41. Harned, *Patience*, 116.

42. Harned, *Patience*, 122.

43. For example, see part III of Catholic Church, Sacred Congregation for the Doctrine of the Faith. *Declaration on Euthanasia* (Washington, D.C.: United States Catholic Conference, 1980).

44. Harned, *Patience*, 122–23.

45. Jacqueline Grant, "The Sin of Servanthood and the Deliverance of Discipleship," in *A Troubling in My Soul: Womanist Perspectives on Evil and Suffering*, ed. Emilie Townes (Maryknoll, N.Y.: Orbis, 1993), 199–218. Grant's article also considers the factor of race, arguing that notions of servanthood or selflessness would be even more undesirable for African American women than for caucasian women. For an analysis of how liturgy (the liturgies of the Triduum and the emphasis on the sacrifice of Christ one finds there is the specific focus) see Ann Patrick Ware, "The Easter Vigil: A Theological and Liturgical Critique," in *Women at Worship: Interpretations of North American Diversity*, ed. Marjorie Procter-Smith and Janet R. Walton (Louisville, Ky.: Westminster John Knox Press, 1993), 83–106. Finally, for a related body of literature that speaks to the use of the household codes of Paul (the *Haustafel*) as proposing an inappropriate servant- or slave-

master marital relationship see Elisabeth Schüssler Fiorenza, "Discipleship and Patriarchy: Early Christian Ethos and Christian Ethics in a Feminist Theological Perspective," in *Feminist Ethics and the Catholic Moral Tradition*, ed. Charles Curran, Margaret Farley and Richard McCormick (New York: Paulist Press, 1996), 33–65. Schüssler Fiorenza's work supplies an ample bibliography for more extensive exploration.

46. See Timothy Quill, *A Midwife through the Dying Process: Stories of Healing and Hard Choices at the End of Life* (Baltimore: Johns Hopkins University Press, 1996), 163–67.

47. Quill, *Midwife*, 165.

48. Susan M. Wolf, "Gender, Feminism and Death: Physician-Assisted Suicide and Euthanasia," in *Feminism and Bioethics: Beyond Reproduction*, ed. Susan M. Wolf (New York: Oxford University Press, 1996), 282–317. James F. Keenan, "The Case for Physician Assisted Suicide?" *America* 179, no. 15 (14 November 1998): 14–20.

49. For two recent monographs, see Eugene LaVerdiere, *The Eucharist in the New Testament and the Early Church* (Collegeville, Minn.: Liturgical Press, 1996), and George Ossom-Batsa, *The Institution of the Eucharist in the Gospel of Mark* (New York: Lang, 2001).

50. Karris, "Luke," 179.

51. Karris, "Luke," 179.

52. Joseph A. Fitzmyer, *The Gospel According to Luke*, vol. 28a, *The Anchor Bible* (New York: Doubleday, 1985), 1443. Fitzmyer chooses to omit the verses in his own translation for reasons stated on page 1444, although he admits, "for Roman Catholics, they are, however, generally considered to be canonical verses."

53. Brown provides substantial bibliographic references on this matter. See Brown *Death of the Messiah*, 115–16.

54. Brown cites G. Schneider, "Engel und Blutschweiss (Lk 22,43-44)," *Biblische Zeitschrift* 20 (1976): 112–16, as a significant article supporting Lucan authorship of these verses. See also the much earlier work, A. Harnack, "Probleme in Texte der Leidensgescichte Jesu," *Sitzungberichte der (königlichen) Preussichen Akademie der Wissenschaften* (1901): 251–55. Their arguments are summarized in Brown, *Death of the Messiah*, 181–82.

55. Brown, *Death of the Messiah*, 181.

56. Brown, *Death of the Messiah*, 181.

57. Brown, *Death of the Messiah*, 181.

58. Bart Ehrman and Mark Plunkett, "The Angel and the Agony: The Textual Problem of Luke 22:43-44," *Catholic Biblical Quarterly* 45 (1983): 413–14.

59. Neyrey, *Passion According to Luke*, 55–57.

60. Karris accepts this interpretation as legitimate, and presents it as the preferred reading in his commentary. See Karris, "Luke," 184.

61. It is the same for Jesus and Paul except for the fact that for Jesus the love of God is through God as *Abba* rather than as Christ.

62. Neyrey, *Passion According to Luke*, 58. Neyrey shows that Philo contrasts agony as a virtue to grief. One combats grief by engaging in struggle against it. Thus, agony is characterized as active and opposed to despair or paralysis that is the mark of grief.

63. Brown, *Death of the Messiah*, 189. For a treatment of this athletic sense of *agonia*, Brown refers the reader to G. Gamba, "Agonia di Gesù," *Rivista Biblica* 16 (1968): 159–66.

64. These words are more of an expression of thanksgiving in their original context in Psalm 31, where the writer or speaker is giving thanks for actually having been redeemed by God in the events of history.

65. The hope here is personal and intimate. Jesus calls out "Father," not to "God" as is called for in the Psalm (and as he is depicted as doing in both Matthew and Mark), indicating a consistent level of trust and connection to God that stretches from his prayer in the garden to his final moments. See Brown, *Death of the Messiah*, 1068.

66. Throughout the passion narrative, Luke softens the material he found in Mark and Matthew that reflected poorly on the disciples. For example, Luke removes the repetition of the scene in which Jesus finds the disciples asleep during his agony in the garden (Lk 22:46). They fall asleep just once instead of three times as they do in Mark and Matthew (see Mk 14:37-41 and Mt 26:40-44).

67. Karris, "Luke," 185.

68. Jon Sobrino, *Christology at the Crossroads: A Latin American Approach* (Maryknoll, N.Y.: Orbis, 1978), 357.

69. For an excellent theological interpretation of the miracle stories, see Edward Schillebeeckx, *Jesus: An Experiment in Christology* (New York: Crossroad, 1979), 179–200.

70. Vigen Guorian notes that in addition to this meaning, the miracles of Christ "foreshadow his victory over death on the cross. See Vigen Guorian, *Life's Living Toward Dying: A Theological and Medical-Ethical Study* (Grand Rapids, Mich.: Eerdmans, 1996), 65.

71. Karris, "Luke," 186.

72. Brown, *Death of the Messiah*, 608.

73. Karris says simply, "The Lord's glance is one of compassion." See Karris, "Luke," 186. Brown concurs. See Brown, *Death of the Messiah*, 622.

74. Brown, *Death of the Messiah*, 622.

75. An additional scene that one might consider under the heading of Jesus' compassion is Lk 23:28ff, where Jesus instructs the "Daughters of Jerusalem" not to weep for him but for themselves. Consideration of that scene is omitted here because it raises a number of complicated issues (e.g., the destruction of the Temple and its significance, culpability and punishment with regard to the blood of Jesus and all prophets, etc.) that do not shed light on the shape of compassion. We can derive from that scene further evidence that Jesus (as portrayed by Luke) remains concerned for others even while he himself is suffering. For a thorough treatment of this scene, consult Brown, *Death of the Messiah*, 918–27. See also Jerome H. Neyrey, "Jesus' Address to the Women of Jerusalem (Lk 23.27-31)–A Prophetic Judgment Oracle," *New Testament Studies* 29 (1983): 74–86.

76. Again, Brown provides a very helpful, succinct treatment of these controversies. See Brown, *Death of the Messiah*, 973ff.

77. Karris, "Luke," 192.

78. Of course, there is a very extensive debate about the meaning of paradise here. A diversity of views existed in Judaism at the time the NT texts were being written; therefore, a precise meaning is ambiguous. See George Nickelsburg, *Resurrection, Immortality and Eternal Life in Intertestamental Judaism* (Cambridge, Mass.: Harvard University Press, 1972). Karris and Neyrey agree that "paradise" here seems to refer both to eternal life with God after death and the restoration of the Divine-human fellowship that existed

before the Fall (i.e., paradise refers not only to a heavenly life after death, but also to the paradise of the Garden of Eden). In this way a connection is made between the sins of Adam and Jesus Christ as the "new Adam." See Karris "Luke," 192. See Neyrey, *Passion According to Luke,* 181ff. Additional controversies include debate over whether Luke and/or Jesus and the criminal he portrays understood Jesus' promise to refer to the coming of an eschatological kingdom or an ascension that was to take place for those two individuals immediately upon their deaths. See Brown, *Death of the Messiah,* 1005–8. For additional works, consult Brown's ample bibliography on the scene in Brown, *Death of the Messiah,* 889.

79. Neyrey, *Passion According to Luke,* 135.

80. Neyrey, *Passion According to Luke,* 135.

81. Brown, *Death of the Messiah,* 1004. The criminal's proclamation is like that of the Roman centurion that comes immediately after Jesus' death: "Certainly, this man was innocent" (Lk 23:47).

82. Brown accurately speaks of this gesture of forgiveness and compassion as being of the type described by Paul in Romans 5:8, "God demonstrated His love for us in that while we were still sinners, Christ died for us." Love and forgiveness are offered prior to conversion.

83. Alasdair MacIntyre highlights this distinctiveness in *After Virtue* where he argues that medieval Christian proponents of Aristotle's ethics modified his thought by proposing virtues such as charity and practices such as forgiveness of sinners that Aristotle would not have recognized as virtues. Not only were terms such as charity, sin, and repentance nonexistent in the Greek of Aristotle's day, the concepts themselves go against Aristotle's understanding of the way in which friendship and community sustained virtue. In Aristotle's conception, those who were good sought out friendship with the good and structured their community to make outcasts of those whose actions were counterproductive to the development of a good society. See MacIntyre, *After Virtue: A Study in Moral Theory,* 2nd ed. (Notre Dame, Ind.: University of Notre Dame Press, 1984), 174ff.

84. William Perkins, *A Salve for a Sicke Man,* in *The English Ars Moriendi,* ed. David William Atkinson (New York: Peter Lang, 1992), 149 and 157.

85. Neyrey develops a very extensive argument along this line. He argues that in many ways, Jesus saves not as a result of his own personal power, but rather via the depth of his faith in God to save. Thus, Jesus is a very fitting model for Christians as they approach death, for both Jesus and Christians today find themselves at God's mercy—at the mercy of a loving power that is outside of themselves. Jesus is savior, but he becomes so only after being saved himself. See Neyrey, *Passion According to Luke,* 156–92.

Chapter 5

Toward an *Ars Moriendi* for Our Time

Since the morning of Tuesday, September 11, 2001, Americans have been told by the news media again and again that "everything has changed." The exact meaning of that phrase has yet to be made clear. However, it is certain that at least one thing did change on that tragic day: death came out of the hiding place in which it has long been kept in American society.

The events of September 11 revealed the fact that death was not something under technological, medical control. Death was revealed again as a force to be reckoned with existentially. It was right here in our "homeland." It had taken thousands of people in one fell swoop. It did not discriminate on the basis of race or class, taking everyday folks like the wait staff at "Windows on the World," and wealthy New York financial types alike. In the faces of the dead that appeared for months after the tragedy in the *New York Times*, there was someone among the victims with whom each of us could identify.[1] As the focus shifted from the World Trade Center attack to anthrax, loose nukes, and "what could be next," the message many had already grasped in their identification with the 9/11 victims became more explicit: "I could be next. I could die too."[2]

Coming to a conscious knowledge of the fact that death will one day come calling for us, perhaps sooner rather than later, did bring about at least a momentary change of perspective for many Americans. It was observed that many people chose to stay closer to home and to spend time with family during the Thanksgiving and Christmas holidays of 2001.[3] Apparently, the proximity of death called to mind in many people "what is truly important in life," most notably our personal, loving attachments to one another.

The tragedy of September 11 has reminded us again that there is something potentially transformative that comes with the true realization of one's own mortality. Catholic Christians have long recognized this fact. It is in an effort to harness that power that Roman Catholics begin Lent, the time of year most consciously devoted to repentance and renewal, by hearing: "Remember that you are dust, and to dust you shall return." The Christian writers examined in chapter 2 were also aware of the importance of the practice of *momento mori*, or "remembering death." William Perkins and Jeremy Taylor were particularly emphatic on the importance of this practice.[4] These authors saw it as an important source of motivation to live each day as if it were one's last (i.e., to live a life of holiness and repentance). At the same time, these authors also recognized that a momentary flash of insight into the fact of mortality was not enough to "change everything" for an individual. Remembering death was not the solution to the challenge of dying well. This remembrance served as only one way in which people could be called back to the more difficult tasks that were at the heart of a conscious preparation for dying well.

A moment of possibility perhaps exists today in America. Death seems nearer now; the question is open as to how this new proximity of death and tragedy is to be integrated into our approach to life. In these days when we Americans are constantly called to be "on watch" and to be prepared for another round of violence, a corresponding sense of the need to find a way to be prepared for death presents itself.

In this conclusion, I will offer two main points that highlight what the reflection on patience, compassion, hope, and dying well of the last three chapters might offer toward the process of constructing an *ars moriendi* for our time. I began this book with the assertion that insufficient attention has been paid to the experiences ordinary people have of dying. Recent scholarship in bioethics and even theological ethics has offered little advice regarding how people might meet the existential challenges presented in dying. In answer to my own criticism, I want to end on a very practical note by suggesting two steps that can be taken to make dying—ever tragic and difficult—into something that can be endured. Together these suggestions constitute an effort to reintegrate dying into its place as a part of the full experience of human living.

Living Well is the Key to Dying Well

In his introduction to the volume containing Erasmus's *Preparing for Death*, John O'Malley wrote that one of Erasmus's greatest contributions to the *ars moriendi* tradition was to transform it from a collection of techniques that could be employed to thwart the devil on one's deathbed into a body of literature that focused on living well as a preparation for dying well. This key insight of Erasmus, Perkins, Taylor, Bellarmine, and many of the other authors of the *ars moriendi* tradition is one that needs to be heard once again today, some 450 years later. It is by a lifelong effort to nurture faith, hope, patience, compassion, and all the virtues of the good Christian life that we best prepare ourselves for the time of our dying.

Of course, the full shape of the virtuous Christian life is something too comprehensive to describe even briefly in this conclusion. Therefore, I will focus exclusively on the virtue whose development I see as most urgently needed today. Patience as I described it in chapters 3 and 4 is perhaps the hardest virtue for American contemporary men and women to learn. As the portrait of Jesus in Luke's passion narrative makes clear, learning "to hand oneself over" is at the center of the practice of Christian patience. Jesus is a model of patience for Christians in his willingness to cede absolute control over his own fate by recognizing God's intimate guiding presence in his life and by recognizing his deep relationship to the people around him.

I have singled out patience as the key virtue to be practiced over a lifetime because it is the inability to be patient that makes dying a horror for so many Americans today. In the stories of the patients of Timothy Quill I retold in chapters 3 and 4, and in the stories of many dying people living in fear of death told by the journalist Bill Moyers in his PBS television documentary, *On Our Own Terms*, it becomes clear that what makes dying so hard is the inevitable loss of control that accompanies it.[5] It is the inability to care for oneself, or have enough control to determine exactly when one is to die that many people find intolerable.

How is one to learn patience today? As I remarked in chapter 3, very little attention has been paid to patience in recent years, leaving few resources from which to draw in answer to this question. Therefore, it seems wise to turn again to the writers of the historical *ars moriendi* tradition for guidance. William Perkins suggests that there are two components to growing in patience. First, one must build endurance. He writes:

> He that would be able to beare the crosse of all crosses, namely death itselfe, must first of all learne to beare small crosses, as sicknesses in body & troubles in mind, with losses of goods and of friends, of good name, which I may fitely tearme little deaths . . . wee must first of all acquaint our selues with these little deaths before we can well be able to beare the great death of all.[6]

This suggests a need to build up one's stamina and coping mechanisms. Death is difficult and painful; in Perkins's view one will be unable to endure its magnitude of suffering, loss, and pain if one has no experience with learning to endure in the face of these evils.[7]

The second half of Perkins's approach to learning patience is to learn obedience. He writes that one should be "willing and ready and desirous to go out of this world whensoever God shall call him, and that without murmuring or repining, at what time, where, and when it shall please God."[8] He names this disposition toward death "dying in obedience" (to God) and sees Jesus as a paradigm for it. Perkins cites Jesus' words, "Father, if you are willing, remove this cup from me; yet, not my will but yours be done" (Lk 22:42), as exemplary of a will-ingness to embrace suffering and even death as God's will.[9] Erasmus agrees with Perkins on this twofold approach to patience, but he is even more emphatic about the need to *embrace* suffering or difficulties. He writes:

> Misfortunes become profit if, free of sins, we bear them with endurance, giving thanks to the Lord for all; they become medicine if anything resides in us that has to be purged either by surgery or cautery or by bitter drugs. Such misfor-tunes are disease, poverty, old age, loss of our loved ones, and the other count-less troubles by which all human lives are beset on all sides. . . . If we accept these misfortunes with compliance and even with an expression of thanks—as if they come from the hand of a kindly disposed parent—and consider that we have deserved much more grievous things and the Christ, though innocent, suf-fered horribly for our sins, these are no longer afflictions but either health-giving remedies or the means of increasing our heavenly rewards.[10]

Erasmus goes beyond Perkins's advocacy of obedience by recommending a dis-position of thanks to God for the suffering one must endure.

The approach that predominates in the *ars moriendi* literature presents both evident flaws and promise as one attempts to appropriate their insights today. Let me begin by naming the flaws.

I would not dispute the basic insight of the first piece of the traditional *ars moriendi* approach to developing patience. Unquestionably, one is better pre-pared to deal with great matters of suffering, pain, and loss when one has al-ready overcome similar travails earlier in life. However, there is an excessive focus upon the physical dimension of suffering in all of these authors. This em-phasis is mislaid, particularly for contemporary readers because the main diffi-culty to be endured in dying is no longer pain so much as vulnerability or a sense of meaninglessness. Thus, the image of bearing the cross throughout life—a very physical image—can easily distract contemporary men and women from the task of learning the patience required for dying. It suggests that what we must prepare for is to endure pain—to carry a cross—when in fact what we must prepare for is to be handed over to the care of others. What we must pre-pare for is to accept the loss of our independence.

The traditional *ars moriendi* approach is further flawed by the fact that it implies (particularly in the quote from Erasmus cited above) that Jesus *em-braced* suffering and it is this embrace that is to be imitated by contemporary Christians. This approach is at odds with two insights I developed in chapter 4. First, Jesus' prayer in the garden that God might take away the cup before him (Lk 22:42) indicates that he does not embrace suffering for moral edification as Erasmus would have us do. Jesus takes a very negative view of suffering and clearly does not offer up thanks to his Father for it. Second, this approach to patience fails to connect it to compassion. Jesus is portrayed as obedient to God's will, but his is not a completely blind obedience. As I demonstrated in chapter 4, Luke's portrayal of Jesus at the Last Supper suggests that he had some sense that the suffering he was about to endure was for the good of others. Thus, Jesus practices patience so that he can both be obedient to what he perceives God's will to be and so that he can be compassionate toward those he loved.

What this suggests is that it was not toughness and indifference to pain and suffering that were crucial to Jesus' practice of patience in dying. Instead, it was a learned attentiveness to God's call and presence, and a willingness to hand himself over to that calling and finally into the hands of others. It is this type of patience that was crucial not only for Jesus' way of dying, but characteristic of his whole way of living. As Donald Senior has remarked, what made Jesus' dying as portrayed by Luke such a powerful example is the cohesion between how he lived and how he died.[11] He remained faithful to God, merciful toward enemies, and compassionate toward all those around him even in the midst of suffering and death. His patience functioned to protect the integrity of the other virtues he had developed and exhibited throughout life and preserve them through his dying as well.

In the same way, Christians today should pursue patience throughout life in a way that is consistent with the demands that will be placed upon them in dying. They must learn to be attuned to God's presence and practice discerning the good that God might be calling them to serve in any given situation. More importantly, Christians must practice ceding absolute control of their lives. Today, what so many people find it impossible to admit is that they are not autonomous islands but creatures that cannot flourish without other people. This is a fact that it will take a lifetime to learn. But it is only if we learn this truth that we will be able to hand ourselves over patiently to the care of those we love when death draws near.

The task of dying is not that of learning to bear misfortune without grimacing. It is to learn the truth about ourselves—that we are not the center of the universe, able to exist indefinitely and independently by the sheer force of our own will. We are social creatures ultimately dependent upon God. We are called to share our destiny with God in God's presence and by God's grace. To come to know this truth is at the heart of the Christian life, and in this way the *ars moriendi* will always be linked to the *ars vivendi*.

Let me offer one anecdote that illustrates how patience, compassion, and hope can at once be developed and be of use in contexts of suffering besides death. As William Perkins remarked, it is by learning to deal with life's "little deaths" (moments of suffering on a much smaller scale) that our patience, compassion, and hope are developed throughout life to a point where they might be strong enough to face a tragedy as great as dying.

I hope that an analogy from my own experience will illuminate the point I am trying to make. I found writing my doctoral dissertation to be a time of intellectual growth and satisfaction, but also to be a time of some suffering. I eventu-

ally learned to deal with that suffering by growing in patience. I did so by culti-
vating a sense of God's Providence and by being more attentive to the possibilities for meaning and service in my work. I propose that my experience is suggestive of the way in which patience, compassion, and hope can have a lifelong
usefulness.

Quite obviously, writing a dissertation and dying are not the same thing.
Anyone who has lost a loved one knows that nothing really compares to the
magnitude of sadness that comes with that experience. To love someone who is
dying or to face death oneself are perhaps life's most bitter and painful trage-
dies. There is nothing else really like it. At the same time, dying can be classi-
fied within the category of experiences of suffering. In that sense dying relates
to other moments of suffering in our lives such as professional setbacks or loss
of employment, broken relationships, and so forth. Insights derived from those
other experiences therefore may yield some insight into how to deal with the
much more profound suffering of dying. I relate the following analogy to suggest in a very simple but experiential way how patience, compassion, and hope
can be applied to other areas of life, and to suggest that what is learned there
might offer some small insight into practicing these virtues in the context of
dying.

I remember several times over the course of the two long years that I was
writing when I reached a particularly exasperating moment and asked myself,
"Why bother??!? What am I doing? I am spending years writing something that
few people will ever read in order to acquire credentials for a job I'll never get!
Why endure this suffering? What is the point?!?" I know from some partners in
commiseration that I was not unique in my experience of these sentiments and
frustrations. I know from these same friends that neither was I alone in the "solution" I found for these moments of difficulty.

I recall one occasion when I was at an especially low point in my writing
efforts. I had spent months writing a chapter that still had not come together to
my satisfaction or that of my director. I had finished a full round of job inter-
views, visits, and the inevitable months of waiting for an answer only to come
up completely empty at the end. I was facing another year of trying to help support my family on a graduate student's stipend. I was giving serious consideration to giving up and changing career paths. I was suffering. I was suffering
from the frustration that accompanies failure, but suffering even more from an
enveloping sense of meaninglessness. There seemed no point in going forward. I
could not conceive of any benefit to myself or the world that might come by my
continued effort.

A friend of mine pointed the way out of my suffering. She told me to think
about why I had originally set off to pursue graduate studies in theology. She
told me to try to remember the way in which I had discerned God was calling
me to an academic vocation. She encouraged me to pray—to bring my suffering
before God and to seek to find comfort there. Most importantly, she suggested

that I contemplate God's providence and the presence and need for God's grace in my life. Thus, her proposed solution went something like this: remember that God has called you to this work, that God has called you to it for some purpose and that by grace God will give you the means to accomplish what it is you must do.

As a theologian, I am ashamed to admit that I had not already thought of this way of addressing my suffering and sense of hopelessness. The truth is that I had become so involved in my writing and the details of its progress that I had forgotten any inner connection I had once made between my work and my efforts to live as a faithful disciple of Jesus Christ. I had begun to fail and to experience a deep sense of hopelessness and meaninglessness because I had ceased to see my work as a service to God, or as a response to God's calling. I had stopped turning to God as a source of the strength and means to accomplish what was before me in life. My work finally began again to progress when I made a conscious effort to restore this connection. My anxiety, my previous sense of the meaninglessness of my work, and my sense of my own inadequacies before the challenge of writing all diminished when I came to see my work as a difficult task carried out in the presence of God, as a witness to God in the presence of God's grace. I learned patience by grounding that virtue in faith in God's presence and in hope that my efforts were not ultimately in vain and God would provide the means to accomplish this task

A few months later, I found an additional support for the patience required to write and pursue a theological vocation. My suffering had already subsided to the extent that I could again think and write productively. I had finished another chapter, and I was meeting with someone to discuss the draft. At that meeting, this person told me that he really had appreciated what he had read. He read it at a time when a friend of his was dying, and he had found what I had written to be helpful, comforting, and insightful. Upon learning this, I was quite moved. That day I found an answer to some of the exasperated questions I raised above ("Why bother spending years to write something that few people will ever read?!?! What's the point?!?!"). That day I saw my writing as an activity of compassion. In a very small way, I had helped to ease someone's suffering. I had found in compassion further support for the patience I needed to persist in writing.

The transformation of my experience from frustration, suffering, and even despair into a difficult, but meaningful and worthwhile task is analogous to the way in which someone's dying might be transformed from a meaningless period of suffering into something that can be endured and in which one might find meaning. As I have said, there are some significant differences between the two experiences. Most notably, dying is a tragic event that ultimately brings about the end of one's life on earth and all the positive experiences that go along with it. Writing a dissertation is difficult, but not life threatening and has an intrinsic worth. No one would pursue dying as a good *in se*. However, these facts are not debilitating to the point that I wish to make. I am not trying to prove that writing a dissertation and dying are both good things nor even that we are called to our dying in the same way that we are called to a vocation. I would not go so far as to suggest either of these. My point simply is to call attention to the potentially transformative effects of the practice of patience and the pursuit of the virtues of compassion and hope in situations otherwise predisposed to despair.

My experience of writing was not changed by anything inherent in the process of writing itself. I did not come to see putting words on a page as in itself a joy; it remained difficult work that many times I would have preferred to avoid. What changed was the context of meaning in which I experienced the writing of my dissertation. I came to see it as a calling—as something from which good would come. I came to see it as a deepening of my own understanding and even an opportunity to help others.

Perhaps in a similar sort of way, a patient's dying can be transformed from one of pointless suffering into something tolerable and worth attending to by a conscious choice to seek out something meaningful and worth suffering for in the midst of dying. In my experience of writing, I was able to accomplish that task by seeing my work as a mode of service to God—as something to which God had called me as a unique avenue for growth in self-understanding, for service and witness to God, and for the expression of compassion or service to others. Perhaps analogously one's own dying can be seen as an opportunity to prayerfully grow in self-understanding, in trust in God, and in love and compassion with those around us. This is not the same thing as saying that God wants us to suffer or that God wants us to die. God calls us not to the experience of suffering itself, but to what might be accomplished in the midst of suffering.

Integrating Dying Within the Life of the Christian Community

What I have advocated so far is advice directed toward individuals. We individual Christians should seek to imitate Jesus in the way that he nourished his hope and his practice of patience by linking those virtues to a prayerful faith in God, trust in Providence, and compassion for others. But a change of consciousness within any number of individuals will not be enough to transform the contemporary experience of dying from an unspeakable horror into an endurable tragedy. The efforts of individuals must be supported by communal practices in order to bring about noticeable change.

The variety of ways in which the Christian community could support people in their dying is too wide to describe here. Therefore, I want to suggest just one possibility: a parish-based program of lay ministry to the dying. This would be a ministry that trains lay people in the ways of Christian compassion as I have described it in chapter 3. That is, participants would learn to listen to the voice of the one suffering, to seek to enter into that suffering and feel it as their own, and to act on behalf of and in concert with the dying. This ministry would itself serve as the embodiment of the fourth dimension of Christian compassion, namely integrating and connecting the dying to the Christian community.

Volunteers are already an important part of the support offered by most hospice agencies. Agency volunteers perform tasks varying from simply sitting and talking with a lonely patient, to running errands, to ensuring that a patient is safe at home while his or her primary caregivers leave for a few hours of respite.[12] Some volunteers also perform what is known as "vigil service," agreeing to be called to the home of a patient who is "actively dying" (i.e., approximately in the last twenty-four to forty-eight hours of life) to ensure that someone is constantly at a person's bedside at the very end.

The fact that a network of volunteers already exists increases the viability of my suggestion that a parish-based network of volunteers should be instituted. Hospice agency volunteers typically receive at least six weeks of relatively intensive training. By collaborating with these agencies, church-based groups could find ready access to much of the expertise required to take on this sort of volunteer initiative. But if such services and opportunities to volunteer already exist, why undertake a new parish initiative?

The overall theme of my concluding remarks is that dying needs to be reintegrated into life. An important step in bringing this about is to decompartmentalize care for the dying. Great hospice care is being delivered to the dying every day, but unless you personally know someone receiving such care you would probably never realize that fact. Adding care for the dying to the social ministry of parishes is one possible way to mainstream such care and to see it as a part of life. Everyone lives, everyone dies, and everyone should play a role as a member of the community in supporting and caring for those who are dying.

An analogy can be found in the model of the Rite of Christian Initiation for Adults (RCIA). For years before the RCIA, people were entering the church, often catechized individually by a priest or another member of a parish's pastoral staff. Services were being delivered, but in a way cut off from the life of the parish. It was a service delivered by specialists (priests, etc.) to unusual individuals. The RCIA model performs the same work of catechizing new members of the community, but does so in a way that shares responsibility for that task and integrates its performance into the liturgical life of the community. The task of welcoming new members now often is undertaken by a lay team in concert with a member of the parish's pastoral staff (thus a small group of dedicated volunteers perform the bulk of the work of catechizing and sharing the faith). The congregation as a whole too is involved, however. They are made aware of the process of ongoing catechesis liturgically when candidates and catechumens are dismissed after the homily. They stand as witnesses and confirm their own faith alongside these newcomers at scrutinies during Lent, receiving the implicit message (sometimes explicitly preached) that catechesis is a very public matter for which the whole community shares responsibility.

Similar opportunities might exist for communicating the fact that ministry to the dying is a public matter for which the whole community is responsible. I have been present at a liturgy where those who bring the Eucharist to the sick and dying are called to the front of church near the end of the mass, blessed and then sent forth in the congregation's name. The community was then also asked to pray for those dying and to "remember them" (i.e., as "one of us"). My expertise is not in the area of liturgy, but it seems to me that the possibilities in this area would be rich.

The benefit of this ministry of compassion toward the dying is at least three-fold. First, it institutionalizes the connection between dying and the rest of life. Second, it makes concrete some of the fundamental understandings of a Christian anthropology, namely that human beings are essentially relational creatures who retain their full dignity even in situations where their independence and physical capacities are impaired. Keeping the dying in our thoughts and in our care affirms their ongoing worth as human beings. It makes clear that even when dying they remain "one of us." In this ministry, by its words and actions, the Christian community assures the dying (and everyone else) that the eventual debilitation of our physical capacities, our aging, and our dying are all part of the very meaning of being human, and therefore not a source of shame. Such a move affirms a place in the human community for those facing imminent death and places caregivers in solidarity with them. In this way, compassion supports the development of patience in the dying as well as their efforts to see their dying as an integral part of the life they have been called to lead as Christians.

Third, this type of ministry provides an opportunity for people to prepare for their own death by serving the dying. Both Erasmus and William Perkins suggested that it was important for Christians frequently to be at the bedside of the dying. This practice served as a way of being reminded regularly of the fact that the life of each person will someday end in death. Furthermore, the purpose of these visits was not only to support brothers and sisters in their faith, but also to serve as a moment of learning about dying and how to face it well oneself at some later date. Erasmus believed that seeing the example of others dying well would provide concrete inspiration for oneself at one's own dying.[13] Perkins believed that the process of inspiring faith and hope in the dying would serve visitors to the dying well in health and as a prelude to their own effort ultimately to remain hopeful in dying.[14] Ministry to the dying can be a significant way of putting preparation for dying on the moral and spiritual agenda of contemporary Christians. It is also an important way in which they can learn that a "Good Death" is actually possible.

Recently, Libby Purves noted how far this idea of a good death has drifted from the consciousness of most people today. Her insight is keen and worth quoting at some length:

> Today's brave, chippy books on fighting cancer offer no conception of hoping for the Good Death. Only the weakness, the absence, the horror

and the pity are anticipated so that a hideous yawning unspeakableness lies between the "brave fight" in the hospital and the "celebration of life" in the memorial service. . . . Whether you go like a soldier, or a martyr, or a mystic, or simply from your bed like [former Beatles star George] Harrison, "conscious of God and fearless of death," you have won the last battle. But somehow our culture has lost the ability to consider it that way. Fighting means resisting, denying, seeking pointless and agonizing treatments and clutching tightly at the fripperies of life. . . . The only hope for a Good Death that you ever hear is the common one of, "I don't want to know anything about it . . ." The only report we value is "It was instantaneous, he can't have known anything."[15]

Purves's observation is much the same one that I have made in this book, namely that many Christians today see death as something always to be avoided. Few have any sense that their deaths might be redemptive for themselves or others, or any sense that they might find God or a deeper self-understanding via the experience of dying.

It is my hope that the reflections I have offered and the proposals I have made here might begin to lead men and women today toward entertaining again the possibility that Purves proposes. Death is always tragic, but not always devoid of meaning. It is possible to experience a "Good Death." It is possible to leave the world at peace with those we love and in their embrace, to die with faith in God and hope that our attachment to the Divine will endure beyond the grave. To die in this way is the best ending that we mortal, fallen humans can hope for. It is a goal worth striving toward.

Notes

1. The *New York Times* published obituaries with memorial photos of victims of the WTC attack at a rate of about a dozen a day, beginning shortly after the tragedy. Even at this generous rate, the *Times* did not print a profile of each victim until late spring 2002.

2. Bill Nichols and Peter Eisler, "The Threat of Nuclear Terror Is Slim but Real," *USA Today*, 29 November 2001. Lester Paldy, "The Nuclear Threat Can't Be Ignored," *Newsday*, 19 November 2001. "As Anthrax scare grows, Perspective gets lost," *USA Today*, 18 October 2001.

3. Kathryn Matthews, "Thankful for Being Together," *Newsday*, November 21, 2001. Julie Poppen, "Many Students Flying Home for Thanksgiving this Year," *Rocky Mountain News*, 21 November 2001.

4. See especially William Perkins, *A Salve for a Sicke Man*, in *The English ars moriendi*, ed. David William Atkinson (New York: Peter Lang, 1992), 137–41, and Jeremy Taylor, *Holy Dying*, vol. 2, *Holy Living and Holy Dying*, ed. P. G. Stanwood (Oxford: Clarendon Press, 1989), 49–50.

5. Bill Moyers, *On Our Own Terms*, WNET PBS television, 2000.

6. Perkins, *Salve for a Sicke Man*, 141.

7. Jeremy Taylor agrees. He encourages readers to avoid a "soft, delicate life" in favor of a life lived "under the sign of the cross." See Taylor, *Holy Dying*, 51–52.

8. Perkins, *Salve for a Sicke Man*, 158.

9. Perkins, *Salve for a Sicke Man*, 158.

10. Desiderius Erasmus, *Preparing for Death* (*De praeparatione ad mortem*), trans. John N. Grant, in *Spiritualia and Pastoralia*, vol. 70, *Collected Works of Erasmus*, ed. John W. O'Malley (Toronto: University of Toronto Press, 1998), 409–10.

11. Senior suggests that what is implied in the centurion's comment, "Truly this man was just" (Lk 23:48) is that Jesus lived his whole life faithful to the mission given to him by God and remained equally faithful to that mission in death. Thus, "just" here implies that Jesus had integrity and that his character in the midst of suffering was consistent with how he conducted himself throughout his public ministry. See Donald Senior, *The Passion of Jesus in the Gospel of Luke* (Wilmington, Del.: Glazier, 1989), 146.

12. See "The Hospice Homepage Great Ideas . . . Volunteers," Santa Clara University Hospice Homepage, www.scu.edu/Hospice/10volunt.html (5 Jan. 2004).

13. Erasmus, *Preparing for Death*, 447.

14. Perkins, *Salve for a Sicke Man*, 146-48.

15. Libby Purves, "Something in the way he died," *The Tablet*, December 8, 2001, 1734.

Bibliography

Angell, Marcia. "The Quality of Mercy." *New England Journal of Medicine* 306, no. 2 (Jan. 14, 1982): 98–99.

Ariès, Philippe. *Western Attitudes Toward Death: From the Middle Ages to the Present*. Baltimore: Johns Hopkins University Press, 1974.

———. *The Hour of Our Death*. New York: Knopf, 1981.

Atkinson, David W. "*A Salve For A Sicke Man*: William Perkins' Contribution to the *ars moriendi*." *Historical Magazine of the Protestant Episcopal Church* 46, no. 4 (December 1977): 409–18.

———. "Erasmus on Preparing to Die," *Wascana Review* 15, no. 2 (1980): 10–21.

———. "The English *ars moriendi*: its Protestant Transformation," *Renaissance and Reformation* 6, no. 1 (1982): 1–10.

———, ed. *The English Ars Moriendi*. New York: Lang, 1992.

Beaty, Nancy Lee. *The Craft of Dying: A Study in the Literary Tradition of the Ars Moriendi in England*. New Haven, Conn.: Yale University Press, 1970.

Beck, Brian E. "*Imitatio Christi* and the Lucan Passion Narrative." In *Suffering and Martyrdom in the New Testament*, edited by William Horbury and Brian McNeil, 28–47. Cambridge: Cambridge University Press, 1981.

Becker, Arthur H. "Compassion: The Foundation of the Care of the Sick." *Trinity Seminary Review* 5:1 (spring 1983): 14–21.

Becon, Thomas. "The Sicke Man's Salve." In *The English Ars Moriendi*, edited by David W. Atkinson, 87–126. New York: Lang, 1992.

Bellarmine, Robert. *Robert Bellarmine: Spiritual Writings*, edited and translated by John Patrick Donnelly and Roland J. Teske. New York: Paulist Press, 1989.

141

Bergant, Dianne, and Paul J. Wadell. "Compassion." In *The Collegeville Pastoral Dictionary of Biblical Theology*, edited by Carroll Stuhlmueller, 154–58. Collegeville, Minn.: Liturgical Press, 1996.

Bietenholz, Peter G. "Ludwig Baer, Erasmus, and the Tradition of the 'Ars bene moriendi.'" *Revue de littérature comparée* 52 (1978): 155–70.

Bozak, Barbara A. "Suffering and the Psalms of Lament: Speech for the Speechless, Power for the Powerless." *Eglise et Théologie* 23 (1992): 325–38.

Bregman, Lucy. "Current Perspectives on Death, Dying, and Mourning." *Religious Studies Review* 25, no. 1 (January 1999): 29–34.

Breshahan, James. "Catholic Spirituality and Medical Interventions in Dying." In *On Moral Medicine: Theological Perspectives in Medical Ethics*, 2nd ed., edited by Stephen E. Lammers and Allen Verhey, 642–47. Grand Rapids, Mich.: Eerdmans, 1998.

Brodrick, James. *Robert Bellarmine: Saint and Scholar*. London: Burns & Oates, 1961.

Brody, Howard. "Assisted Death: A Compassionate Response to a Medical Failure." *New England Journal of Medicine* 327 (November 5, 1992): 1384–88.

Brown, Raymond E. *The Death of the Messiah: From Gethsemane to the Grave*. New York: Doubleday, 1994.

Brownlee, Annette Geoffrion. "The Dark Night of Hope." *Journal of Religion and Aging* 1, no. 2 (winter 1984): 9–25.

Brueggemann, Walter. *The Message of the Psalms: A Theological Commentary*. Minneapolis, Minn.: Augsburg Fortress Press, 1984.

Bulka, Reuven P. *Judaism on Illness and Suffering*. Northvale, N.J.: Aronson, 1998.

Burghardt, Walter J. "Aging, Suffering and Dying: A Christian Perspective." In *Aging*, edited by Lisa Sowle Cahill and Dietmar Mieth, 65–71. London: SCM Press, 1991.

———. "Preaching Christian Hope." *Church* 12 (autumn 1996): 5–10.

Byock, Ira. *Dying Well: Peace and Possibilities at the End of Life*. New York: Riverhead Books, 1997.

Cahill, Lisa Sowle. "'Embodiment' and moral critique: A Christian social perspective." In *Embodiment, Morality and Medicine*, edited by Lisa Sowle Cahill and Margaret A. Farley, 199–215. Dordrecht: Kluwer Academic Publishers, 1995.

———. *Love Your Enemies: Discipleship, Pacifism and Just War Theory*. Minneapolis, Minn.: Fortress Press, 1984.

Callahan, Daniel. *False Hopes: Why America's Quest for Perfect Health is a Recipe for Failure*. New York: Simon & Schuster, 1998.

———. *The Troubled Dream of Life: In Search of a Peaceful Death*. New York: Simon and Schuster, 1993.

Callanan, Maggie, and Patricia Kelley. *Final Gifts: Understanding the Special Awareness, Needs, and Communications of the Dying.* New York: Poseidon Press, 1992.

Campbell, Alastair V. "Caring and Being Cared For. On Dignity and Death." In *On Moral Medicine: Theological Perspectives in Medical Ethics*, edited by Stephen E. Lammers and Allen Verhey, 266–72. Grand Rapids, Mich.: Eerdmans, 1987.

Carmody, John T., and Denise L. Carmody. "The Body Suffering: Illness and Disability." In *Embodiment, Morality and Medicine*, edited by Lisa Sowle Cahill and Margaret A. Farley, 185–97. Dordrecht: Kluwer Academic Publishers, 1995.

Carni, Ellen. "Issues of Hope and Faith in the Cancer Patient." *Journal of Religion and Health* 27 (1988): 285–90.

Carroll, Thomas K., ed. *Jeremy Taylor: Selected Works.* New York: Paulist Press, 1990.

Carse, James P. *The Silence of God: Meditations on Prayer.* New York: Macmillan, 1985.

Casey, Juliana. "Suffering and Dying with Dignity." In *Suffering and Healing in Our Day*, edited by Francis A. Eigo, 136–66. Villanova, Penn.: Villanova University Press, 1990.

Cassel, Eric J. "The Nature of Suffering and the Goals of Medicine." *New England Journal of Medicine* 306, no. 11 (March 18, 1982): 639–45.

Cates, Diana Fritz. *Choosing to Feel: Virtue, Friendship and Compassion for Friends.* Notre Dame, Ind.: University of Notre Dame Press, 1997.

Catholic Church, Sacred Congregation for the Doctrine of the Faith. *Declaration on Euthanasia.* Washington, D.C.: United States Catholic Conference, 1980.

Cohen, Charles Lloyd. *God's Caress: The Psychology of Puritan Religious Experience.* New York: Oxford University Press, 1986.

Committee on Improving Care at the End of Life. *Approaching Death: Improving Care at the End of Life*, edited by Marilyn J. Field and Christine K. Cassel. Washington, D.C.: National Academy Press, 1997.

Conzelmann, Hans. *The Theology of Saint Luke.* Translated by Geoffrey Buswell. London: Faber and Faber, 1960.

Cunningham, Agnes. "The Dark Night of the Soul–When Only Hope Remains." *Chicago Studies* 33 (August 1994): 111–23.

Davies, P. E. "Did Jesus Die as a Martyr Prophet?" *Biblical Research* 19 (1974): 34–47.

Demos, John. "From This World to the Next: Notes on Death and Dying in Early America." In *Facing Death: Where Culture, Religion and Medicine Meet*, edited by Howard M. Spiro, Mary G. McCrea Curnen, and Lee Palmer Wandel, 160–65. New Haven, Conn.: Yale University Press, 1996.

Donnelly, John Patrick, ed. *Robert Bellarmine: Spiritual Writings*. New York: Paulist Press, 1988.

Dorff, Elliot N. "Assisted Death: A Jewish Perspective." In *Must We Suffer Our Way to Death? Cultural and Theological Perspectives on Death by Choice*, edited by Ronald P. Hamel and Edwin R. DuBose, 141–73. Dallas, Tex.: Southern Methodist University Press, 1996.

Downing, John. "Jesus and Martyrdom." *Journal of Theological Studies* n.s. 14 (1963): 279–93.

Duntley, Mark A. "Covenantal Ethics and Care for the Dying." In *On Moral Medicine: Theological Perspectives in Medical Ethics*, 2nd ed., edited by Stephen E. Lammers and Allen Verhey, 663–65. Grand Rapids, Mich.: Eerdmans, 1998.

Dupré, Louis, and Don E. Saliers, eds. *Christian Spirituality*. Vol. 3, *Post-Reformation and Modern*. New York: Crossroad, 1989.

Dwyer, J. W., and R. T. Coward. "A Multivariate Comparison of the Involvement of Adult Sons vs. Daughters in the Care of Impaired Parents." *Journal of Gerontology: Social Sciences* 46 (1991): S259–69.

Ehrman, Bart, and Mark Plunkett. "The Angel and the Agony: The Textual Problem of Luke 22:43–44." *Catholic Biblical Quarterly* 45 (1983): 401–16.

Eire, Carlos M. N. "*Ars Moriendi*." In *The Westminster Dictionary of Christian Spirituality*, edited by Gordon S. Wakefield, 21–22. Philadelphia: Westminster Press, 1983.

———. *From Madrid to Purgatory: The Art and Craft of Dying in Sixteenth-Century Spain*. New York: Cambridge University Press, 1995.

Emanuel, Ezekiel J. "What is the Benefit of Legalizing Assisted Suicide?" *Ethics* 109 (April 1999): 629–42.

Erasmus, Desiderius. *Preparing for Death (De praeparatione ad mortem)*. Translated and annotated by John N. Grant. In *Spiritualia and Pastoralia*. Vol. 70, *Collected Works of Erasmus*, edited by John W. O'Malley, 389–450. Toronto: University of Toronto Press, 1998.

Farley, Wendy. "Natural Suffering, Tragedy and the Compassion of God." *Second Opinion* 18, no. 3 (October 1992): 23–29.

———. *Tragic Vision and Divine Compassion: A Contemporary Theodicy*. Louisville, Ky.: Westminster John Knox Press, 1990.

Fiorenza, Francis Schüssler. *Foundational Theology: Jesus and the Church*. New York: Crossroad, 1992.

Fitzmyer, Joseph A. *The Gospel According to Luke*. Vol. 28a, *The Anchor Bible*. New York: Doubleday, 1985.

Foley, K. M. "The Treatment of Cancer Pain." *New England Journal of Medicine* 313, no. 2 (1985): 84–95.

Frank, Arthur. *At the Will of the Body: Reflections on Illness*. Boston: Houghton Mifflin Company, 1991.

Frankl, Viktor. *Man's Search for Meaning: An Introduction to Logotherapy.* New York: Pocket Books, 1963.

Friedman, Barry W. "Spiritual Growth through Care of the Dying." *Journal of Religion and Health* 22 (1983): 268–77.

Gadamer, Hans-Georg. *Truth and Method.* 2nd Rev. Ed. Translation by Joel Weinsheimer and Donald G. Marshall. New York: Crossroad, 1991.

Gilleman, Gérard. *The Primacy of Charity in Moral Theology.* Translated by William F. Ryan and André Vachon. Westminster, Md.: Newman Press, 1959.

Glick, Shimon. "The Jewish Approach to Living and Dying." In *Jewish and Catholic Bioethics: An Ecumenical Dialogue,* edited by Edmund D. Pellegrino and Alan Faden, 43–53. Washington, D.C.: Georgetown University Press, 1999.

Grant, Jacqueline. "The Sin of Servanthood and the Deliverance of Discipleship." In *A Troubling in My Soul: Womanist Perspectives on Evil and Suffering,* edited by Emilie Townes, 199–218. Maryknoll, N.Y.: Orbis, 1993.

Greshake, Gisbert. "Towards a Theology of Dying." In *The Experience of Dying,* edited by Norbert Greinacher and Alois Müller, 80–98. New York: Herder and Herder, 1974.

Groopman, Jerome. *The Measure of Our Days: New Beginnings at Life's End.* New York: Penguin Books, 1997.

Gula, Richard M. *Reason Informed by Faith: Foundations of Catholic Morality.* New York: Paulist Press, 1989.

Gunderman, Richard. "Illness as Failure: Blaming Patients." *Hastings Center Report* 30, no. 4 (July–August 2000): 7–11.

Guroian, Vigen. *Life's Living Toward Dying: A Theological and Medical-Ethical Study.* Grand Rapids, Mich.: Eerdmans, 1996.

Gustafson, James M. "The Conditions for Hope: Reflections on Human Experience." *Continuum* 7 (1970): 535–45.

Gutiérrez, Gustavo. *A Theology of Liberation.* Maryknoll, N.Y.: Orbis, 1987.

Hale, John. *The Civilization of Europe in the Renaissance.* New York: Simon and Schuster, 1993.

Hall, Douglas J. "Beyond Cynicism and Credulity: On the Meaning of Christian Hope." *Princeton Seminary Bulletin* 6, no. 3 (1985): 201–10.

Hambrick-Stowe, Charles. "Puritan Spirituality in America." In *Christian Spirituality.* Vol. 3, *Post-Reformation and Modern,* edited by Louis Dupré and Don E. Saliers, 338–53. New York: Crossroad, 1989.

Hamel, Ronald P., and Edwin R. DuBose. *Must We Suffer Our Way to Death? Cultural and Theological Perspectives on Death by Choice.* Dallas, Tex.: Southern Methodist University Press, 1996.

Harned, David Baily. *Patience: How We Wait upon the World.* Cambridge, Mass.: Cowley Publications, 1997.

Harrington, Daniel. *Why Do We Suffer? A Scriptural Approach to the Human Condition.* Franklin, Wis.: Sheed and Ward, 2000.

Hauerwas, Stanley, and Charles Pinches. *Christians Among the Virtues: Theological Conversations with Ancient and Modern Ethics.* Notre Dame, Ind.: University of Notre Dame Press, 1997.

Hauerwas, Stanley. "Care. On Dignity and Death." In *On Moral Medicine: Theological Perspectives in Medical Ethics,* edited by Stephen E. Lammers and Allen Verhey, 262–66. Grand Rapids, Mich.: Eerdmans, 1987.

———. *Character and the Christian Life: A Study in Theological Ethics.* Notre Dame, Ind.: University of Notre Dame Press, 1994.

———. *Naming the Silences: God, Medicine, and the Problem of Suffering.* Grand Rapids, Mich.: Eerdmans, 1990.

Hays, Richard B. "The Church as a Scripture-Shaped Community: The Problem of Method in New Testament Ethics." *Interpretation* 44, no. 1 (1990): 42–55.

Hebblethwaite, Margaret. "Patience." *The Furrow* 36 (1985): 139–47.

Hellwig, Monica. "Eschatology." In *Systematic Theology: Roman Catholic Perspectives,* edited by Francis Schüssler Fiorenza and John P. Galvin, vol. 2, 347–72. Minneapolis, Minn.: Augsburg Fortress Press, 1991.

———. *What Are They Saying about Death and Christian Hope?* New York: Paulist Press, 1978.

Hirsch, Eric D. *Validity in Interpretation.* New Haven, Conn.: Yale University Press, 1967.

Imhof, Arthur E. "An *Ars Moriendi* for Our Time: To Live a Fulfilled Life; to Die a Peaceful Death." In *Facing Death: Where Culture, Religion, and Medicine Meet,* edited by Howard M. Spiro, Mary G. McCrea Curnen, and Lee Palmer Wandel, 114–20. New Haven, Conn.: Yale University Press, 1996.

———. "From the Old Mortality Pattern to the New; Implications of a Radical Change from the Sixteenth to the Twentieth Century," *Bulletin of the History of Medicine* 59, no. 1 (spring 1985): 1–29.

John Paul II, Pope. *Dives in Misericordia (On the Mercy of God).* Boston: St. Paul Editions, 1980.

Jung, Patricia Beattie. "Dying Well Isn't Easy: Thoughts of a Roman Catholic Theological on Assisted Death." In *Must We Suffer Our Way to Death? Cultural and Theological Perspectives on Death by Choice,* edited by Ronald P. Hamel and Edwin R. DuBose, 174–97. Dallas, Tex.: Southern Methodist University Press, 1996.

Karris, Robert J. "The Gospel According to Luke." In *The New Jerome Biblical Commentary,* edited by Raymond E. Brown, Joseph A. Fitzmyer, and Roland E. Murphy, 625–721. Englewood Cliffs, N.J.: Prentice Hall, 1990.

Keenan, James F. "Listening to the Voice of Suffering." *Church* 12 (autumn 1996): 41–43.

————. "The Case for Physician-Assisted Suicide?" *America* 179, no. 15 (14 Nov 1998): 14–20.

————. "Cases, Rhetoric, and the American Debate about Physician Assisted Suicide." In *Das medizinisch assistierte Sterben zur Sterbehilfe aus medizinischer ethischer, juristischer und theologischer Sicht*, edited by Adrian Holderegger. Freiburg: Universitätsverlag, 1999.

————. "Catholic Moral Theology, Ignatian Spirituality, and Virtue Ethics: Strange Bedfellows," *The Way* suppl. 88 (spring 1997): 36–45.

————. "Proposing Cardinal Virtues." *Theological Studies* 56 (1995): 708–29.

————. "The Meaning of Suffering." In *Jewish and Catholic Bioethics: An Ecumenical Dialogue*, edited by Edmund D. Pellegrino and Alan I. Faden, 83–95. Washington, D.C.: Georgetown University Press, 1999.

————. "The Virtues and Imagination." *Church* 11 (Spring 1995): 41–43.

————. *Virtues for Ordinary Christians*. Kansas City, Mo.: Sheed & Ward, 1996.

————. "What's New in the Ethical and Religious Directives?" *Linacre Quarterly* 65, no. 1 (February 1998): 33–40.

————. "William Perkins (1558–1602) and the Birth of British Casuistry." In *The Context of Casuistry*, edited by James F. Keenan and Thomas A. Shannon, 105–30. Washington, D.C.: Georgetown University Press, 1995.

Kleinman, Arthur. *The Illness Narratives: Suffering, Healing, and the Human Condition*. New York: Basic Books, 1988.

Kloppenborg, John S. "*Exitus Clari viri:* The Death of Jesus in Luke." *Toronto Journal of Theology* 8, no. 1 (1992): 106–20.

Kotva, Joseph J. *The Christian Case for Virtue Ethics*. Washington, D.C.: Georgetown University Press, 1996.

Kübler-Ross, Elisabeth. *Death: The Final Stage of Growth*. New York: Simon & Schuster, 1986.

————. *On Death and Dying*. New York: Macmillan, 1969.

Kurz, William S. "Luke 22:14-38 and Greco-Roman Biblical Farewell Addresses," *Journal of Biblical Literature* 104 (1985): 251–68.

Kuykendall, George. "Care for the Dying: A Kübler-Ross Critique." *Theology Today* 38 (1981): 37–48.

Lammers, Stephen E. "How do we Wish to Die? The Controversy over Assisted Death." *Religious Studies Review* 25, no. 1 (January 1999): 35–41.

Lammers, Stephen E., and Allen Verhey. *On Moral Medicine: Theological Perspectives in Medical Ethics*. Grand Rapids, Mich.: Eerdmans, 1987.

————. *On Moral Medicine: Theological Perspectives in Medical Ethics*. 2nd ed. Grand Rapids, Mich.: Eerdmans, 1998.

Lauritzen, Paul. "Reflections on the Nether World: Some Problems for a Feminist Ethic of Care and Compassion." *Soundings* 75, no. 2-3 (summer/fall 1992): 383–402.

Lebacqz, Karen. "The Virtuous Patient." In *Virtue and Medicine: Explorations in the Character of Medicine*, edited by Earl E. Shelp, 275–88. Dordrecht: Reidel, 1985.

———. "The Weeping Womb: Why Beneficence Needs the Still Small Voice of Compassion." In *Secular Bioethics in Theological Perspective*, edited by E. E. Shelp, 85–96. Dordrecht: Kluwer Academic Publishers, 1996.

Lebacqz, Karen, and Shirley Macemon. "Vicious Virtue? Patience, Justice and Salaries in the Church." In *Practice What You Preach: Virtues, Ethics and Power in the Lives of Pastoral Ministers*, edited by James F. Keenan and Joseph Kotva. Franklin, Wis.: Sheed & Ward, 1999.

Longaker, Christine. *Facing Death and Finding Hope: A Guide to the Emotional and Spiritual Care of the Dying*. New York: Doubleday, 1997.

Lovelace, Richard C. "The Anatomy of Puritan Piety: English Puritan Devotional Literature." In *Christian Spirituality*, Vol. 3, *Post-Reformation and Modern*, edited by Louis Dupré and Don E. Saliers, 294–323. New York: Crossroad, 1989.

Lund, Eric. "Second Age of the Reformation: Lutheran and Reformed Spirituality." In *Christian Spirituality*, Vol. 3, *Post-Reformation and Modern*, edited by Louis Dupré and Don E. Saliers, 213–39. New York: Crossroad, 1989.

Luria, Keith P. "The Counter-Reformation and Popular Spirituality." In *Christian Spirituality*, Vol. 3, *Post-Reformation and Modern*, edited by Louis Dupré and Don E. Saliers, 93–120. New York: Crossroad, 1989.

Lynch, William F. *Images of Hope: Imagination as Healer of the Hopeless*. Notre Dame, Ind.: University of Notre Dame Press, 1965.

Lynn, Joanne. "Caring for Those Who Die in Old Age." In *Facing Death: Where Culture, Religion, and Medicine Meet*, edited by Howard M. Spiro, Mary G. McCrea Curnen, and Lee Palmer Wandel, 90–102. New Haven, Conn.: Yale University Press, 1996.

Lysaught, M. Therese. "Patient Suffering and the Anointing of the Sick." In *On Moral Medicine: Theological Perspectives in Medical Ethics*, 2nd ed., edited by Stephen E. Lammers and Allen Verhey, 356–63. Grand Rapids, Mich.: Eerdmans, 1998.

MacIntyre, Alasdair. *After Virtue: A Study in Moral Theory*. Notre Dame, Ind.: University of Notre Dame Press, 1984.

MacRae, George. "With Me in Paradise." *Worship* 35 (1960–1961): 235–40.

Matera, Frank. *Passion Narratives and Gospel Theologies*. New York: Paulist Press, 1986.

May, William F. "Moral and Religious Reservations about Euthanasia." In *Must We Suffer Our Way to Death? Cultural and Theological Perspectives on Death by Choice*, edited by Ronald P. Hamel and Edwin R. DuBose, 103–19. Dallas, Tex.: Southern Methodist University Press, 1996.

Mayer-Scheu, Josef. "Compassion and Death." In *The Experience of Dying*, edited by Norbert Greinacher and Alois Müller, 111–25. New York: Herder and Herder, 1974.

McGill, Arthur C. *Death and Life: An American Theology*. Philadelphia: Fortress Press, 1987.

———. *Suffering: A Test of Theological Method*. Philadelphia: Westminster Press, 1982.

Meyer, Michael J. "Dignity, Death and Modern Virtue." *American Philosophical Quarterly* 32 (1995): 45–55.

Miller, Richard B. "Moral Sources, Ordinary Life, and Truth-telling in Jeremy Taylor's Casuistry." In *The Context of Casuistry*, edited by James F. Keenan and Thomas A. Shannon, 131–58. Washington, D.C.: Georgetown University Press, 1995.

Mohrmann, Margaret E. *Pain Seeking Understanding: Suffering, Medicine, and Faith*. Cleveland, Ohio: Pilgrim Press, 1999.

———. "Stories and Suffering." In *On Moral Medicine: Theological Perspectives in Medical Ethics*, 2nd ed., edited by Stephen E. Lammers and Allen Verhey, 347–55. Grand Rapids, Mich.: Eerdmans, 1998.

Moltmann, Jürgen. "Resurrection as Hope." *Harvard Theological Review* 61 (1968): 129–47.

———. *Is There Life After Death?* Milwaukee, Wis.: Marquette University Press, 1998.

Mui, Ada C. "Caring for Frail Elderly Patients: A Comparison of Adult Sons and Daughters." *The Gerontologist* 35, no. 1 (1995): 86–93.

Müller, Alois. "Care of the Dying as a Task of the Church." In *The Experience of Dying*, edited by Norbert Greinacher and Alois Müller. New York: Herder and Herder, 1974.

Murphy, Robert F. *The Body Silent*. New York: Henry Holt and Company, 1987.

National Conference of Catholic Bishops (USA). *A Ritual for Laypersons: Rites for Holy Communion and the Pastoral Care of the Sick and Dying*. Collegeville, Minn.: Liturgical Press, 1993.

———. *Ethical and Religious Directives for Catholic Health Care Services*. Washington, D.C.: United States Catholic Conference, 1995.

New, John F. H. *Anglican and Puritan: The Basis of their Opposition 1558–1640*. Stanford, Calif.: Stanford University Press, 1964.

Neyrey, Jerome. *The Passion According to Luke: A Redaction Study of Luke's Soteriology*. New York: Paulist Press, 1985.

———. "Jesus' Address to the Women of Jerusalem (Lk 23.27–31)–A Prophetic Judgment Oracle." *New Testament Studies* 29 (1983): 74–86.

Nickelsburg, George W. E. *Resurrection, Immortality and Eternal Life in Intertestamental Judaism*. Cambridge, Mass.: Harvard University Press, 1972.

Nossen, Robert. "Jeremy Taylor: Seventeenth-Century Theologian." *Anglican Theological Review* 42 (1960): 28–39.

———. "A Critical Study of the Holy Dying of Jeremy Taylor." Ph.D. diss., Northwestern University, 1951.

Nuland, Sherwin. *How We Die: Reflections on Life's Final Chapter*. New York: Alfred A. Knopf, 1994.

O'Connor, Mary Catherine. *The Art of Dying Well: The Development of the Ars moriendi*. New York: Columbia University Press, 1942.

O'Malley, John W. Introduction to *Spiritualia and Pastoralia*. Vol. 66, *Collected Works of Erasmus*. Toronto: University of Toronto Press, 1988.

———. Introduction to *Spiritualia and Pastoralia*. Vol. 70, *Collected Works of Erasmus*. Toronto: University of Toronto Press, 1998.

Ogden, Schubert M. "The Meaning of Christian Hope." *Union Seminary Quarterly Review* 30 (1975): 153–64.

Olthuis, James H. "An Ethics of Compassion: Ethics in a Post-Modern Age." In *What Right Does Ethics Have? Public Philosophy in a Pluralistic Culture*, edited by Sander Griffoen. Amsterdam: VU University Press, 1990.

Parsons, Susan Frank. *Feminism and Christian Ethics*. Cambridge: Cambridge University Press, 1996.

Pauw, Amy Plantinga. "Dying Well." In *Practicing Our Faith: A Way of Life for a Searching People*, edited by Dorothy C. Bass, 163–77. San Francisco: Jossey-Bass, 1997.

Perkins, William. *A Salve for a Sicke Man*. In *The English Ars Moriendi*, edited by David W. Atkinson, 127–63. New York: Lang, 1992.

Pilch, John J., and Paul J. Wadell. "Hope." In *The Collegeville Pastoral Dictionary of Biblical Theology*, edited by Carroll Stuhlmueller, 435–42. Collegeville, Minn.: Liturgical Press, 1996.

Plantinga, Cornelius, Jr. "Contours of Christian Compassion." *Perspectives* 10 (fall 1995): 9–11.

Pohl, Christine D. "Hospitality from the Edge: The Significance of Marginality in the Practice of Welcome." *Annual of the Society of Christian Ethics* (1995): 121–36.

Porter, Jean. "Virtue Ethics." In *The Cambridge Companion to Christian Ethics*, edited by Robin Gill, 96–111. New York: Cambridge University Press, 2001.

Purves, Libby. "Something in the way he died," *The Tablet*, 8 December 2001, 1734.

Quill, Timothy E. *Death and Dignity: Making Choices and Taking Charge*. New York: W. W. Norton, 1993.

———. "Doctor, I want to die. Will you help me?" *Journal of the American Medical Association* 270, no. 7 (Aug. 18, 1993): 870–3.

———. "Incurable Suffering." *Hastings Center Report* 24, no. 2 (Mar-Apr, 1994): 45.

——. *A Midwife through the Dying Process: Stories of Healing and Hard Choices at the End of Life*. Baltimore: Johns Hopkins University Press, 1996.

Quill, Timothy E., and Christine K. Cassel. "Nonabandonment: A Central Obligation for Physicians." *Annals of Internal Medicine* 122, no. 5 (1 March 1995): 368–74.

Quill, Timothy E., Christine K. Cassel, and D. E. Meier. "Care of the hopelessly ill. Proposed clinical criteria for physician-assisted suicide." *New England Journal of Medicine* 327, no. 19 (Nov 5, 1992): 1380–4.

Rahner, Karl. "Towards a Theology of Hope." *Concurrence* 1 (1969): 23–33.

Ramsey, Paul. "Death's Pedagogy." In *Death, Dying and Euthanasia*, edited by Dennis J. Horan and David Mall, 331–43. Washington, D.C.: University Publications of America, 1980.

Reich, Warren T. "Speaking of Suffering: A Moral Account of Compassion." *Soundings* 72 (spring 1989): 83–108.

Ricoeur, Paul. *Hermeneutics and the Human Sciences: Essays on Language, Action and Interpretation*. Edited and translated by John B. Thompson. Cambridge: Cambridge University Press, 1981.

Riley, James C. *Sickness, Recovery and Death: A History and Forecast of Ill Health*. Iowa City: University of Iowa Press, 1989.

Sachs, G. A., J. C. Ahronheim, J. A. Rhymes, L. Volicer, and J. Lynn. "Good Care of Dying Patients: The Alternative to Physician-Assisted Suicide and Euthanasia." *Journal of the American Geriatric Society* 43 (1995): 553–62.

Saint-Laurent, George E. "Christian Spirituality and the Virtue of Hope." *Epiphany* 4, no. 2 (winter 1983): 3–9.

Scarry, Elaine. *The Body in Pain: The Making and Unmaking of the World*. New York: Oxford University Press, 1985.

Schiffhorst, Gerald J. "Christian Patience and Stock Responses." *Spiritual Life* 30 (fall 1984): 163–68.

Schillebeeckx, Edward. *Jesus: An Experiment in Christology*. New York: Crossroad, 1979.

Schuman, Walter H. "Midwives for the Dying: The Role of the Church in Death Care." *Currents in Theology and Mission* 21 (June 1994): 213–17.

Segers, Mary C. "Feminism, Liberalism, and Catholicism." In *Feminist Ethics and the Catholic Moral Tradition*, edited by Charles E. Curran, Margaret A. Farley, and Richard McCormick, 586–615. New York: Paulist Press, 1996.

Senior, Donald. *The Passion of Jesus in the Gospel of Luke*. Wilmington, Del.: Glazier, 1989.

Smith, David H. "Suffering, Medicine, and Christian Theology: On Dignity and Death." In *On Moral Medicine: Theological Perspectives in Medical Ethics*, edited by Stephen E. Lammers and Allen Verhey, 255–61. Grand Rapids, Mich.: Eerdmans, 1987.

Sobrino, Jon. *Christology at the Crossroads: A Latin American Approach.* Maryknoll, N.Y.: Orbis, 1978.

Sölle, Dorothy. *Suffering.* Philadelphia: Fortress Press, 1975.

Spiro, Howard M., Mary G. McCrea Curnen, and Lee Palmer Wandel, eds. *Facing Death: Where Culture, Religion and Medicine Meet.* New Haven, Conn.: Yale University Press, 1996.

Spohn, William S. *Go and Do Likewise: Jesus and Ethics.* New York: Continuum, 1999.

———. "The Return of Virtue Ethics." *Theological Studies* 53 (1992): 60–75.

Stannard, David E. *The Puritan Way of Death: A Study in Religion, Culture, and Social Change.* New York: Oxford University Press, 1977.

Steinburg, Avraham. "The Meaning of Suffering: A Jewish Perspective." In *Jewish and Catholic Bioethics: An Ecumenical Dialogue,* edited by Edmund D. Pellegrino and Alan Faden, 77–82. Washington, D.C.: Georgetown University Press, 1999.

Talbert, Charles H. *Reading Luke: A Literary and Theological Commentary on the Third Gospel.* New York: Crossroad, 1982.

Taylor, Jeremy. *Holy Living and Holy Dying.* Edited by P. G. Stanwood. Oxford: Clarendon Press, 1989.

Throckmorton, Burton H. *Gospel Parallels: A Synopsis of the First Three Gospels.* 4th ed. Nashville, Tenn.: Thomas Nelson Publishers, 1979.

Tobin, Daniel R. *Peaceful Dying: The Step-by-step Guide to Preserving Your Dignity, Your Choice and Your Inner Peace at the End of Life.* Reading, Mass.: Perseus, 1999.

Verhey, Allen. "Assisted Suicide: A Biblical and Reformed Perspective." In *Must We Suffer Our Way to Death? Cultural and Theological Perspectives on Death by Choice,* edited by Ronald P. Hamel and Edwin R. DuBose, 226–65. Dallas, Tex.: Southern Methodist University Press, 1996.

———. "Suffering and Compassion: Looking Heavenward." *Perspectives* 10 (fall 1995): 17–21.

Wadell, Paul. *Friendship and the Moral Life.* Notre Dame, Ind.: University of Notre Dame Press, 1989.

Wakefield, Gordon S. *Puritan Devotion: Its Place in the Development of Christian Piety.* London: Epworth Press, 1957.

Wakely, Robin. "From Fear to Hope: The Riddle of Death and the Hope of Eternal Life." *Journal of Theology for Southern Africa* 59 (July 1987): 73–83.

Ware, Ann Patrick. "The Easter Vigil: A Theological and Liturgical Critique." In *Women at Worship: Interpretations of North American Diversity,* edited by Marjorie Procter-Smith and Janet R. Walton, 83–106. Louisville, Ky.: Westminster John Knox Press, 1993.

White, Helen C. *English Devotional Literature [Prose] 1600–1640.* New York: Haskell House, 1966.

Wolf, Susan M. "Gender, Feminism, and Death: Physician-Assisted Suicide and Euthanasia." In *Feminism and Bioethics: Beyond Reproduction*, edited by Susan M. Wolf, 282–317. New York: Oxford University Press, 1996.

Yearly, Lee H. "Recent Work on Virtue." *Religious Studies Review* 16 (1990): 1–9.

Zehnle, Richard. "The Salvific Character of Jesus' Death in Lucan Soteriology." *Theological Studies* 30 (1969): 430–44.

Index

155

About the Author

Christopher Vogt is assistant professor of theology and religious studies at St. John's University in New York. He received a Ph.D. in theological ethics from Boston College in 2002. His research interests lie at the intersection between virtue ethics and Catholic social ethics. He has presented his work at the Society of Christian Ethics and the annual International Conference Promoting Business Ethics, sponsored by the Vincentian universities in the United States. He serves in an advisory capacity on the ethics committee of Good Shepherd Hospice, Port Jefferson, New York.

Before undertaking graduate studies in theology, Dr. Vogt worked as a lay member of the pastoral staff at a small parish in the Roman Catholic diocese of Rochester, New York. He served there as catechetical coordinator and as a pastoral visitor to the homebound and hospitalized, which gave him the opportunity to experience and witness firsthand the challenges of ministering to the dying and their caregivers.

He is married to Jennifer Vogt, a registered nurse who specializes in hospice care. They live together with their children on Long Island.